Composition in the Twenty-First Century

Composition

IN THE TWENTY-FIRST CENTURY

CENTURY

CRISIS

AND

CHANGE

EDITED BY

Lynn Z. Bloom

Donald A. Daiker

Edward M. White

Southern Illinois University Press   Carbondale and Edwardsville

Library of Congress Cataloging-in-Publication Data

Composition in the 21st century : crisis and change / edited by Lynn
  Z. Bloom, Donald A. Daiker, Edward M. White.
    p. cm.
    Includes bibliographical references and index.
    1. English language—Rhetoric—Study and teaching.
2. Twenty-first century. I. Bloom, Lynn Z., 1934–   . II. Daiker,
Donald A., 1938–   . III. White, Edward M. (Edward Michael), 1933–   .
PE1404.C6255   1996
808′.042—dc20   95-1147
ISBN 0-8093-2128-9 (pbk.)   CIP

This book is dedicated to the memory of

James A. Berlin, teacher, scholar, citizen, friend.

Contents

Editors' Preface

Crisis and change, academia's faithful though not always welcome consorts, are nowhere more apparent than in the arena of composition. Composition, even as variously defined as the contributors in this book interpret such an amorphous and protean discipline, is currently undergoing major changes in concept, theory, and research, which invariably affect pedagogical theory and practice. These changes, in turn, have profound implications for public policy, reflected in such matters as (national) standards (what does it mean to be able to read and write? at what level?), school funding, and assessment of students and programs.

At the approach of the turn of the century—a phrase that itself will require major readjustment among those of us who associate the notion with the Victorian and Edwardian sensibilities of the turn of the last century—it seemed fitting to do what academicians are wont to do in order to focus on significant issues: hold a conference. In one sense, the Conference on Composition in the 21st Century: Crisis and Change, of which this book is the published version, has been in process throughout all of our personal and professional lifetimes as we experience and try to understand what it means to be able to read and write as human beings, students, teachers, and researchers.

In a more limited sense, the conference was three years in the making. Preliminary planning involved consultations among the three organizers—Lynn Z. Bloom, Donald A. Daiker, and Edward M. White—who had worked together for a decade with the national Council of Writing Program Administrators, an organization so new that it had few precedents or procedures. This flexibility allowed us, in consultation with the Modern Language Association (MLA) and the National Council of Teachers of English (NCTE—and thus with its Conference on College Composition and Communication, CCCC), as well as with representatives from two-year and four-year institutions across the nation, to replicate the writing process by inventing the conference and revising it as the initial text developed. It would be sponsored by the Council of Writing Program Administrators, with support from both Miami University, home of the WPA, and the University of Connecticut. It would be held 8–10 October 1993 at Miami University, where facilities would permit large and small group discussions among the 400 teachers, researchers, administrators, and graduate students we expected to attend (they did). It would focus on seven of the questions central to the future of composition, such as "What is composition and why do we teach it?" and "Who should teach composition and what should they know?" And it would incorporate audience response, as does this book through the commentaries following each set of paired essays.

We particularly wanted a format that would enable intense and active discussion of these key issues among all the conferees, invited speakers and participants alike. Thus, each of the seven sessions began with two speakers, invited because of their significant contributions to the field in the past quarter century, addressing a major question for half an hour each. We expected their talks, like the hour-long plenary addresses by Andrea A. Lunsford and Linda Flower, to provoke discussion and debate that would move the field along, and they did. During the second hour, participants gathered in groups of 8 or 10 to address the topic, with a designated discussion leader presiding and taking notes that would eventually be delivered to the invited session respondent. We hoped this participatory format would not only allow for varied and spontaneous voices in this volume but also present a positive model for teaching and learning as well. Conferees validated this interactive approach with comments like, "There were more voices heard, more ideas circulating, and more ideas aired than at most conferences," and, "It's the first time I felt that a conference was truly dialogic!"

By organizing the Conference on Composition in the 21st Century: Crisis and Change with an eye to the book that would emerge from it, we hoped to be able to address the world as well as the conferees. So we are particularly grateful to the 16 speakers and 7 respondents whose presentations have been revised into the essays that appear here.

Behind the scenes, an equally essential supporting cast contributed intelligence and hard work, along with goodwill and good cheer, to the success of the conference and the making of this book:

- Conference National Planning Committee: Miriam T. Chaplin, Rutgers University-Camden; Carol Petersen Hartzog, UCLA; Jesse Jones, North Texas Community and Junior College Consortium; and Phyllis Roth, Skidmore College—with help from Phyllis Franklin and David Laurence, MLA, and Miles Myers, NCTE.
- Conference Co-Director and Program Organizer: Jeff Sommers, Miami University-Middletown.

- Conference Coordinators: Jim Dubinsky, Risa P. Gorelick, Edwina Helton, John Krafft, Rich Lane, Jim McFadden, Malea Powell, Diana Royer, and Shannon Wilson, all of Miami University.

- Conference Organizing Committee: Debbie Bertsch, Bob Broad, Katy Charles, Shannon Fairchild, Johy Heyda, Cindy Lewiecki-Wilson, Maggy Lindgren, LuMing Mao, Max Morenberg, Kim Murray, Karen Powers-Stubbs, Erica Scott, and Janet Ziegler, all of Miami University.

- Conference Secretary: Debra Nixon.

- Conference Administrative Support: Barry Chabot, chair, English department, and Leta Carmichael, Kathy Fox, Jackie Kearns, and Trudi Nixon, secretaries, all of Miami University. John Gatta, chair, English department; Sarah Aguiar and Ning Yu, research assistants; and Denise Beaudoin and Lori Corsini-Nelson, secretaries, all of the University of Connecticut.

- Conference Session Moderators: Richard Bullock, Wright State University; Winifred Bryan Horner, Texas Christian University; David A. Jolliffe, University of Illinois at Chicago; Mary Jane Schenck, University of Tampa; Robert A. Schwegler, University of Rhode Island; William E. Smith, Western Washington University; and Nancy Sommers, Harvard University.

- Conference Session Introducers: Barbara Cambridge, Indiana University-Purdue University, Indianapolis; Edward P. J. Corbett, Ohio State University; Theresa Enos, University of Arizona; Richard Gebhardt, Bowling Green State University; Jesse Jones, North Texas Community and Junior College Consortium; Ben W. McClelland, University of Mississippi; Elizabeth Nist, Anoka-Ramsay Community College; Linda Peterson, Yale University; Helon Raines, Casper Community College; Dawn Rodrigues, Kennesaw State College; Phyllis Roth, Skidmore College; Jeffrey Sommers, Miami University-Middletown; Irwin Weiser, Purdue University; and Art Young, Clemson University.

- Conference Discussion Leaders: Karen J. Allanson, Chris M. Anson, Susan O. Bachman, Betty Bamberg, Pat Belanoff, Lynn Z. Bloom, Grant Boswell, Patricia P. Buckler, Richard Bullock, Kathy Burton, Mary Ann Cain, Jo Ann Campbell, Ayne Cantrell, Lee Ann Carroll, Thomas Clemens, William Condon, Elizabeth Cooper, Beth Daniell, M. Francine Danis, Marvin Diogenes, Ann B. Dobie, Dean Elkins, Rebecca Blevins Faery, John Fallon, James P. Farrelly, Ruth Fennick, Evelyn M. Finklea, Jane Frick, Richard Fulkerson, Toby Fulwiler, Alice Gillam, Barbara Gordon, Risa P. Gorelick, Claude Greenwood, Judy Hannekin, Kristine Hansen, Phyllis Hastings, Carol Peterson Haviland, Gail E. Hawisher, Shirley Brice Heath, Marguerite Helmers, Carol Heskett, Sylvia Holladay, Winifred Bryan Horner, Christine Hult, Margaret N. Hundleby, Joseph Janangelo, Richard Jenseth, David A. Jolliffe, Libby Falk Jones, George Kalamaras, Elaine Allen Karls, Mary King, Joyce Kinkead, Sarah L. Larson, Harriet Malinowitz, LuMing Mao, Richard Marback, Micheael Steven Marx, Ben W. McClelland, James McFadden, Claudie McIsaac, Margaret A. McLaughlin, Philip Miner, George Moberg, Clyde

Moneyhun, Joan Mullin, Deborah Mutnick, Beth S. Neman, W. Webster Newbold, Cynthia Novak, Gloria J. Owen-Roddy, Judy A. Pearce, Michael A. Pemberton, Linda Peterson, Virginia G. Polanski, Margaret B. Racin, Ruth Ray, Marjorie Roemer, Duane H. Roen, Phyllis Roth, Alice Roye, Diana Royer, Jean Sanborn, Mary Jane Schenck, Lucille M. Schultz, Charles Schuster, Robert A. Schwegler, Erica Scott, Nancy Shapiro, Courtenay Smith, Mark Smith, William E. Smith, Judith A. Stoffel, Barbara Stout, Pat Sullivan, Thomas Thompson, Elizabeth R. Turpin, Michael Vivion, Barbara Walvoord, George L. Ware III, Alison Warriner, Heidemarie Z. Weidner, Irwin Weiser, Stephen Wilhoit, Shannon Wilson, Rosemary Winslow, Virginia Young, and Betty Youngkin.

- Organizational Sponsors: the Council of Writing Program Administrators, especially Barbara Cambridge and Ben W. McClelland (then current and past presidents); the Aetna Endowment through the Aetna Chair of Writing (Lynn Z. Bloom), University of Connecticut.

- Indexer: Tama Sogoian, a skilled and meticulous graduate student in English composition at California State University at San Bernadino.

- Publishers: Southern Illinois University Press, especially former editor-director Kenney Withers and associate director Curtis Clark.

- Our families: Martin Bloom, and especially Paul Alexander Bloom; the patient White and Daiker households.

Our collaboration, conducted cross-country by phone, fax, computer disk, e-mail, and courier service, was the most fun in person, during lively discussions at professional meetings and on Miami University's thoroughly hospitable campus. We were friends when we started; that we remain friends is due, in part, to the human network, resilient and resourceful, feisty and good-humored, whose support provides much more than technology ever can.

Introduction: The New Geography of Composition

DONALD A. DAIKER

We are in a different place.
—Carol Petersen Hartzog

On her evaluation form for the Conference on Composition in the 21st Century: Crisis and Change, one participant wrote: "I leave this conference with more doubts about composition's future than I have felt in the last 10 years. The future, as the speakers at this conference have painted it, does not seem as hopeful as I once thought it would be."

I can well understand why participants might have left the conference in discomfort. After all, Stephen M. North began his invited address by announcing the "death of paradigm hope," the utter collapse of the research enterprise articulated by Richard Braddock, Richard Lloyd-Jones, and Lowell Schoer in the book that for many marks the beginning of modern composition studies, *Research in Written Composition*. According to North, there really is no future for research in composition as Braddock, Lloyd-Jones, and Schoer characterize it: research in composition is not destined to be transformed into a science. What also may be discomforting to some is North's obvious glee in the demise of scientific composition research.

Perhaps even more disturbing is Sharon Crowley's contention that the shift from product-oriented to process-oriented instruction in the 1970s and 1980s did not represent anything as significant as a paradigm shift because it failed to change the epistemological and rhetorical assumptions that undergird our teaching. Crowley argues that current-traditional rhetoric continues to hold sway largely because of its compatibility with academic notions of authority. While some see process pedagogy as revolutionary, for Crowley it is—in the most important sense—business as usual.

Robert J. Connors is not much more hopeful. In "The Abolition Debate in Composition: A Short History," Connors traces cycles of abolition and reform within the required first-year composition course. Ever since 1890, by which time most American universities had followed Harvard's lead in establishing a required freshman course in composition, national efforts to abolish the course have alternated with national efforts to improve it. In times of political, social, and economic calm, cries for the abolition of the requirement are not only heard but also taken seriously. But in times of upheaval, especially when new populations of students enter the university or when there is a perceived "literacy crisis," abolitionist sentiment is replaced by calls for reform. That this alternating pattern has repeated itself decade after decade throughout the 20th century might well suggest that composition in the 21st century will be characterized by the same turbid ebb and flow of conflicting energies.

But Connors, like Crowley and North, finds reason for optimism that some conferees may have missed. He believes that our knowledge of the past gives us "more of a chance today than ever before to rethink in a serious and thoroughgoing way the best methods for working on student literacy issues." Crowley, while denying a paradigm shift, nevertheless believes that "enormous changes" have occurred in our profession. She believes it is our professional identity that has changed, and it changed when we discovered a subject matter for composition studies: the writing processes of our students. So, as C. Jan Swearingen reports, some promising paths lead out of both the abolitionist-reformist cycle and the process/product epistemological abyss. For North, the death of scientific research in composition will have many salutary effects, such as expanding the range of our research, enabling us to write in a wider variety of forms, encouraging alternative publishing opportunities with alternative criteria for acceptance, and changing the way research is valued: in the absence of "truth" we will now value "plausibility and utility."

North predicts that "the landscape of college literacy instruction will change rapidly" in the years ahead, and it is this geographical metaphor that, for me, best captures the spirit and thrust of the conference and of the essays in this volume. At one small discussion session, Betty Youngkin of the University of Dayton suggested that we take our lead from Carlos Fuentes, the Mexican writer, who speaks of the "new geography of the novel." She proposed that we begin speaking of the "new geography of composition." To a large extent, this volume seeks to map and chart that new geography.

Perhaps the central fact of the new geography of composition is that the most exciting things are happening outside and away from the college classroom. Or to put it another way, the college classroom is in the process of expanding to include segments of the larger community, both on and off campus.

Nowhere is the expansion of the field of composition more imaginatively presented than in Shirley Brice Heath's "Work, Class, and Categories: Dilemmas of Identity." Heath cites examples from an inner-city youth organization, a collaborative venture between industry and community colleges, and a university benefits program to illustrate that people use reading and writing to satisfy their perceived personal needs, and many institutions of higher learning are adapting to meet those needs. Given the shifting uses of reading, writing, speaking, and listening, Heath argues that composition and other courses in the 21st century will have to be quite different than they are today: they will need to be tied much more closely to vocational, personal, and community-building goals. College courses and programs, including composition, will have to intersect with employment, physical and mental health, and civic and ethical concerns. Programs once labeled "extracurricular" or relegated to offices of continuing education will become increasingly central to 21st century institutions.

For James A. Berlin, it is the compression of time and space as a result of rapid travel and communication that has created a new geography for education in general and composition in particular. In "English Studies, Work, and Politics in the New Economy," Berlin points to the inadequacy of the old college curriculum in preparing workers for new and and more challenging responsibilities. He argues that within a democratic society, English studies, including both literature and composition, must have an expanded educational role. We must take the lead in preparing students not only as excellent communicators but also as quick and flexible learners and as cooperative collaborators. We must foster an openness to the differences of other cultures, at home and abroad, by expanding the literary canon and by taking cultural difference as the subject of writing courses.

Linda Flower explains in "Literate Action" how she expanded the horizons of her undergraduate seminar in composition and rhetoric by moving its site from the campus of Carnegie Mellon University to Pittsburgh's Community Literacy Center. The seminar was based on compelling invitations to literate action such as the following:

> How do you, a relatively privileged, white, middle-class, academically successful college student, go about entering into a meaningful conversation with an inner-city African American teenager who has not been nurtured by academic institutions, who is skeptical about the power of writing, and is probably uncertain about you? How do you open up the cross-cultural inquiry you both want into the reality of each other's lives?

Flower proposes that we broaden the schoolroom vision of literacy—with its emphasis on textuality and its concern with correctness, convention, and style—to include intellectual action and social involvement. By the same token, she suggests moving beyond the conflict between academic or textual literacy on the one hand and expressive literacy on the other to embrace what she calls "rhetorical literacy," which focuses on social practices and personal acts. Flower's pedagogy for the 21st century invites students to test theory through involvement in real situations, to apply participation- and observation-based reflection to their own writing, and thus to build working theories of their own.

Within this expanded geography of composition, teaching and teachers occupy an even more important location than in the past. In Flower's pedagogy of literate action, for example, literacy educators must in addition to their traditional expertise and talents be skilled negotiators at sites of social, political, and academic conflict. For Sylvia A. Holladay, teachers of composition—especially at community colleges—must be democratic educators, waging war in the name of egalitarianism against elitism, prejudice, and injustice: they must teach composition to empower students to liberate themselves. For Sandra Stotsky, editor of *Research in the Teaching of English*, it is teachers rather than other researchers who must become the primary audience of educational research. Stotsky asserts that educational research is justifiable only if made intelligible to teachers and only if made relevant to practice.

Anne Ruggles Gere urges teachers who are writing program administrators to reconceive their writing programs as research sites. Because of what Gere calls composition's "tradition of amateurism"—composition courses entrusted to inexperienced graduate students or untrained literature specialists, WPAs without expertise in composition and without tenure—writing programs have been perceived as merely administrative units without the power and prestige accorded to scholarship. Reconceived and restructured as research sites, writing programs support and conduct "action research," research that embodies transformative power because it combines investigation with attempts to effect change. At their research site, WPAs and composition instructors become reflective practitioners who simultaneously teach and thoughtfully examine teaching and learning.

It is not only teachers but also students who occupy a more prominent site in the new geography of composition. Action research, in contrast to the "scientific" research of the old paradigm, encourages teachers to see students as collaborators and partners rather than as subjects. Miriam T. Chaplin challenges teachers to try to understand how students think as well as what they know. Kurt Spellmeyer's question is even more challenging: are we helping "to strengthen our students' sense of agency and self-worth while . . . replenish[ing] the fragile historical sources of compassion and mutual assistance"?

In his powerful and persuasive essay "Disciplining Students: Whom Should Composition Teach and What Should They Know?," James F. Slevin signals the new importance accorded students by transposing the original conference title "Who Should Teach Composition and What Should They Know?" Slevin brilliantly argues for a redefinition of the valorized term "discipline": he proposes that we understand discipline not as the knowledge of a particular subject and not as professional conversation about that subject but rather as the act of inviting and enabling others to join our conversation. Thus, it is transmission and transformation—the *activity* of passing on knowledge and nurturing the powers that enable it—that constitute a discipline. Understood this way, the discipline includes everyone engaged in transmission and transformation, students as well as teachers:

> Our discipline is about the encounter of ordinary people with different ways of reading and writing; our discipline exists in acts of instruction and discussion, not as a bounded field of knowledge expanded by research. When *we* discuss expanding the canon, we usually discuss a process originating in encounters with new student populations and new ways of reading and thinking and persuading brought into our classrooms by our students. The research we do in part arises from that encounter; the encounter does not simply follow from and get defined by the research, as it might in other fields. Our discipline arises from the need and the desirability of promoting and enriching a dialogue already underway.

Students have also become more central to the field of assessment. As Brian Huot perceptively observes, both Peter Elbow and Edward M. White implicitly qualify the traditional definition of validity as the degree to which a test measures what it purports to measure; both Elbow and White assert that any test that has a negative effect on teaching or on students' learning can no longer be considered valid.

Significantly, virtually every speaker and respondent urges that boundaries be crossed, expanded, or broken down entirely. White insists that only if writing teachers bridge the gap between the education community and the assessment community can they influence the future of testing and evaluation. Elbow's avowedly "utopian view" of writing assessment in the 21st century dissolves many barriers, including what he calls "the stranglehold link" between helping unskilled writers and segregating them into basic writing courses. He argues that these students be given extra help without quarantining them from other writers. For Elbow, the decline of tracking as well as the growth of both mainstreaming and peer tutoring are positive signs that we are coming to recognize the advantages of heterogeneity.

By the same token, Carol Petersen Hartzog, Erika Lindemann, Sarah Warshauer Freedman, and Andrea A. Lunsford all endorse dissolving academic boundaries and enlarging the academic community. For Lunsford, composition studies now embraces issues of intellectual property and its relation to human subjectivity and information. Lunsford challenges traditional notions of "author" and "work" because they neglect "the largely collaborative and dispersed nature of most creative endeavors." An example from medical research is among her most telling of problems engendered by a narrow definition of intellectual property:

> Centuries of cultivation by Third World farmers produce wheat and rice strains with valuable quality—in the resistance to disease, say. . . . The biologists/agronomists and genetic engineers of a Western chemical company take samples of these strains, engineer them a little to add a greater resistance to fungus or a thinner husk. The chemical company's scientists fit the paradigm of authorship. The farmers are everything authors should not be—their contribution comes from a community rather than an individual, tradition rather than innovation, evolution rather than transformation. Guess who gets the intellectual property rights? Next year, the farmers may need a license to re-sow the grain from their own crops.

The converse of Lunsford's explosion of conventional boundaries is John Trimbur's "Writing Instruction and the Politics of Professionalization." Trimbur warns us not to remove the field of composition and rhetoric from the world of ordinary people lest we create a stratified class system and the more egalitarian Conference on College Composition and Communication becomes an elitist Modern Language Association. He asks that instead we celebrate a "unity of difference" and accept composition studies as a "mobile and decentered intellectual project."

In his provocative response, "Inventing the University Student," Kurt Spellmeyer argues that the sites of learning—the classroom, the college, the library—have become increasingly separated, both spatially and symbolically, from the tasks of everyday life. He further asserts that both modern mass education and the professions have taken from ordinary citizens the power to create knowledge and to effect change. Truth, knowledge, and even facts are now the property of the specialists, and it has become the role of the professions to close off avenues of inquiry to nonspecialists. Because teachers of composition-level reading and writing are positioned at the threshold between the specialists and the laity, Spellmeyer invites us to make our classrooms more democratic by recognizing nonspecialists—our students—as genuine collaborators in the making of knowledge.

For David Bartholomae, too, composition is bound to the ordinary. Like Spellmeyer, he laments the disciplinary specialization that has produced the compositionist who teaches courses in composition research, composition theory, and composition pedagogy—but not composition itself. He believes that composition must focus on the texts of "unauthorized" writers, that student writing is its starting point and central emphasis, and that the essential work of the composition course is, in the broadest sense, revision. To be "in" composition, according to Bartholomae, requires a fundamental commitment to exploring the critical problems of language, knowledge, and culture through the work of ordinary or novice writers. The field of composition asks us, above all, "to be willing to pay attention to common things."

Bartholomae acknowledges that he is increasingly drawn to the metaphor of space in discussing composition, including the space a writer needs to fill as well as the space a writer needs to occupy. Sarah Warshauer Freedman invites us to consider how we use space within our classrooms, while others—especially Shirley Brice Heath and Linda Flower—urge us to follow the example of Stephen Spender's "An Elementary Classroom in the Slum" and "Break, O break open" the windows, walls, and other boundaries that divide us from our students, our colleagues, and our communities.

Composition in the 21st Century: Crisis and Change consists of a series of invitations to move into new spaces.

Part 1 What Is Composition and Why Do We Teach It?

1 What Is Composition and (if you know what that is) Why Do We Teach It?

DAVID BARTHOLOMAE

A Disclaimer

I will not be presenting a theory paper here. Nor do I want to argue for a particular kind of program or set of practices. I have no desire to be comprehensive. I have, however, been "in" composition for some time; more recently, I
have done a good bit of traveling to evaluate departments and programs. I
would like to offer something like a report from the field and to write about
some places where composition has shown its face in interesting or surprising
ways. I need to be clear: the composition I am talking about is not a consensus
or a specific professional (or "disciplinary") agenda; it is not in the control of
composition professionals; it is not represented by the conflicts that take place
at meetings or in journals. It is, rather, a set of problems produced by a wider,
more diffuse set of practices and desires, usually brought into play by instances
of language change or variety (or by the possibility that writing might change
or be various). In a sense, the history of composition has been the record of
institutional and professional responses to challenged standards, challenges to
a standard of writing produced by writers who were said to be unprepared.
Composition marked the people and places charged to prepare those students
and/or to defend and rationalize their "unauthorized" writing.

I am interested in composition as it is represented in both its institutional
and more broadly cultural setting. When I refer to composition, I mean the
institutionally supported desire to organize and evaluate the writing of unauthorized writers, to control writing in practice, and to define it as an object
of professional scrutiny. Composition, then, refers to what goes on across the
grades and across academic departments. It refers to curricular agendas (stated
and unstated), to daily pedagogical encounters of all sorts and varieties, to the
marketing of careers and materials, to institutional arrangements and negotia-

tions, sponsored research, the importing and exporting of theory and method (where, for example, writing is organized or valued off campus through a vague memory of what English teachers thought and said)—an array of often competing desires for order and control, sometimes meeting out in the open, sometimes not; sometimes meeting on shared terrain and even terms, often not. Composition is not, then, the same thing as the combined desires and practices of the members of the Conference on College Composition and Communication on any given day. It is not summed up in the journals, and it has an off-and-on-again relationship with the "key figures" in the field.

Curriculum

Let me begin with a local example, an excerpt from a student essay that won first prize in the University of Pittsburgh's undergraduate writing competition. I want to use it to think for a minute about the sources and uses of writing, particularly writing in schooling, where schooling demands/enables the intersection of tradition and the individual talent and provides the point of negotiation between a cultural field and an unauthorized writer. As you read this piece, notice the traces of at least two sources: a student and an academic discipline.

> Initially, such early steel entrepreneurs like Andrew Carnegie and Henry Clay Frick used the technique of vertical integration to control all factors of steel production. This necessitated the construction of massive bureaucratic organizations to take advantage of economies of scale in the procurement of the required natural resources and the subsequent production of the steel itself. Each organization was a textbook bureaucracy, with its fixed areas of managerial jurisdiction and supervisory hierarchies consisting of numerous layers of management personnel. At the same time, in order to achieve strict control over these new, huge bureaucratic operations, management adopted techniques which minimized human variability and uncertainty in the production process. Most of these techniques were derived in large part from Frederick W. Taylor's philosophy of "scientific management." Taylor believed that standardization of work procedures and division of labor in mass-production industries would enable firms to achieve optimal levels of output and increased revenues. For example, on the question of organizing work Taylor expressed the following views: "All possible brainwork should be removed from the shop. . . . Each man [should receive] complete written instructions describing in detail the task which he is to accomplish. This task specifies not only what is to be done, but how it is to be done and the time allowed for doing it. . . . " Taylor's philosophy was quite influential in the early 1900s and, consequently, the steel industry

implemented many of his principles. The firms enacted bonus and wage incentive plans designed to appeal to the greed of the "economic man," defined jobs within very narrow boundaries, and instituted highly detailed shop rules and procedures which the floor supervisors were instructed to enforce through a system of rewards and punishments.

It is easy to see why this was an award-winning essay. For a moment, I would like to turn its success against itself and against those practices it represents. For a moment, I would like to think of this essay as too good, too finished, too seamless, too professional. This is not a hard critique to imagine—instead of talking about writing in the disciplines, we can talk about writing and discipline, as in discipline and punish, the reproduction of disciplinary boundaries and disciplinary authority. It has become easy to get this kind of critical purchase on the texts of contemporary life.

In this sense, you could think of the essay as providing the terms of its own critique: the writing is an example of the techniques of vertical integration as they are part of the university curriculum. The writing is Taylorized, organized to minimize human variability and uncertainty in the production process. "All possible brainwork should be removed from the shop." "Rules and procedures are enforced through a system of rewards and punishments."

I do not want to dismiss the accomplishment represented here, either on the part of the student, or his teacher, or the institution. But I do want to open up the essay to question. The best way to do that is for me to imagine other possible narratives, other histories that are being displaced here. Here, for example, is the story I might tell. The writer, since this is Pittsburgh, is the son of an unemployed steel worker—or the daughter of a middle manager in what is now USX, a multinational corporation no longer primarily making steel. They would also have other stories to tell about management and labor in the steel industry, and other ways of telling the story, but that story and those methods are silenced by the "official" disciplinary history, one couched in the rhetoric of "objectivity" or one that deals in terms of Great Men and Great Ideas.

There are dangers here. I am clearly idealizing the student who is silenced. Or the danger is that I will paint a portrait of too complete a victim (a writer for whom this essay is simply shameful, a loss, a writer who has no control, no sense of himself or herself as a writer). But with these dangers in mind, let me push ahead.

Because we have had students write family histories and neighborhood histories, and because we teach some of the published and unpublished narratives of life in the Monongahela Valley, I am aware of the ways in which a nexus of knowledge and desire that I will (problematically) name "the student" could be excluded from this narrative of "The Adversarial Relationship Between

Management and Labor in the American Steel Industry." I want to insist upon the ways in which, at least in this document, the historical narrative excludes this writer as a source and defines her position, rather, as someone who assembles materials according to a master plan.

But there are other narratives suppressed by this master narrative of industrial organization. I am increasingly drawn to the metaphor of space in talking about writing. Some sentences create spaces a writer has to fill; some sentences are careful to hide or overlay a writer's space, the space where the writer needs to come forward to write rather than recite the text that waits to be written. Here the key space for me comes both before and after the block quotation. There is the student who, having read Taylor, says, "Huh? What made this so powerful? so convincing? How was this read in the Monongahela Valley?" or the student who says, "This is terrible! How did they get away with that? Why would anyone have bought this argument?"

But there is also another silence represented by those spaces: it is, in Gerald Graff's terms, the silence the disciplines maintain in the face of students, like parents hiding their fights from the children. That is, one can imagine in those spaces all of the second thoughts that belong, not to the student working with the material, but to the discipline and its work—other readings of labor relations in the early periods of the steel industry; other ways of doing history, with numbers or with diaries and newspapers and letters, let us say, rather than with great men and great ideas. One could imagine a different text, one much less finished; and one could imagine that this countertext would imply a different form or goal to a writer's education: for an undergraduate to ask difficult questions about the "official" work of history, and to ask these questions from the inside, while doing it; for the official work of history to maintain space for second thoughts, including the musings or sidetracks of an amateur; for a writer to produce a text that is, in a sense, less finished and less professional. It is hard to imagine, for example, the institution sending this student back to this essay with any other motive than to perfect it—to make it even more perfectly what it already is. It is rare to find an individual, either inside or outside an English department, teaching protocols for revision whose goal is to call the discourse into question, to undo it in some fundamental way. The problem here is not departmental or disciplinary. It is derived from a larger conception of the academy and intellectual labor, particularly as it involves students. As a faculty, we do not have a way of saying to a student, "Make that essay a little worse, not quite so finished, a little more fragmented and confused," and to say this in the name of learning. The institution is designed to produce and reward mastery, not to call it into question.

And what about composition professionals—those of us "in" composition? I would like to say that the turn toward criticism and critical theory was leading to work in this direction, but I do not think that is the case. The essays on Mikhail Bahktin or Hélène Cixous in our journals make only the faintest connection to the history paper (even the "composition" paper). This is partly an intellectual problem—what *is* the connection? And it is partly the legacy of the liberal tradition in composition. The structures of support produced in the name of composition (tutorials, the composing process, journals, Writing Across the Curriculum) allow us to identify with the student as an individual without taking notice of or responsibility for the forms of knowledge being produced through their writing.

Here is a brief second example. I include it because it is more familiar to English teachers. This, too, was a prize-winning essay in a university writing contest. The excerpt comes from a paper on Dylan Thomas's poem "Fern Hill":

Through the structure of the last stanza, Thomas reveals that there is no peaceful sleep for the narrator. The dream parallels the nightmare of reality. Time has indisputably flown with the fields. The choice of the verb "wake" completes the tragic mood. Its harsh, clipped sound recalls other meanings: "to hold a funeral," or "to keep a vigil over." The masterful duality in the sleep sequences works toward one goal: to appeal to the basic human fear of death and loss. It is horrifically successful. The contrast between the peaceful sleep of the child and the uneasy half-asleep older man is extremely saddening.

This was the unanimous first choice by every judge except the one from the English department, for whom the piece was the worst example of a student reproducing a "masterful" reading (that is, reproducing a reading whose skill and finish mocked the discipline and its values). It is too good and finesses key questions: what, you want to say to the writer, allows you to believe that you can speak for all readers of the poem? Or—"sad and horrific," "the nightmare of reality"—come on, it is just a poem. The poem may appeal to these emotions, but it is another thing to say that the poem creates them. Or—in whose interests is this story of youth and age and death? Why do we tell it over and over again?

It is not hard for us to think about how to get a critical purchase on this text. But, imagine what it would take to explain your position to your colleague in chemistry when he says that this sounds just like an English paper is supposed to sound, "you know—flowery." How would you explain to your colleague that he is exactly right and that is exactly why the paper, even if it marks some kind of achievement, does not deserve a ribbon?

But this is not a one-sided dilemma. In the story I am telling, the problem with the English paper was replicated with papers from other disciplines. The rest of us loved the lab report the chemistry professor said was just mechanical, uninspired. The rest of us loved the case study of the underground economy of a Mexican village that the sociologist said was mostly cliché and suffering from the worst excesses of ethnography.

Our inability to talk with each other about writing, about the student text and what it represents —as that writing reflects on the fundamental problems of professional writing, writing that negotiates the disciplines, their limits and possibilities—our inability to have that kind of discussion leads us (or our institutions) to give awards to papers we do not believe in and to turn away from the papers we do, papers most often clumsy and awkward but, as we say to each other, ambitious, interesting, a sign of a student for whom something is happening. In spite of our positions as critics, as teachers we are trapped within a discourse of error that makes it impossible to praise the student paper that is disordered and disorderly.

The chemistry professor and the English professor do not have these conversations because they are not prepared to and because they want to respect disciplinary boundaries and because they want to keep certain secrets secret. Their silence is a version of the silence in composition, where we are extraordinarily hesitant to argue about what writing is good and what is bad, what is worth doing and what is not; where we can talk for hours about empowering writers without raising the fundamental questions of power as they are represented in discourse. We move the furniture in the classroom, collaborate on electronic networks, take turns being the boss, but we do not change writing. It is still the same old routine.

But I want to focus attention on the students' writing, the Taylor essay and the Dylan Thomas essay, and to think about what achievement they represent. Here, as a way of working toward that discussion, is Paul Bové on Stephen Toulmin, one of the key figures in composition's "new" rhetoric:

> We might say that Toulmin's expansion of reason is one of the latest forms of error, that always found among traditional intellectuals as they tell stories about and to themselves and their masters. . . . Toulmin's own thinking leads us nowhere near these questions, for as a traditional intellectual there is no reflective origin to be found in his work. He makes no effort to understand his own position within the regime of truth, that is to say, the space within which he practices is taken for granted, assumed to have natural status within the discourses of truth and judgment. The result, in part, is that his work goes on untroubled by any implications it might have within the apparatus of power/knowledge, especially as this affects those less empowered by this very apparatus. In effect, I take Toulmin to exemplify in-

tellectual irresponsibility, a disregard for extension of the regime of truth across society and national borders, and a carelessness toward interrogating one's own intellectual function within such an apparatus. ("Rationality," 66)

Now for a moment, I would like to imagine Bové providing the terms for a practical criticism. I would like to imagine how an instructor might be prepared to write at the end of the student's essay something along these lines: "Next time, don't be so careless about interrogating your intellectual function within the regime of truth." How would one phrase this so that it could be read? What sort of context would make the ensuing work both possible and valued? If composition is in any way going to be a critical practice, instructors will need to be prepared to imagine such forms of commentary.

I want to force this equation of Toulmin and the two student writers because I think it is not a comparison any member of the academy is prepared to make. I want you to imagine that one important way of saying "don't be careless" to student writers is as that term is used by Bové. I want you to imagine that the same critique can (and should) be applied to the student writer. It is too convenient to say that students, because they are students, do not share in the general problems of writing (like writing history or writing literary criticism, like the problem of the writer's relationship to the discourse that enables his or her writing). It enables us to produce thousands of writers (and professors) who think that writing is trivial unless it comes prevalued through channels of publication. The version of writing we sell shrinks from the comparison of Stephen Toulmin and a freshman; it gathers its authority from the representation that writing problems are unique to beginners, to students.

I want to use Bové as a way of capturing a simple word, "carelessness," and deploying it in the critique of writing untroubled by its relationship to "tradition" and to discursive habits and their status in the distribution of knowledge/power in the institution. That is, we can imagine that the goal of writing instruction might be to teach an act of criticism that would enable a writer to interrogate his or her own text in relationship to the problems of writing and the problems of disciplinary knowledge. (This is not, needless to say, the same thing as promoting Writing Across the Curriculum.)

Let us think for a moment in utopian terms about the future of student writing. Composition—or, those professionals willing to work on student writing—has a particularly valuable (or, perhaps "novel" or "unexploited") way of imagining criticism as something to be learned in practice, perhaps learned at the point of practice. This is different from studying the work of critics or theorists. Composition—or, the space within English studies where student writing is a central concern—is positioned to promote practical criticism because of its historic concern for the space on the page and what it might mean to do work there and not somewhere else.

Criticism

So, since this is a book about the next century, what is the future for this kind of work? How might we imagine the role of composition in the 21st century?

Here is Bové again, this time at the end of his book *Intellectuals in Power: A Genealogy of Critical Humanism*:

> Critical scholarship should seize the power function of "truth" and sophistically enlist it for political work intended not only to reveal the dark side of humanism's oppression but also to knock the underpinnings from humanism and the dominant regimes it supports. Criticism must be negative, and its negation should be of two sorts: invested with knowledge and the skills to produce more, it should destroy the local discursive and institutional formations of the "regime of truth," but this local negation will be most effective when aimed at necessary conditions for the extension of that regime, at those nodal points upon which humanism rests its own power and banks its own reserves. But this "negation" must have a "positive" content; it must carry out its destruction with newly produced knowledge directed not only against the centers of the anthropological attitude but, with an eye to its utility, to others in one's own locale and elsewhere. (309–19)

The project of critical scholarship, as it is defined here, could be said to be opposed to composition. That is, if we take composition to stand for the most common representation of writing in the required composition course, where the writer is figured as an individual agent making decisions governed by genre and convention and by a desire to be correct, then the composition course could be seen as one of those nodal points "upon which humanism rests its own power and banks its own reserves."

The "negation" of composition, or what is labeled composition, goes on daily in the workings of English departments—in personnel decisions, in the ebb and flow of goodwill and status that is part of a department's everyday life. This is news to no one, although in the last decade the terms of the negation have changed as the source of the critique has passed across areas in the department, roughly from literature to theory. Given the potentially shared institutional histories and ideological programs, the failure of an alliance between "theory" and "composition" is, for some at least, disappointing. It is possible, in other words, to see both as similar attempts to reimagine what it means to "do" English. Their presence as areas of professional definition in

English was initially defined in opposition to the traditional use and status of literature and the forms of reading and writing promoted by a "literature" faculty. Both were renegotiating (with other new areas in English studies) the representation of high and low, the understanding of language as a problem in the undergraduate curriculum, the fragility of the traditional figure of the "author," and "official" accounts of the production and reproduction of knowledge, including disciplinary knowledge.

Composition has almost been nonexistent, however, in recent critiques and histories of English studies. When composition is figured into these accounts, it is figured negatively, said to represent a naive understanding of the problematics of language (see for example J. Miller), and to actively promote a purely functional literacy in service of or sponsored by late or postindustrial capitalism (as in Ohmann). The most recent version of this account is written into the introduction to Wlad Godzich's *Culture of Literacy*. According to Godzich, the 1980s featured both the spread of theory and, with Reaganomics and the recession, a push toward the "new vocationalism"—"a utilitarian conception of the university which foreshadowed its current transformation into a production site for the new force of production in a postindustrial society: knowledge" (1). These phenomena unfolded, according to Godzich, "in curious ignorance of each other, not last because they occupied different habitats: theory, the elite research institutions which continued to recruit students from milieux for the most part unaffected by the new illiteracy; composition, the rest, including the large land-grant universities" (1–2). Writing programs established their autonomy by promoting "a new differentiated culture in which the student is trained to use language from the reception and conveyance of information in only one sphere of human activity: that of his or her future field of employment" (5).

Godzich argues that composition profited when university resources were reallocated in the 1980s, getting funds and faculty lines at the expense of literature and theory. It is true, I think, that over the last 20 years federal and local monies have supported composition as an area of research and curriculum development and that composition "faculties" (although broadly defined to include nontenure-stream instructors) have increased.

It is useful, however, to also see this phenomenon as a coherent expression of *English's* desires; it is not simply the clever or lucky advancement of one subgroup at the expense of another. While I cannot cite figures and it would be unethical to name names, I have seen records of hiring patterns in departments that I think are representative. What these patterns show is that the effect, and in some ways the intent, of growth in English departments has been to divert money from tenure-stream faculty lines in order to provide increased funding for graduate study through the creation of a larger pool of teaching and research assistants. The growth in composition has been accompanied by a growth in the size of graduate programs, programs of literature and theory and cultural studies. It is not unusual to find a department, at least in large universities, where the faculty teaches only majors and graduate students. English, then, has spent its money on the graduate rather than the undergraduate curriculum, providing specialized courses for the faculty to teach and turning introductory courses and general education over to teaching assistants and fellows. I was recently on a campus where both a dean and a department chair acknowledge this as part of the ways decisions were made to allocate salary monies. The history department had spent its money on assistant professors, the English department on TAs and, to a lesser degree, part-timers. Specialization within the field and the values determining appropriate work for the professoriat have produced "composition" as it is realized in the formation of careers and the organization of resources in relation to the lower-division courses. The creation of the slot for the "critical theorist" and the slot for the "composition specialist" has both produced a curriculum that relies on part-timers and graduate students in the writing courses. The movement toward specialization has also determined who gets to use and practice criticism in the academy.

While I would argue with some other details in Godzich's account (composition, at least as it is represented by what goes on at professional meetings, was preoccupied with theory in the 1980s, not ignorant of it), what I have wanted to suggest is the importance of distinguishing between the various material practices, institutional pressures, habits, and conventions that govern writing and schooling. Godzich argues that in the 1980s, programs and careers were made in the name of what could be called the "new vocationalism." It is important to note, however, that the interests being served by the reallocation of resources in the 1980s included those that could be lumped under the name "critical theory," by "freeing" faculty from basic instruction and providing graduate students to take the seminars taught instead. It is misleading to imagine that the conflict was between critical theory and composition (as it was once misleading to argue that it was between literature and composition). The lines of interest separated those committed to basic instruction (across programs of composition, literature, and cultural studies) from those interested in "advanced" work. While it is true that some of those courses in basic instruction were promoting only instrumental uses of language, it is not a useful way of generalizing composition. (At least it is not useful if one wants to imagine the potential for English departments' involvement with introductory and general education. It is, of course, possible to argue that English departments should only serve to produce English majors and/or Ph.D.'s.) An argument like Godzich's forces the profession to overlook courses, programs, and projects developed in opposition to the institutional and cultural pressures to promote a functional literacy.

Composition as Reaganism or last-gasp humanism is a convenient reading of the 1980s. Without attention to the "local," it can be said to have both historical and empirical truth. Composition, however, has radically divergent relations to the "regime of truth" (and, I would say, has had such divergence since it became a school subject in the 19th century). My desire, however, is not to make a case for composition as "critical scholarship." As I understand what composition is, it could not be composition and be identical with this project. Composition—that is, the term I want to preserve to enable a certain kind of thinking about writing, local and institutional—is concerned with how and why one might work with the space on the page, and, in this sense, it is not the same thing as Theory. It is, rather, a way of committing professional time and energy to the revision of the Taylor essay—both as it is the product of institutional goals and practices (composition, then, is a commitment to study, critique, and change writing in the schools) and as the product of a particular writing at a particular point in time (composition, then, is a commitment to intervene in and direct the practice of individual writers). Composition would take its work to be revision; the form of composition I am willing to teach would direct the revision of the essay as an exercise in criticism (even, I think I would say, cultural criticism—that is, I would want students not only to question the force of the text but also the way the text positions them in relationship to a history of writing).

This binds composition to the ordinary in ways that are professionally difficult. It takes as its subject the writing of the Taylor essay rather than Toulmin, and this buys less in the academic marketplace. And it ends with revisions that are small, local, and difficult to value. It assumes the direct intervention in specific projects where (from a certain angle of vision) the gains are small. If it teaches criticism, it is practical criticism (or criticism-in-practice). Composition produces hundreds of thousands of writers every year; if there is composition in the 21st century, by the midcentury it will have produced millions. In this sense, the stakes are high. The worst that could happen, to my mind, is that English would give up its stake in a direct intervention with the production of writing.

Career

Composition currently serves as a term that justifies and produces certain career paths in English. This is commonplace; people talk regularly about the number of composition jobs on the job list. I am not sure this is simply a matter of a growing demand for writing teachers. It is (or it might also be said to be) a way the profession is choosing to allocate its resources—maintaining the viability (and exclusivity) of some careers by choosing to cluster a certain set of curricular responsibilities under the name "composition" (and, in composition, producing the category of the "specialists" that, in turn, justifies the use of part-time or adjunct teachers to do the daily work of instruction).

There was a time, for example, when it was possible to make the argument that everyone in English should teach composition, that it was part of everyone's mission and preparation. Composition—that is, the set of career interests represented by the term—assisted the division of the labor pool by arguing that not everyone could teach composition, not everyone was prepared, that it required a certain kind of training and orientation. I have never been convinced by this argument (having never been trained in composition, at least as that training is now defined in graduate programs across the country). I see composition as a professional commitment to do a certain kind of work with a certain set of materials with a general commitment to the values and problems of English. (And, therefore, I see composition courses properly housed in an English department.) The route "into" composition, then, was once like the route into film studies or women's studies, and like these, composition has become professionalized, so that the routes of entry have become more predictable, "disciplinary," and formalized.

It seems clear to me that composition professionals continue to provide rationale for the argument that establishes their identity and necessity in the English department by promoting the disciplinary status of the field. I find it hard to support or endorse this, even as I want to support the common enterprise. I refuse to encourage graduate students to define a professional identity solely through CCCC and the composition journals. It is, however, getting harder and harder for me to maintain this position, not because of a changed sense of what it means to be professionally committed to composition, but because of the battering people are taking when they try to work outside of disciplinary boundaries that organize the field of English.

The most surprising thing I have noticed as I travel and monitor the development of composition as an area of professional identification is the consistency, virulence, and direction of the attack on composition and those in it. Composition has never been a route to status in the profession. The surprising thing is the degree to which the programs most visibly under attack are those distinguished by the seriousness of their commitment to research and theory. (The criticism of programs at Texas, Syracuse, Carnegie-Mellon, and Pittsburgh is public knowledge.)

These programs have differing ideological commitments, and the attacks have come from both the right and the left. What is most striking is that it is the more thoughtfully organized and highly funded programs (in terms of commitment to faculty) that are being called into question, and this by English, not from the outside. It is not, in other words, a case of the faculty in political science questioning why the composition program is not teaching students how to write term papers. It is faculty in English attacking composition programs on ideological grounds. In fact, a visible and critically oriented program is more likely to be criticized than one whose approach to writing is fairly old-fashioned (teaching topic sentences as the key to writing) or simply poorly run. That is, it is not inconsistent to find "careless" programs housed in high-powered, critically aware English departments. Or, it is not uncommon to find English departments more troubled by an ambitious composition program than a mediocre one.

Now, there are many ways to explain this. When programs make themselves visible and invite ideological critique, they get what they ask for. There are also material bases to the conflict, as I have argued above. It could be said that what is at stake are the hearts and minds and bodies of graduate students. This, too, is what composition is; it is the term used to justify or to front the widespread support of graduate study in English. It is a rare English department that hires, promotes, or rewards graduate teaching assistants with an eye to their participation in the undergraduate curriculum. The more faculty involved with a composition program, the greater the potential conflict over the understanding and distribution of support for graduate study. Composition asks for a commitment of time (the time spent teaching and preparing to teach) that can easily seem to graduate students and graduate faculty as time that has nothing to do with their professional goals or professional preparation.

If I speak, now, as the traveler who has visited and evaluated departments and programs, the second most surprising thing I have noticed in the profession is the production of a kind of career I once could never have imagined. And that is the career of the composition specialist who never teaches composition. I may date myself by my surprise at this, but it seems to me to be increasingly common to find a specialist whose professional identity keeps him or her from the scene of instruction that defines his or her specialty. Composition has produced and justified a career that has everything to do with status and identity in English and little to do with the organization, management, and evaluation of student writing, except perhaps as an administrative problem.

These careers are not inevitable. I am going to use my career as an example (I will be either the chump or the hero of this story), but I have in fact taken my cue from others and could point to similar cases at a variety of institutions. There are senior faculty "in" composition who regularly teach the introductory composition course, and by regularly I mean every term. To the degree to which I am speaking for myself, I want to make it clear what I want this to stand for. I teach the course every year, often every semester. This is not a sacrifice. It is not a statement about solidarity with the masses (either the TAs or the students). It is not a commitment to teaching (as opposed to research). It is, rather, a fundamental commitment to a certain kind of intellectual project—one that requires me to think out critical problems of language, knowledge, and culture through the work of "ordinary" or "novice" or student writers. It is a way of working on the "popular" in relation to academic or high culture.

Courses

Here, at the end of this paper, I find myself trying to articulate a position for composition between critical negation and carelessness. Or, to put it another way, I want to try to imagine a way for composition to name a critical project, one that is local, one whose effects will be necessarily limited, but one, still, of significant consequence. I think of the question this way—what does it mean to accept student writing as a starting point, as the primary text for a course of instruction, and to work with it carefully, aware of its and the course's role in a larger cultural project?

Let me think this through by means of a final example, a student paper:

A few summers ago, I accompanied my church youth group on a mission trip to St. Croix, in the Virgin Islands. We were to clean up damage from a hurricane which passed through the summer before. To tell you the truth, I really wasn't looking forward to working, but rather I was excited to visit the Virgin Islands. But, by the end of my trip, I would not have traded my experience for anything in the world.

Our group flew from Philadelphia to Puerto Rico, and then to St. Croix. After arriving from a long plane trip we were driven to the place which for the next couple of weeks we would call "home." We stayed on an old plantation which was located in the lower class part of St. Croix. The plantation was surrounded by a 15 foot high stone wall, but on the other side of the wall were the slums. As we entered the driveway leading to the plantation, adults as well as children lined up. They all watched carefully, probably trying to figure out why we were on their island.

On the first day of our journey, we started by picking up trash and tree limbs which had fallen to the ground from the hurricane the year before. It was so incredible how much damage was done and how it appeared that the hurricane had just passed. This task took several days to accomplish, even in a small area. There were just so many things covering the ground it was just unbelievable.

From day to day, we came in contact with lots of people who had lived on the island for many years. Quickly, we learned how many of the islanders felt about people from the "States." Once, while we were working, a group of islanders approached us and inquired why we were there. They asked why we were intruding on their land when we had a land of our own which was better. It was almost as if they were afraid that we were trying to take their island from them. I could tell by their voice of inquiry that they felt threatened. Even after we tried to explain that we were trying to help them in a time of need, they still wanted to know what we expected in return. At this point in time, I felt shut out. They would not except that the only reason that we were there was to help them.

Over the weeks we accomplished several tasks. These tasks included digging up five foot in diameter tree stumps, rebuilding roofs of homes which were blown off, picking up trash, and helping run a coffee shop for the homeless and less fortunate. All of these tasks were time consuming and entailed much work. As we went to the different locations, I found the chance to talk to a lot of the islanders. They seemed very anxious to know my reasons for helping them. I explained that all my work was volunteer and that I liked to help others. Slowly they started to except the fact that I, as well as the others, just wanted to befriend them. I witnessed their feelings starting to change toward us and soon they appreciated the work we had done.

As our time of service came to an end, I looked back on the huge difference which we had made on the island. After these several weeks, the islanders came to realize that we did not expect anything in return for our work, except their friendship. In the beginning, this concept was hard for them to understand, but as they watched the changes occur, they learned to appreciate our help. In fact, by the end, the many people which at one time had questioned our existence were the ones to tell us how sad they were to see us leave. They graciously thanked us over and over for our help. Their appreciation was unbelievable. They just constantly asked how they could pay us back. They praised the work which we had done and expressed their undying gratitude.

This change in our position in such a short amount of time was incredible. We went from being the unacceptable in their community to the heros of the community. We were once looked down and frowned upon, but after working hard to prove our position we were more than accepted. Our efforts proved to change our position in that particular society and we became well respected guests on the island. (unedited student paper)

In the spirit of the Conference on Composition in the 21st Century, I want to end by provoking discussion, so let me end quickly and without taking responsibility for conclusions. I recently taught an introductory composition course where students wrote travel narratives, at least for starters, and read Mary Louise Pratt's *Imperial Eyes*. I chose Pratt's book because I thought it a good introduction to the problems of writing as they preoccupy the professoriat, and I chose it because it was difficult. Part of the point of the course was to teach students how and why they might work with difficult texts. The course was divided into three sections. The first dealt with revision, the second with a writer's use of Pratt's book, the third with sentences (revision exercises asking students to translate their sentences into and out of a style that might loosely be called "Pratt-like," somewhat in imitation of the exercises in Joseph Williams's *Style: Ten Lessons in Clarity and Grace*).

I used Pratt in the course as an example of a writer working on a project similar to the students' (learning how to articulate a critical reading of travel narratives) but also to help make the point that writers need to understand the degree to which their writing is not their own. In this case, students were invited to see their writing as part of a tradition that began with travel narratives of the 18th and 19th century and that implicated them in the same general cultural project, here taking possession of worlds not their own. This is part of what a writer needs to know in order to revise. Or, to put it another way, this historical perspective is as important for composition, it seems to me, as seeing today's textbooks or classroom rhetorics in relation to their 18th- and 19th-century counterparts. I say this not to argue against the current work on composition's history. I do, however, want to argue that the profession has not yet found a way to make composition a name for a critical/historical study of student writing.

I want you to imagine, then, a course that takes the St. Croix essay as its central text. The question for the writing teacher, then, is "What next?" As I am imagining composition, the job of the teacher is to prepare students to work on that text. It is not, as it might be in other courses, to set it aside. I want to make this point because I have seen many courses, often offered as "cultural studies" composition courses, that provide a knowledge of the problems of writing only by erasing student writing. In such courses, for example, students would learn to produce arguments about American imperialism or arguments against the "missionary" narrative; they would perhaps summarize Pratt's argument. The central work of the course would not, however, be work on the very discourse within which the students, as writers, operate. They would not revise the essay because the essay would be seen as irredeemably corrupt or trivial. And, of course, the results of that revision would be up for grabs—the final product may be more of the missionary narrative, not less. In fact, I can say from experience that students who learn how to produce the critique of the narrativizing of the other will, when they write a narrative, easily produce the very discourse they have learned to critique. Students learn to be critical of their writing (to understand how and where they are implicated in questionable ways of speaking) long before they learn to change it. (This is demonstrated, I think, in William E. Coles's *The Plural I*.)

The course put the St. Croix narrative (with some others also written by students) as primary texts. (The St. Croix narrative can stand for all of the narratives the students wrote. It is the narrative that ordinarily writers cannot *not* write.) The problem for the course was how to imagine its revision, particularly if revision was to be made possible by and to enact a critical reading of the text, and where that critical reading was not merely a critique of the formal properties of the text—where a writer would have to ask about and think about, say, the history of North American relations with St. Croix. Through this discussion, students were to imagine the revision of their own opening essays.

In a strange displacement, revision is not usually taught as criticism. In fact, as a result of the "writing process movement," criticism was removed from the writing course, where it was seen as counterproductive (a "barrier" to writing) and characterized in the figure of the maniacal English teacher with the red pencil. There was, then, a "correction" of writing that was deliberately blind to questions of value. The process movement, for example, produced forms of evaluation, like holistic scoring, where the evaluative judgment was comparative (one could not appeal to considerations outside the boundaries of what most writers would produce) and where readers were taught *not* to read closely.

Within the terms of the process movement, the primary goal was the efficient production of text. Students learned to produce writing; questions of value seldom, if ever, came up, at least as value is imagined as social value. And within this field of vision, revision was primarily addition and subtraction—adding vivid details, for example, and taking out redundancies. The result (or the goal) was to perfect and, by extension, preserve the discourse. Within these protocols for revision, the missionary narrative may become more finished, but it will remain the missionary narrative. Details can be added, but they will have the status of the details in the essay (as local color). It would be inappropriate to ask questions of the discourse as a discourse: What is its history? Whose interests are served? What does the scene of the plantation mean? What does it mean in terms of the history of St. Croix? What does it mean that it is offered as background and color? Why don't the people of St. Croix get to speak? How might one *not* write a missionary narrative and yet still tell the story of a missionary trip to St. Croix? The writing process curriculum, at least as I have characterized it here, produces good writing without asking questions about "the good."

A course in practical criticism (and I can only begin to suggest its difference) would teach students to question the text by reworking it, perhaps attending to detail in one week, perhaps breaking or experimenting with the narrative structure the next, perhaps writing alternative openings or endings, perhaps writing alternative scenes of confrontation, perhaps adding text that does not fit (a report on the history of St. Croix or a report on the documents preparing students for the trip), perhaps adding different voice or points of view, perhaps writing several versions of who the writer or the St. Croixians might be said to be. In every case, the product would be an essay that was, in a certain sense, less skillful or less finished or less masterful than the original. The key point for me is that a course in practical criticism must return students to their writing. In the context of my example, it requires the ability to understand both Pratt's argument and her way of reading; it assumes (and exercises) the ability to produce a critical reading of the St. Croix essay; but its final work, for each student, is multiple revisions of the travel narratives they have begun.

I have tried to place composition in the context of the curriculum, of debates about the place of criticism in the academy, of careerism, and of a course, one where freshman writers could be thought of as continuous with European travel writers of the 18th century. I want to at least suggest the possibilities for a practical criticism (as opposed to a critical scholarship), one that investigates the problems of writing at the point of production and that investigates representations of writing as a mode of learning. That is what I think composition is or might properly be. It is, I believe, a good field to work in, but you have to be willing to pay attention to common things.

$\mathscr{2}$ Order out of Chaos: Voices from the Community College

SYLVIA A. HOLLADAY

In attempting to answer the questions "What is composition" and "Why do we teach it?" I reviewed rhetorical theory and empirical research; I studied psychology, philosophy, and critical theory. All the voices in my head, my collaborators in anything I write—the theorists, researchers, textbook authors I have read and taught from; the rhetoricians, experts, and practitioners I have heard speak; my teachers and professors; my colleagues; my students—were competing to be heard.

I isolated some familiar answers. To some, composition is self-expression, inner-directed, and we teach it to help students discover themselves. To others, composition is communication, outer-directed, and we teach it to enable writers to influence others. The current rhetorical view is that composing is manipulating a text to achieve a specific purpose for a particular audience, and we teach it to give students power and control of their language and their lives.

Composition is all of these, and we teach it for all of these reasons. In *Textual Power*, Robert Scholes speaks for many of us when he says,

> What students need from us—and this is true of students in our great universities, our small colleges, and our urban and community colleges—what they need from us now is the kind of knowledge and skill that will enable them to make sense of their worlds, to determine their own interests, both individual and collective, to see through the manipulations of all sorts of texts to all sorts of media, and to express their own views in some appropriate manner. (55–6)

I agree with these positions but from the somewhat different perspective of a community college instructor. Students in community colleges desperately need power and control of their language and their lives. The questions for those of us who teach in community colleges and open-door universities are not only "What is composition and why do we teach it?" but also "What is composition in these colleges and why do we teach it here?"

In open-door colleges, we teach composition because we are idealists. Our answer is that we teach composition not only to empower students but also to enable students to use their newly earned knowledge and power to liberate themselves, to free themselves. We cannot do it for them. Most of our students are nontraditional and at-risk and are locked in chaotic, crisis-driven lives. Usually they feel impotent when they enter the two-year college; our goal is not to give them power but to help them develop the ability to think and to write that will give them sufficient self-esteem, confidence, and authority to free themselves, to change their lives. Through making informed choices in language and composing, students gain power to control their lives and to make their lives more pleasant and their individual worlds more humane.

To understand my view, you need to know something about the college where I teach. St. Petersburg Junior College was founded in 1927, 40 years before most community colleges were established. Its purposes then and now are to meet the needs of a growing state population and to provide the opportunity for local access to higher education for all students who choose to enter. Students can live at home, pay low tuition, work full-time or part-time (as 80 percent do), and pursue a quality postsecondary education.

At SPJC we now have 22,000 students, 40 percent male, 60 percent female, taking credit courses on eight campuses throughout the county. Although their average age is 28, 53 percent are under 25, 35 percent are between 25 and 40, and 12 percent are over 40. Eighty-eight percent are white; 6 percent are African American; and the rest are Hispanic, Asian, Native American, and other. Seventy percent are part-time, taking an average of only eight hours per semester. Fifty-five percent are underprepared in writing, 45 percent in reading.

Behind these statistics are human beings. Miriam, a 44-year-old woman who was divorced after 25 years of marriage, has never worked outside the home. She and her children are adjusting to a lower standard of living because she receives inadequate alimony. As she is learning how to do a research paper, she is also learning how to build a bookcase for her 12-year-old daughter because they cannot afford to buy one. Her goal is twofold: to get a job to provide a better life for her children and to become a role model of whom they can be proud.

Michael is a single parent who recently missed several classes because he was in court fighting for custody of his eight-year-old son. His ex-wife's boyfriend was sexually abusing the child. When he won the court case, he requested a change in his schedule so that he could spend more time with his son.

Binh has lost his Vietnamese homeland, after spending two years in refugee camps. He is struggling to become educated in a different language and a different culture. He is thankful that Florida provides a public community college where he can study English as a second language and learn math.

Peter, brain-damaged at birth, can never achieve what his classmates will but works diligently to do what he is capable of so that he can support himself when his mother dies. Latoya, an alcoholic, spent three years in prison for writing bad checks; now she and her daughter live in a halfway house where she receives support and counseling. Luci, a 49-year-old ex-drug addict, did not know until last year when she entered SPJC that she has specific learning disabilities. All her life, drifting from one abusive relationship to another, she thought she just could not learn. Mark, in Desert Storm at 19, cannot relate easily to students or teachers and suffers severe bouts of depression. He escapes by getting high on drugs. Darby, home-schooled because of illness, earned a GED, which some universities do not recognize. Shy and lacking self-confidence, he entered SPJC with a love of reading and writing, one of the few freshmen I know who has read *Jude the Obscure*. After one year, he is now a member of the Student Government Association and one of the best students in our honors program. He intends to become a college English instructor.

For each of these two-year college students, life is a daily struggle—personal, financial, emotional, academic—that few of us can imagine. As I work with them daily, I wonder how they can concentrate enough to learn anything. How petty commas and thesis statements must seem to them!

Because of open admissions at SPJC, we have a history of curricular innovation. If we admit a student, we believe it is our responsibility to provide the appropriate courses and instructional techniques. In our constant search for better methods to help all students succeed in expressing themselves more effectively, we continually review and revise our courses and our methods of assessment.

Our curriculum and instruction have been shaped, not by past practices or theoretical models, but by the students' needs. Before the returning student gained nationwide attention, we had developed techniques for working effectively with adult students. Before K. Patricia Cross wrote about the needs of the nontraditional student, we were using conferences, self-pacing, student tutors, writing labs, and collaborative learning to help underprepared students write more effectively. Before rhetoricians advocated the process approach, we were out of necessity working individually with students on the parts of the process, intervening at strategic points so that they could experience success instead of more failure. Before diversity was politically correct, our student body was multicultural and our teaching materials were noncanonical. Before the new critical and cultural theories were popular, we were implementing their principles in order to show respect for and to reach the diverse students in our composition classes.

What do we do specifically to enable our at-risk students to liberate themselves? I will let my colleagues at St. Petersburg Junior College speak for me and the students. They are a group of realistic idealists dedicated to working with our special student population. We care, we teach, we learn, we enjoy what we do, and we benefit as much as our students do.

Joanne Rodriguez, a colleague and friend at SPJC, makes the point that we care:

> I gave my first F for a research paper last week. Usually we can manage to squeeze a D with extra help in my office. I thought it would bother [the student], but he took it in stride. It bothered me more. I think this is the basis of my teaching—I care. The success of my students is very important to me. I think a teacher has to be dedicated and has to have a real love of the students and the material being taught.

Because we care, we share and we love, points out Evelyn Finklea:

> Robert Fulghum says in *All I Really Need to Know I Learned in Kindergarten*, "Share everything." Share everything! That is my teaching credo. I see my classroom as a unique opportunity for individual and collaborative sharing. I want my students to be successful, not only in my class, but beyond my class. I want them to remember my writing class. I want them to remember that I have a love of words, of language, of thought, and most importantly a love of students.

Richard LaManna indicates that the roots of his caring are in his own college experience:

> Having graduated from a community college [in the early 1970s], I understand very well the impact good teachers can have on their students. I was not encouraged by my family to pursue writing and literature; rather, a few professors recognized [my] talents . . . [and encouraged me] in contemplation and activities of the written word. My philosophy as a community college teacher is expressed in one word: encouragement. Though the community college does serve many utilitarian purposes, I see college as a dynamic expansion of an individual's intellectual, emotional, and, in a broad sense, spiritual life. I encourage all my students, from the young blond beach bum

to the middle-aged fireman, from the timid housewife to the Southeast Asian refugee, to pursue education and specifically to learn to read critically and write well. The benefits cannot be measured simply in terms of skills but in other personal areas such as self esteem, pride, and confidence. I don't penalize for late papers; I encourage the student who lacks confidence to see his ideas to the end and thereby achieve a sense of completion. I resist giving final interpretations of short stories; I encourage my students to think for themselves, much as the author under study did. . . . Value begins with the individual.

David Hartman emphasizes that because we care about our students, we teach—patiently and creatively:

I wonder what more I, as a somewhat more experienced traveler, can do to help my students reach their destinations. It's a precarious position. I need to teach them skills and concepts that will enable them to safely reach their destinations, without dictating these destinations or criticizing their choices. All the while, a voice inside me keeps repeating, "If you can just make them want to travel—if you can just give them sufficient reasons to travel—the rest will take care of itself." I want my students to like to write. I do know that nothing seems to work better than writing when my students need to sort out their often-tangled lives.

As we in two-year colleges teach, we prepare students for their futures, enabling them to free themselves for better lives through better jobs. Some English teachers think that preparing students for the work world is beneath them; however, such preparation is a major function of our role in the community college. Our students need not only knowledge but also the skill to apply knowledge. When those of us who are teaching now were in school, most of us transferred knowledge and made connections on our own, but most of our students today cannot do that when they enter college. Another one of my colleagues, Willie Felton, explained that when we were in college, we were students, but today in community colleges we are creating students.

Dale Parnell, past president of the Association of Community and Junior Colleges, has long been concerned about the neglected majority in education, the individuals who are not going to be doctors, lawyers, senators, executives, and professors but rather those who are going to be the workers—the plumbers, the air-conditioning repair persons, the automobile mechanics, the soldiers, the secretaries, the computer operators; in other words, those who make it possible and pleasant for others to run society or to lead a contemplative life.

In *Dateline 2000*, Parnell challenges us to prepare these people for changes in the nature of work in the future:

> Rapid technological developments are pushing higher education institutions of all kinds into a search for synergy, for systems and disciplines to work together. . . . By Dateline 2000 . . . colleges and universities will be giving much greater attention toward creating application-literate as well as knowledge-literate students. Simulators and simulation experiences will be designed to help the process. Rapid technological change is making the workplace more complex. This fundamental shift in the nature of work requires a worker, at all levels, who is well educated, highly skilled, and highly adaptive, fully able to apply learning in most situations. (251)

What skills will workers need for the jobs of the 21st century? A 1991 survey of Illinois business and labor representatives by the Center for Governmental Studies at Northern Illinois University identified nine areas of basic skills as necessary for the modern workplace:

1) Basic academic skills, including reading, writing, and mathematics.
2) Communication skills, including listening and speaking.
3) Employment readiness skills, including attitudes toward work and knowledge of business operations.
4) Cognitive skills, including critical thinking, decision making, and problem solving.
5) Interpersonal skills, including group and teamwork skills.
6) Personal skills, including self-esteem, goal setting, and personal and career development.
7) Keyboarding and computer literacy skills.
8) Knowledge of technological systems (biotechnology, communication systems, physical technology).
9) Leadership skills for improving organization effectiveness.

(qtd. in Daggett, Appendix A)

Such a study shows that the basics go beyond the students' cognitive and academic development to their personal and interpersonal development in order to prepare them for the world of work. The composition classroom offers an excellent setting to help students develop most of these skills. For the benefit of our students—entry-level employees, experienced employees who need to keep up, dislocated workers who need to be retrained, divorced housewives, single parents, refugees from poverty and political turmoil—as Willard Daggett has said, "We must balance the need to prepare youth for the world of work with preparing them for other adult roles" (34). If we are ethical, we accept the dual function of preparing students academically *and* vocationally.

As we in community colleges teach, preparing students for learning, working, and living, we ourselves learn. A few years ago, I headed a study for the Florida Association of Community and Junior Colleges to define excellence in the classroom. We concluded that excellence in education is students and teachers learning together. As David Galaher, another of my colleagues, says:

> *Learning* is the word that most fully expresses the philosophy and the art of teaching. *Learning* is what we who teach should strive to do everyday both in and out of our college environment. Teaching then becomes an active or interactive collaborative experience that involves students, teachers, the discipline, and the world. Teaching requires that we learn to create an environment that invites the student to participate actively in the shared challenge, to take risks; we thus invite a possible failure of both teaching and learning. Maybe the excitement of taking the risk to learn with enthusiasm and curiosity is what teaching is all about.

As we learn, we change. We must be flexible. We have no choice. As the world of education and our students are changing so rapidly, similar to what is happening in the business world today, we need "an overhaul of our psyches . . . to shrug off past successes and failures and frequently reinvent ourselves to fill the new roles that suddenly replace the old" (Sandroff 52).

We have developed innovative techniques to provide opportunities for all who enter to succeed in learning, and we adapt our teaching materials to reflect respect for everyone. Helping students to attain personal power is a radical act. Says colleague Jeff Hooks: "The community college system is where the educational battle [against elitism, prejudice, injustice] is focused, where these issues are confronted openly. To paraphrase Shaw, the universities talk about multiculturalism, but the community colleges deal with it daily." Another colleague, Julie Nieves, elaborates on the importance of democratic education:

> When I was student-teaching at a Pennsylvania junior high school, a veteran teacher told me she never had her "slow" students turn in essays because writing assignments would only remind them of their weak skills. Attending a workshop at the Southeastern Conference on English in the Two-Year College convention, I heard a community college instructor state that since his composition students were incapable of writing about literature and abstract ideas, he never asked them to. Probably both these individuals saw themselves as great liberals who were protecting students' self-esteem, saving students from the elitism of the traditional composition curriculum. However, I see both as guilty of the worst kind of racism and class discrimination. They've taken it upon themselves to decide that certain groups of

people are not able to deal with the rigors of a liberal arts education and are thereby consigning them to second-class citizenship in a society that will increasingly demand a strong academic background.

Economists foresee the shrinking of the American middle class and the creation of a large "underclass" permanently incapacitated by lack of skills. Whenever educators lower standards in the classroom, they are helping to shape this nightmarish future. In the short term, their call for cultural pluralism sounds like the essence of democratic thinking, but in reality they are the ultimate elitists, believing only a minority are capable of superior work while the rest can be placated with a bare-bones academic experience.

Educational conservatives then become the true liberals. If they challenge undergraduates to move beyond self-imposed boundaries, they widen the circle of achievement, showing young people they do not have to settle for a third-rate education that will predestine them to a third-rate future. When instructors set high standards, they imply students are capable of meeting those standards, and somehow, as if by magic, they usually do.

In the democratization of education through equal access to excellence, the community college has a vital role to play. Most students are capable of reaching demanding goals, but they are not all prepared to reach those goals in the hurried, depersonalized atmosphere of a large university. Some individuals will need more assistance than others; a number will respond to certain teaching methods while others will require different techniques; a few will not be able to succeed within 16 weeks but can perform admirably after 32 weeks. The community college, ideally situated to offer these options, must take advantage of its unique position rather than bend to passing fads, offering educational pabulum to young people who will require solid food to meet 21st-century challenges.

This responsibility creates conflicts, says faculty member Barbara Wahking:

> The diversity of the student body of SPJC does indeed necessitate our increased awareness of pluralities and tolerance for diversity. However, this tolerance does not carry with it a demand that we abandon our own integrity. Our multiplicity is both our strength and our weakness. We must encourage all students to search for and stand upon the strength of their ethnic, racial, sexual, or religious heritage while we continue to uphold and further the tenets of American democracy—life, truth, honor, loyalty, and freedom. We can no longer expect persons to melt into one pot of American stew seasoned with only a measure of the rights and privileges granted under the Constitution, yet neither can we tolerate a pluralism that stresses isolationism and exclusivity of groups. We appreciate individual unique-

ness while enabling a common minimum standard of performance. We reward individual achievement while upholding group processes. Thus we attempt to integrate the rights and freedoms of our republic with the responsibilities and reasonableness of our democracy. God forbid that we shift such values because of pressures from fin de siècle revisionists.

As a result of all that we are and all that we do, we benefit. Helen Bohman expresses our joy in community college teaching:

Teaching defines the person, gives substance to one's world, and laces one's life with exhilaration. One is constantly being surprised by [C. S.] Lewis's "Joy"—sometimes by current students who are inspired by what they have learned and are fired to learn more on their own, and sometimes by students who return by letter or in person 5, 10, 20, 30 years later who still remember and use what they learned in composition class and approach the teacher with pleasure and gratitude. Some come with that sincerest form of flattery to talk about being teachers. Finally, there is that greatest of satisfactions—the knowledge that perhaps one has not let down the best of one's own teachers, that their truths are being perpetuated, and their integrity held in trust for the future.

Linda LaPointe effectively summarizes the joy and the pain my colleagues and I feel teaching composition in a two-year college:

When I ask my students to write, the litany begins. "I can't write." "I hate to write." "I don't have anything to write about"—a painful refrain. How have they "unlearned" the natural human response of story telling? After this, though, we do write—together. Joy replaces the pain. It exists not only in the finished essay or final draft but in the actual movement of pencil, pen, or computer keys. I watch students make ideas visible, slowly and tediously. Joy triumphs when that first student volunteers to read his/her essay to the class. Now, ideas are visible and audible. Other students applaud and react to what they have heard. The student feels the pride, the victory which is a writer's territory.

Yes, we who teach composition in community colleges do so because we care—about our language, about education, about our world, but most of all about our students who are struggling to be free individuals. In *Killing the Spirit*, Page Smith reaffirms the need for the teacher's "personal involvement" with the students' academic and personal concerns: "All the rest is 'instruction' or 'information transferral,' 'communication technique,' or some other . . . antiseptic phrase, but it is not teaching and the student is not truly learning" (7). Teachers can teach only if they are willing to take chances, to "come down from [one's] perch as a professor . . . and be as vulnerable" as the students; "no professorial vulnerability, no real teaching" (216).

All of us as teachers are indeed vulnerable. But we support one another, we listen to one another, and together we seek better ways to help students free themselves from their chaotic lives through effective thinking, writing, and communicating. Our successes and our failures make us humble.

3 Inventing the University Student

RESPONSE BY KURT SPELLMEYER

A hundred years from now, after poring over documents like this collection of essays, historians may remember our century as the Age of Education. The Athens of Pericles, the city of Florence in the age of the Medici, the Empire of Napoleon—none of these offers anything to compare with the system of higher learning that teacher-scholars like Sylvia A. Holladay have helped to perfect: a system that has opened the academy's doors to nearly three out of every four college-age Americans, and not simply to Americans but also to thousands of men and women from places as far away as Yemen and Brunei. And this unparalleled social experiment, which has proven so successful that it now even seems prosaic, might look all the more astonishing to historians if they consider that only 50 years earlier, fewer than 5 out of every 10 Americans ever finished high school (United States, *Biennial* 31). Whatever the academy's detractors allege, historians a century or so from now may describe the growth of higher education as an unqualified success, and perhaps these same historians will even remember us—teachers of composition—as the ones who made it possible in our unassuming way.

But the historians are far more likely, I believe, to regard the last hundred years in a rather different light—as a period of social instability on an unprecedented scale. Like mass public education, mass political upheavals have become so commonplace that we take them more or less for granted, and when people of another time try to understand how we lived, they may think first of these upheavals: the collapse of the last preindustrial empires in Russia, China, and the Ottoman Near East; the appearance of the first truly global wars, together with the ongoing "militarization" of government and economy; and, of course, the increasing frequency of local conflicts whose aim is no longer the extension of territorial sovereignty but the liquidation of entire peoples—the Armenians in Turkey, the Jews in Germany, the Mayas in Guatemala, the ethnic Chinese in Southeast Asia, the Hausa in the Sudan. When we recall that Stalin's "rationalization" of Russian society cost about 20 million lives and that Mao killed roughly twice that number in modernizing Imperial China, we may find it less easy to suppose that the rise of public education will occupy an altogether unchallenged place in collective memory.

Contemplating these two quite dissimilar accounts of our time—one a story of mass enlightenment, the other of mass manipulation—we would probably prefer to think of them as mutually opposing developments, like heroic rivals in a Manichaean struggle. But here again, I suspect, our successors may see things quite differently; they may think of public education and state power as mutually reinforcing. Within premodern societies, the power of the ruling classes did not depend on the cultural normalization of those below them. The Moslem Moguls ruled a largely Hindu populace; the Turkish court spoke its own dialect, part Turkish, part Persian, part Arabic (Giddens 117). The ruling class of medieval Europe sustained a cosmopolitan culture distinctly unlike the local cultures of city dwellers and peasants. And as the Renaissance drew to a close, Charles V ruled over Austrians, Burgundians, Basques, Milanese, Netherlanders, and Sicilians, none of whom knew much, or cared much, about the others. It is only with the emergence of the modern nation-state that we find a concerted effort to maintain control by systematic inclusion rather than by exclusion and by enculturation and surveillance rather than by the selective, infrequent use of force (Giddens; Foucault, *Discipline*).

So completely is mass education caught up in the rise of the nation-state that many fair-minded observers have described the principal function of public schooling as the inculcation of normative values and behaviors rather than the dispersal of knowledge per se. Half a century ago, when most Americans lived by unskilled or semiskilled labor, a 65 percent high school dropout rate troubled absolutely no one, provided that the dropouts left the schools, at least, with the proper respect for their country and its supporting institutions. Not only do mass education and the modern state arise together, in the Marxist East as well as the capitalist West, but both also precede industrialization—a fact that holds as true for communist China, modern Turkey, and "democratic" Thailand as it did for Europe and the U.S. (see for example Schofield). And once we have started to see public education in this role of handmaiden to the covert exercise of power through the administration of human subjects, we begin to understand why there might be a link between the fostering of mass literacy and the suppression of cultural minorities: Native Americans, blacks, Asians, and the even the Amish in the U.S. (Nabokov; Smitherman; Lindholm; Kraybill); Tibetans in China; Native Americans, yet again, across much of Latin America. In the old Chinese empire, a region like Tibet could

remain culturally and even politically self-determining so long as it acknowledged the de jure rule of the emperor in Peking. But precisely because the
purpose of mass schooling is to create a distinctively national subject—the
red-blooded American, the new Soviet man, the Moslem Malay "son of the
soil"—minorities like the Tibetans are never simply different but also always
subversive, an ideological challenge (Avedon 278–319; Burger).

Before the modern system of nation-states emerged, the idea of "the nation"
needed first to be invented, together with the national subject, the individual
"citizen" (B. Anderson). Precisely because modernization overturns long-sanc-
tioned local sources of identity, it demands the active promotion of new subjectivities conducive to the nation-state itself, and for this reason, political
leaders during the periods of rapid modernization often rely on the trait that
Victorians called "force of personality." A Bismarck, a Teddy Roosevelt, a
Sukarno, or, more ominously, a Hitler or a Mao enjoys a fundamentally different relation to the national citizen than a premodern king did to his subjects.
The king personified the kingdom—"L'état, c'est moi"—but the charismatic
national leader provides a model for the individual citizen's self-perception, a
model widely disseminated through the apparatus of public schooling even
where there is no significant public press. One does not simply acknowledge
Mao's sovereignty; one learns, in a sense, to think and act as Mao would himself.

Although societies like ours offer citizens a far greater array of identities
than Mao's China offered young Red Guards—so many, perhaps, that choice
itself may be confounded—identity has still become the principal arena of
struggle between individuals and powerful institutions, a struggle that often
replicates, in the context of a single, isolated life, larger inequalities between
and within groups. It is therefore hardly surprising that what Janet Eldred and
Peter Mortensen have called literacy narratives are often deeply conflicted.
Whether the writer is Richard Hoggart or Richard Rodriguez, James Baldwin
or the students whose work Bartholomae discusses, the movement from the
home to the school and to the world of work almost always involves an untiring
labor of ascetic self-suppression and refashioning. While debates about writing pedagogy have tended to turn on trivial subjects such as the merits of
"clarity" or the need for instruction in "style," literate practices matter as
much as they do because they are essential to the normalization of identity.
Quite apart from *what* books and classroom lectures may profess, these books
and lectures teach people *how* to think and act, how to represent themselves
to themselves and to others.

But we have not truly understood the crucial link between public schooling
and the nation-state until we are willing to recognize the peculiar and "disembodied" character of knowledge in the modern world, which is as different

from knowledge at other times as the nation-state is from the Hellenic polis. Just as the survival of the modern nation depends on the persistent suppression of regional allegiances and "provincial" traditions, so what qualifies as "knowledge" is almost always removed from experience at the local or personal level. In traditional societies, by contrast, knowledge is inseparably tied to the tasks of everyday life, and learning does not occur in a place—the classroom, the college, the library—spatially and symbolically separated from the processes of that life (Erickson). Since the 17th century, however, we have increasingly presupposed that the pursuit of knowledge must begin with an act of voluntary alienation, of radical, Cartesian detachment. Literally and symbolically, knowledge becomes "disembodied," wrenched from the local contexts of its origin and imposed on others as universal (Bordo). While people in every time and place inherit knowledge that must be reshaped in the face of changing circumstances, mass education has typically served to wrest from ordinary citizens the power to effect such a change on their own, in their particular social interests. In our world, the modern world, whatever remains "particular," whatever fails to claim the status of universality, gets dismissed as special pleading, ignorance, or empty sentiment. There is a feeling *or* objectivity, opinion *or* fact. Feelings, opinions, and intuitions may still belong to us in our privacy, but truth, facts, and knowledge are the property of specialists. And the phenomenon of specialization goes a long way toward explaining, in turn, why the teaching of college-level reading and writing has become so complex and contradictory a task.

But how have the agents of the modern nation-state succeeded in convincing many millions of "lay" citizens to surrender the ownership of knowledge—and then to privilege a knowledge made by others over their own experience? The agents of modernity have succeeded, I believe, by erecting the modern system of professions, each of which claims as its exclusive domain large areas of inquiry effectively closed off to nonspecialists. The health of the body, the enjoyment of the arts, the evolution of social life, the various forms of communication, even thinking itself—all of these have been appropriated by specialists who act as mediators (and police) between the dilettantes and the world. And while it is certainly true that the current system of public education furnishes the professions with a venue for the recruitment and training of new members, the primary purpose of a course like Psychology 101 or "Introduction to Political Science" is not to distribute expert knowledge more broadly but to ensure lay support for further specialized inquiry. The point is not to produce 300 or 400 additional colleagues every semester—an economic disaster for any profession—but to persuade another generation of nonspecialists that the subject should be left to those who know it best.

As it goes in the classroom, so it goes in the world. We would do well to remind ourselves that none of the most important global events that we have witnessed since 1986—Gorbachev's declaration of *glasnost*, China's shift to "socialist" consumerism, or the passing of the North America Free Trade Agreement—was decided by the people who will finally pay the price. Instead, these events came about through the efforts of a minute elite who saw it as their mission to decide the course of history, if necessary over the dead body of massive grass-roots resistance. And given the need of such elites to keep the lid on resistance from below, we can scarcely be surprised that such world-historical changes as *glasnost* or NAFTA will register most immediately neither in the workplace nor in the halls of government but in the sphere of education. While a freely elected parliament was still nothing more than an idea, Russian universities dropped their courses on Marxist theory overnight, replacing them with classes on Western business management. And in the U.S., long before anyone has considered transforming the shape of industrial management to meet the "challenge" of the 21st century, business leaders and government officials have already called for a radical restructuring of American education, so radical that the very nature of literacy has been redefined to expose millions of new "illiterates" among the ranks of formerly literate citizens (The Wingspread Group).

At a moment in our history when many observers have remarked on the accelerating breakdown of communities and the spreading mood of cynicism, we need to ask if education as we now imagine it helps to strengthen our students' sense of agency and self-worth while it replenishes the fragile historical sources of compassion and mutual assistance. Or will the calls for reform, even when they come from poststructuralists and the academic left, simply continue the relentless discrediting of local knowledges and "marginal" ways of life on behalf of the administered society? Positioned at the threshold between the specialists and the laity, teachers of college-level reading and writing might begin to explore these questions, as I think Bartholomae has, by acknowledging the divided character of their own situation. Nothing could be less helpful, in my view, than to embrace once again an image of academic intellectuals as representatives of "the people," "the silenced," and so on. Instead, we need to understand that the existence of something called "composition" is itself symptomatic of a persistent and probably widening gap between the concerns of elites who produce what counts as knowledge—Jacques Derrida and Fredric Jameson both belong to this elite—and the needs and fears of those to whom specialized knowledge is strategically parceled out. As someone who believes that a knowledge made for experts is no knowledge at all, I want my students to use the ways of seeing produced by specialists to complicate their own self-understanding, but I also want those students to preserve an attitude of profound skepticism toward the powerful authorities whose job it is, no matter what the ideology of the month may be, to turn out properly tractable social subjects.

The case can be made, although I lack the space to make it here, that the most important social changes of our time are not taking place inside the academy but in the private lives of women and men who have begun to explore new and uncoercive forms of interaction—as couples, families, support groups, "salons," and congregations—and in our courses we too might endorse and explore social forms of this same uncoercive kind. That these experiments are still largely confined to the private sphere only shows how far the so-called public sphere—the classroom perhaps most glaringly of all—has to go before it might be called "democratic" in any credible sense of the word. Yet the freedom that people are pursuing in their private lives they increasingly expect in the public sphere as well. The enormous popularity of Bernie Siegel, a physician who supports patients in the desire for more active control over their own medical treatment, testifies to a significant change in attitudes toward the system of professions. Since medicine has set the pace throughout this century for all the other professions, we may have some reason to be hopeful. But whether academic intellectuals, who have generally taken up the rear guard, will support the more equitable distribution of cultural power remains an open question. Labor reform, the civil rights movement, women's suffrage, and later, feminism—achievements the academy would like to take some credit for—all started first on the "outside." Are we prepared to give up our privileged role as cultural "leaders"? Are we prepared to recognize nonspecialists as genuine collaborators in the making of knowledge? If we are not, then we may lose the little power we now have, as we will so richly deserve.

Part 2 What Have We Learned from the Past and How Can It Shape the Future of Composition?

stopgap until the secondary schools could improve; and second, the teaching of required composition was tiresome, labor-intensive, and a bad use of trained literary scholars.

We see both of these attitudes in William Morton Payne's interesting 1895 collection, *English in American Universities*, which contains 20 reports that had originally appeared in *The Dial* in 1894 on the teaching of college English at different institutions. Though most of the reports detail both literature and composition courses being offered, several are fervid in their triumph at having dispensed with required freshman writing altogether. Payne himself, the editor of *The Dial*, was entirely sympathetic to this movement, and his introduction makes clear why: he was a classic exponent of literature teaching who was in favor of the most stringent entrance requirements possible. He was very doubtful about the Eastern colleges' reliance on the freshman course. "As we go West, we do better and better," he says, noting that Indiana, Nebraska, and Stanford had all abolished freshman composition in favor of strong entrance requirements.

As one examines the reports from those schools, however, it is clear that liberal culture was not the only reason for the abolition. Martin Sampson of Indiana writes that "there are no recitations in 'rhetoric.' The bugbear known generally in our colleges as Freshman English is now a part of our entrance requirements" (93). Melville B. Anderson's report on English at Stanford gives us a genuine feel for the earliest abolitionist sentiments; Stanford, he says, has abolished Freshman English: "Had this salutary innovation not been accomplished, all the literary courses would have been swept away by the rapidly growing inundation of Freshman themes, and all our strength and courage would have been dissipated in preparing our students to do respectable work at more happily equipped Universities" (52). We see here the expected liberal-culture attitudes, of course, but more strongly we see pure self-protection on the part of the tenured faculty. They did not want to teach theme writing, and killing the requirement was the easiest way out of it.

This first wave of abolitionism ebbed after 1900, and Anderson's attitude gives us a key to the reasons why: the growing willingness of universities and colleges to draw on lecturers, instructors, and graduate students to teach their required freshman courses. As I have discussed in more detail in "Rhetoric in the Modern University," the rise of academic specialization and the modern hierarchy of ranks in English departments meant that between 1880 and 1900, most tenured professors were gradually relieved of composition duties by younger and less powerful colleagues or by graduate students. Thus the earliest wave of abolitionism, which had been caused by overwork panic among faculty members, receded because the Andersons and Sampsons no longer had to worry themselves about having to teach freshman composition.

The years between 1885 and 1915 saw a tremendous number of critiques of the freshman course launched, but most of them were oriented toward reforming the course. Not until the end of that period do we see a resurgence of the abolitionist sentiment in the famous article "Compulsory Composition in Colleges," which Thomas Lounsbury of Yale published in *Harper's* in 1911. David Russell, in his essay "Romantics on Writing," has done groundbreaking work on Lounsbury and some of the attitudes that have underlain the early forms of abolitionist argument. Russell describes Lounsbury's abolitionist sentiment as a product of a specific kind of educational idealism that sounds today like liberal-culture literary elitism, tinged throughout by Lounsbury's thinly concealed opinion that undergraduate students were ignorant barbarians. To Lounsbury, the idea that expression could be taught was idiotic, the conception that college students could know anything worth writing about silly, and the position that writing teachers could respond usefully to student writing unlikely. Despite his romantic elitism, Lounsbury makes some telling points against compulsory composition. But Lounsbury was an outsider, a literary scholar. Lounsbury presents an early but completely recognizable version of E. D. Hirsch's cultural literacy argument: writing could not be taught as pure practice-based skill without content. His real and obvious sympathy was with those who had a "cultivated taste begotten of familiarity with the great masterpieces of our literature" (876), and until students' minds were thus furnished, they need not apply, to him at least.

This article caused a small sensation in the English-teaching world, and especially in the still-active circle of composition enthusiasts. Lounsbury had repeated several times in his essay that his was an unpopular minority position, but it was taken very seriously. His article was not followed up in *Harper's*, but it created a long discussion in the *Educational Review* in 1913, and we see here the whole modern reformist/abolitionist debate for the first time. Though some of the *ER* correspondents agreed with Lounsbury, the majority did not. Some commentators saw no problem in the freshman course at all, and they actively praised the course as they had experienced it. Others represented the first wave of what might be called status-quo or modern reformism. These correspondents took the position, as all reformists later would, that the course was imperfect but necessary and that it would be much improved by their suggestions. N. A. Stedman of the University of Texas admitted that freshman English was useful and yielded some good results, but he saw that its "technical" nature created in students "a distaste for English" and proposed that the course be reformed to create more interest in English (53). Lucile Shepherd of the University of Missouri believed that "the course on the whole is admirable" and that with more humanism and a few tinkerings it would be better still (189).

Lounsbury had some clear allies. Carl Zigrosser of Columbia wrote, "In my estimation prescribed work in English is unnecessary" (188), and George Strong of North Carolina huffed, "My own experience with these courses was profitless. It was, in fact, enough to discourage me from continuing the study of English. I failed to derive any benefit whatever from them" (189). In these responses to Lounsbury, we begin to see proposals for that brand of abolition-ism later called Writing Across the Curriculum come hard and fast. Preston William Slosson proposed in 1913 that "the real way to make sure that every Columbia graduate, whatever his other failings, can write whatever it may be necessary for him to write as briefly, logically, and effectively as possible, is not to compel him as a freshman to write stated themes on nothing-in-par-ticular but to insist on constant training in expression in every college course" (408).

But finally, the Lounsbury-based discussion petered out sometime around 1915, after having never attained a solid enough base of agreement from the abolitionists. Reformism began to dominate the professional discussion. At least part of the reason for the failure of abolitionism and the segue we see during the mid-1910s into a clearly reformist period has to do with the grow-ing influence of the ideas of John Dewey. Some of the more widely read teach-ers of composition were beginning to realize that freshman composition could be more than a mere enforcement of mechanical rules. Helen Ogden Mahin, one of the products of Fred Newton Scott's progressive Michigan graduate pro-gram, wrote that she was moved to action by Lounsbury. When she asked her freshman students if they would take the course without the requirement, their answers made her see that "nearly two-thirds of these Freshmen, many of whom had entered the course unwillingly, realized before the end of the first semester that their lives had grown in some way broader and fuller then they had been before" (446). This result, Mahin said, controverted Lounsbury's claims. Required composition could be taught, and should be taught, in such a way that students realize that "writing means simply living and expressing life": "From the testimony of the Freshmen themselves and from the actual results shown in their work the conclusion is very well justified that the stu-dent of writing who does not in the course of his study, if that study is rightly guided, become a happier, bigger, and more socially efficient being is the stu-dent who, unless he is subnormal in intellect, deliberately sets himself against progress" (450). This concept of "English for life skills" and the "more socially efficient being" is instantly recognizable as based in Dewey's ideas. The theory that writing skills *were* humane learning and inherently broadening was to become a staple claim of reformism for decades.

The reformist period that began after World War I lasted throughout the 1920s. In examining the professional articles of that period, we see any number of proposals for improving the required course but none that make any version of the abolitionist case. This is not to say that reform periods contain no grumbling or that no teachers exist during them who wish to see freshman composition eliminated. But abolitionism is submerged during reform periods because the mission of the course comes to seem so important that more of value would be lost than gained by cutting the requirement altogether.

By the end of the 1920s, college demographics were shifting strongly. Enrollments had almost doubled between 1920 and 1930, from 598,000 students to more than 1.1 million, and they were beginning to place heavy staffing demands on the single course that had to serve all students (United States, *Digest* 84). As so often occurs, demographic changes in the student body seem to create strains leading to powerful proposals—either radical reformism or some kind or abolitionism. When abolitionism appeared again after the 1920s, however, it came from a place that Fred Newton Scott would not have suspected: the educational research community, which by 1930 was finding a serious voice within English studies. The debate erupted at the NCTE meeting of 1931, in which Alvin C. Eurich of the University of Minnesota reported findings of a study done there in the late 1920s. In one of the earliest controlled experiments conducted of freshman composition, pretest and posttest compositions were required of 54 freshmen passing through the Minnesota course. The results showed that "no measurable improvement in composition was apparent after three months of practice" (211). Eurich's essay is a research report, written with a complete footnoted literature survey, and his findings indicate that the problem with freshman composition rests on "the inadequacy of the administrative arrangement which is based upon the assumption that the lifelong habits of expression can be modified in a relatively short time" (213). To solve this problem, Eurich proposed a sophisticated system in which English teachers would work with teachers in other fields on writing-based assignments—one of the most serious early Writing Across the Curriculum programs.

Eurich's paper at NCTE was answered by one written by Warner Taylor. Taylor's essay is an archetype of reformist objection to abolitionism. Should the course be abolished? he asks. It is problematical, he says, but "as for me, I do not consider the course futile. I do consider it, in general, open to several changes for the better" (301–2). Taylor goes on to discuss a survey he had done that shows freshman courses relying overwhelmingly on handbooks and rhetorics and making a claim that such methods were themselves to blame for the poor showing the course made in Eurich's research. He proposes instead a course that gets rid of rhetorics and handbooks and mixes composition with literature.

This willingness to admit problems and propose reforms rather than agree to abolitionist ideas is a continuing entropic strand in composition discourse from the 1930s forward. It represents a sort of argumentative jujitsu, using the strength and cogency of any abolitionist argument against abolitionism as a position. "The freshman course is problematical, is hated, is boring, does not work? Absolutely true," reformists typically say, "and proof positive that it needs reform—needs, in specific, the reform I am about to propose."

We see here, of course, a certain amount of vested interest on the part of composition reformers. Even as early as 1930, there were teachers and scholars whose careers were primarily concerned with writing pedagogy, and these people associated freshman composition as a course very clearly with "their discipline." It would be almost unnatural for them to admit that the course that was their primary responsibility and interest was so hopelessly compromised and ineffective that abolishing it was the best solution. There is no doubt that reform rather than abolition served the professional needs of most composition specialists best.

The decade of the 1930s saw more lively discussion of reform and abolition than had ever before occurred. The decade of *English Journal* from the 1930s is filled with debates that sound almost incredibly contemporary—proposals for English as training for social experience, for Marxist critique in the classroom, for Writing Across the Curriculum, for research-based reforms of various kinds, for more or less literary influence on composition, for better conditions for teachers. In 1939, the strong liberal-culture side of the abolitionist argument popped up again in Oscar James Campbell's now well known article, "The Failure of Freshman English." Russell has dealt very effectively with the major part of Campbell's position in his "Romantics on Writing," and here we might merely note that literary elitism was not the entirety of Campbell's position. He, too, put forward a Writing Across the Curriculum agenda, at least tacitly. As Russell describes, Campbell also makes the familiar claim that composition cannot be taught apart from content, that it is intellectually dishonest as well as futile. He blames freshman composition for teacher disaffection and for reducing the usefulness of literary education.

Campbell's position, though probably sympathetic to most literature teachers, received far less support than Lounsbury's had 25 years before. Unlike Lounsbury, Campbell was facing a composition establishment that was already entrenched and was even building the beginnings of a scholarship and a discipline. Though Campbell was respected, he was not agreed with, and all the responses to his essay were essentially reformist. In 1941, Andrew J. Green's "Reform of Freshman English" took Campbell's arguments on directly, stating squarely that "Freshman English is ubiquitous, inevitable, and eternal" (593).

Campbell also found himself in the unfortunate position of opening a battle immediately before the nation's attention became caught up in an all-consuming world war. Instead of the debate that Campbell had no doubt hoped to produce, the entire issue of the worth of freshman composition slipped away, as did what had been other engrossing issues of the 1930s—experience curriculum, social conditions, Marxism—in the intellectual conflagration that was the war effort. After 1941, his complaints seem to have been forgotten, and reformism itself was almost blunted for the duration of the war as the needs of the military came to the fore and stressing any American problems seemed somewhat defeatist. Throughout the war years, overt criticism of the course almost disappeared as scholars betook themselves to serve the war effort by keeping up morale.

The postwar world was a different place, one in which the debate that had been damped down during the war emerged in many forms. Particularly hotly debated was the question of the mission and purpose of liberal arts colleges, a question that was always tied in powerfully to the issue of required freshman composition. Ironically, it was not the abolition sentiment of the Campbells but a kind of accelerated reformism that had the greatest abolitionist effect after World War II. The general education movement, which proposed that college curricula since the introduction of the elective system had become too specialized, was first widely enunciated in the Harvard Report of 1945, and, gaining power rapidly after 1948, it produced widespread withdrawal from the traditional freshman composition course.

The general educationists wished to meld the "heritage" model of traditional education with the more recent pragmatic insights of the followers of Dewey and William James (Harvard Committee 46–7), and to do so they proposed that the specialized introductory courses of the freshman and sophomore years be supplanted by much broader general courses, one each in the humanities, the social sciences, and the sciences. The Harvard Committee specifically proposed that the traditional course in freshman composition be replaced by more emphasis on writing in these new general education courses. The static acceptance of required freshman composition courses that had for so long been tacit educational policy was suddenly shaken as "communication" courses replaced the older composition model.

The communication movement, which was the working out of general education ideas in an English context, proposed to unify what had been separate fields of English and speech by rolling together all four of the "communication skills"—speaking, listening, reading, and writing—and creating a new course around them, the communication course. This movement began to take hold in earnest in the late 1940s and prospered through the mid-1950s, when it lost momentum. During that time, however, many traditional freshman writing courses were converted into communication courses, often team-taught by English and speech professors.

It is important to note several things about these communication courses. First, they were not part of anyone's abolitionist agenda. The general education movement itself was not at all against required courses; it was essentially about widening and adding requirements, especially during the first two years of college. Second, the changes that came down during these years came down from on high as part of a sweeping mandate reaching all the way from Harvard to the federal government. Traditional freshman courses were not transformed by liberal-culture romantics of the old literary sort or even by the kind of Writing Across the Curriculum-oriented attitude we see in Eurich but rather by a temporary enthusiasm for a new sort of reform. This was a specifically successful brand of reformism, perceiving the freshman course in need of change, rather than abolitionism, which perceives the course as hopeless or its change as impossible. It was a reform that changed the name and some of the methods of the traditional freshman composition class in many places but that removed not a jot of requirement anywhere.

Despite the critiques, freshman composition and communication courses flourished throughout the early and middle 1950s. Only at the end of the decade did abolitionism resurge, with the famous statement made in 1959 by Warner G. Rice, chair of the Michigan Department of English, at the NCTE convention of that year and published in *College English* in 1960. Rice's essay, "A Proposal for the Abolition of Freshman English, As It Is Now Commonly Taught, from the College Curriculum," is a classic product of its period; the late 1950s were for colleges a low-stress time during which fewer but much better prepared students were seeking admission. We might think of the period as the antithesis of a literacy crisis: there was no press of new student populations, test scores were rising every year, and there were fewer bachelor's degrees conferred in 1960 than in 1950 (United States, *Digest* 84). The postwar GI boom had not quite been succeeded by the baby boom in colleges, and thus at that moment the need for a required course to remedy freshman literacy problems seemed to many less pressing.

Rice's stance is by now familiar. He made the same claims that abolitionists had always made: basic literacy should be a prerequisite for college; freshman composition in a semester or a year tries to accomplish the impossible and does not really "take"; students are ill-motivated; the course is a financial drain on colleges; English teachers would be happier teaching other courses (361–2). And as Alvin C. Eurich had been answered by reformist Warner Taylor at the NCTE convention 28 years earlier, Rice was answered by reformist Albert R. Kitzhaber in 1959. Kitzhaber's essay, "Death—or Transfiguration?"

admits immediately that "no one would want to make an unqualified defense of the present Freshman English course" and goes on to catalog its shortcomings: overambitious aims, lack of agreement about course content, poor textbooks and methods, and impossibility of proving success (367). But Kitzhaber then proceeds to state positive aspects of the course: it subsidizes graduate study, lets young teachers gain experience, and often gets clearly positive results. He also believes that a writing-based course is worthwhile in and of itself (368). Kitzhaber contests Rice's main points, arguing that abolishing freshman composition would not be cheaper to colleges, that faculty in other disciplines would not take up any great part of literacy responsibilities, that the high schools were not equipped yet to handle the responsibilities themselves, and that a more rhetorically oriented freshman English course would help solve the problem (372).

With the eruption of the New Rhetoric in the early 1960s and the gradual growth of composition studies as a scholarly discipline with its own books and journals, its own disseminative and reproductive mechanisms, we entered a new era. It is an era in which reformism was immensely strengthened, becoming, indeed, the backbone of an ever-larger professional literature. Improving the freshman course (through the New Rhetoric, or invention, or classical rhetoric, or Christensen paragraphing, or sentence combining) became the essential purpose of the books and essays that appeared in always-greater numbers.

Abolition sentiment, however, does not die easily, and there was a short period during the late 1960s when the iconoclasm of that time caused the usual reformist consensus to be disrupted again by arguments against the required freshman course. The most interesting abolitionist attack was made in 1969 by Leonard Greenbaum in his article "The Tradition of Complaint." Greenbaum's essay is a piece of historical research on abolitionism written by an author who takes pains to situate himself outside the field of English. (Thus, his stance as an abolitionist himself is easier to understand because he had no professional stake in reform.) In spite of the slapdash nature of Greenbaum's historical research and his tone of classic late-1960s snottiness, his essay is still worth reading, and his essential point goes beyond the liberal-culture self-interest of many other abolitionists: "Freshman English is a luxury that consumes time, money, and the intelligence of an army of young teachers and of younger teaching fellows. . . . It would be better to stop what we are doing, to sit still, to rest in the sun, and then to search for the populations whose problems can be solved by our professional skills" (187). Greenbaum's position as an outsider to composition kept him from having any of the kind of background that could lead to more detailed ideas about what sort of writing instruction he *could* support.

Greenbaum seemed to expect no followers. As his historical survey had shown him, "Freshman English flourishes; its opponents die, retire, languish in exile" (187). But a number of people agreed with him, and for a few years after his essay, as the general cultural upheaval of the late 1960s and early 1970s produced more obvious dissatisfaction with the status quo in American education than had been seen, one of the institutions interrogated most strongly was freshman composition. Ron Smith conducted a survey in 1973 that found that the number of colleges and universities requiring some form of freshman English had dropped from 93.2 percent in 1967 to 76 percent in 1973 (139). Regina M. Hoover published "Taps for Freshman English?" in 1974, making the point that "among the many confusing and often conflicting currents sweeping through considerations of the status of Freshman English these days is one that may make all the rest irrelevant: that the discipline is dying" (149). And Smith, who admired Greenbaum's positions, saw so many continuing changes in the world of academia—"uniform equivalency testing, *true* three-year degree programs, the general elimination or streamlining of lower-division requirements, systems approaches, performance- or competency-based instruction, open-admissions policies, adjustments to booming and then declining enrollments, and even 'accountability' "—that he was certain that the trend toward deregulation of freshman composition would certainly continue (139). "The change that has occurred these past several years is not going to end very soon," he wrote in 1974. "All signs point to more schools dropping the composition requirement" (148).

Look upon my works, ye mighty, and despair. In direct contradiction to Smith's forecast, we see no more of abolitionism after the early 1970s. In the research for this essay, I could not find anything written between 1975 and 1990 in the field of composition that called for general abolition of the course. Now and then a teacher may write about why he or she does not want to teach it anymore, but the requirement itself seems little questioned in the professional literature, and it gradually grew back in the colleges. There can be found every flavor of reformism—the theorizing, the experimental pedagogies, the complaining, the throwing up of hands, the proffering of every sort of solution to the problems that always recur. But abolitionism peters out after 1974, much as it had done after both world wars.

Reasons for the change are complex. Some are culturally bound. The general military draft ended, and the Vietnam War wound down. The last great antiwar protests were rigorously quashed by the Nixon administration in 1971. The antiwar movement imploded into quarreling factions, and the sudden deflation of campus radicalism after 1972 left schools extremely quiet. There was a gas crisis and an economic recession. It was not a propitious time for any proposal for change.

Professionally, the most obvious reason for the decay of abolitionist senti-ment was, of course, the rise of open admissions, the movement of a whole new demographic sector into college classrooms, and the resulting "literacy crisis" of the middle 1970s. There is nothing like a new population or a perceived problem of lack of student preparation to put energy back into a composition requirement, and by 1976 we had both in plenty. The "Johnny Can't Write" furor of 1976 was at least as potent as the "Illiteracy of American Boys" furor had been 90 years before, and any chance that abolitionist ideas might have had in the early 1970s was swamped by mid-decade. The "back to the basics" movement, the rise of basic writing as a subdiscipline, even the writing process movement all presumed a required freshman course.

Just as important to the decline of abolitionism, I believe, was the matura-tion of the discipline of composition studies and its increasing ability to turn out doctoral specialists who could direct and defend programs. The natural tendency early on was for such specialists to talk reform and defend the course, but their very existence tempered the conditions that had made some literary specialists argue for abolition. With the growing availability of a class of tenure-track composition specialists to handle oversight of the course, lit-erary members of English departments could rest increasingly secure from ever having to do *anything* associated with composition unless they chose to do so. Those overseeing required courses had a rising professional stake in them, and thus reform ideas came hard and fast—but not proposals for aboli-tion. So things went, through the later 1970s and most of the 1980s.

This dearth of abolitionist sentiment, by now lasting almost 20 years, makes the historian with even a slight tinge of Toynbeeism begin to expect that the wheel must turn again, and turn again toward abolitionism. And, true to form, we are now seeing a New Abolitionism. The founding statement of the New Abolitionism was made in 1991 by Sharon Crowley in "A Personal Essay on Freshman English," which details her gradual realization that re-quired freshman composition courses implicated her and all composition spe-cialists with any program oversight in structures that could *not* be signifi-cantly reformed. The course is simply too tied up with institutional and professional baggage to be amenable to serious reform. "In short," she writes, "I doubt whether it is possible to radicalize instruction in a course that is so thoroughly implicated in the maintenance of cultural and academic hierar-chy" (165). Crowley's solution is abolition, not of the course but of the require-ment. "Please note," she writes, "that I am NOT proposing the abolition of Freshman English. I am not so naive as to think that the course can be abol-ished. But it can be made elective" (170). Crowley goes on to argue that elimi-nating the requirement would get rid of admissions exams, prevent any sort of indoctrination of first-year students, offer administrative control over enrollments in freshman courses, and control teaching assistantships more effectively. She then takes on what she considers good arguments, that is, student needs-based, and bad arguments, that is, institutionally or ideologically based, that can be made against her position.

Crowley's deliberately provocative essay led to the proposal of a roundtable session at the 1993 Conference on College Composition and Communication in San Diego titled "(Dis)missing the Universal Requirement." From the quick sketch I have given here of traditional responses to abolitionist arguments over the last century, we might have expected the standard response: reformism. Reformism of a very high standard, no doubt, but, still, reformism: protests that the freshman requirement does more good than harm, or that its methods must be changed to fill-in-the-blank so that it can reach its potential, or that fill-in-the-blank will certainly arrive soon and make it all worthwhile.

But no. No Helen Ogden Mahin or Warner Taylor or Albert R. Kitzhaber stood forth to disagree with Sharon Crowley. Instead, three of the most respected composition scholars and theorists rose, and each one, in his or her own way, agreed with Crowley that the universal requirement should be rethought. Lil Brannon of SUNY at Albany reported that her university had abolished the standard freshman course in 1986 because "a group of faculty from across the curriculum successfully made the case that a 'skills' concept of writing—the very idea of writing that caused the faculty to require Freshman Composition—had no professional currency" (1). David Jolliffe, making an argument based on his historical study, asked whether such a "skills"-based course was a reflection of late-19th-century perceptions. "I wonder if freshman composition isn't a metaphor for a time long passed. I wonder if we shouldn't rethink the position of requiring all incoming students to be 'skilled' in this anachronistic fashion" (1). Calling regular freshman courses "literacy calisthenics," Jolliffe goes on to argue that they should be replaced with a writing-based sophomore-level elective course that would concentrate on writing about content of their choice. And Charles I. Schuster spoke from the point of view of a practicing composition administrator, saying that freshman composition is the Third World of English studies, "a bleak territory within which students have little power to choose" and in which faculty are underpaid and overworked. Teaching writing is foundational, says Schuster, but "either Freshman Composition has to matter to our departments, or we have to get rid of it—or get rid of our colleagues" (6).

The discussion that followed these three presentations was spirited, and though there was by no means unanimity of opinion, many session attenders agreed with the central points made by the presenters. Within a few weeks, the grapevine of hallway conversations, telephone calls, workshop and presentation discussions, and electronic mail was buzzing with word of the session, and the issue even had its name: the New Abolitionism. This "Dismissing" panel was answered in 1994 by a panel called "Dissing Freshman English: At What Risk?" I am sure the conversation will go on.

We have come a long way from 1893 to 1993, from the oldest to the newest abolitionism movements. Are there any conclusions we can draw from what we have learned? Can our understanding of the past inform our sense of the present—or even the future? Is the New Abolitionism any different from previous similar arguments?

The observer of abolition arguments cannot help noting some salient similarities. The New Abolitionism is like previous versions in its condemnation of the required course as often futile, as a disliked hinterland of English studies, as expensive to run, exhausting to teach, and alienating to administer. Many New Abolitionists are present and former course administrators, as were a large number of abolitionists throughout history. The alternatives proposed by the New Abolitionism are not too dissimilar to alternatives proposed by Slosson in 1913 and Eurich in 1932 and Campbell in 1939: make composition the responsibility of the whole faculty.

The differences between the New Abolitionism and the older movements are, however, even more striking than the similarities. Most obviously different is the professional forum in which the argument is playing itself out. The New Abolitionism is a product of a newly scholarly and professionalized discipline of composition studies, one with many national journals and a constant and ongoing conversation. "Composition people" today are not just course administrators or pedagogy enthusiasts but are increasingly visible in English departments as scholars and researchers with their own claims to respect. The New Abolitionism is the work of insiders—people trained as compositionists from an early point in their careers—and it is based on exactly the opposite conclusion: that writing can be taught, and that experts are needed to teach it, but that the required freshman course is not the most effective forum for attaining the ends we seek.

The intellectual and pedagogical backgrounds for the argument have shifted dramatically as a result of these changes in institutional and disciplinary cultures, and this background shift will be another important element in any success the New Abolitionism may have. From a very early point, abolitionists have been claiming that freshman composition should be replaced with one or another system that would take responsibility for literacy off English teachers and place it on all faculty members. These were voices crying in the wilderness through much of this century, however. There were no institutional structures that would have helped faculty members in other disciplines make writing more central to their courses, and there was no extant part of English studies with enough credible expertise to do such outreach work. All that has now changed radically with the advent of the Writing Across the Curriculum movement. For the last decade and longer, writing professionals have, with the blessing and help of administrators, been forging professional links that never existed before with extradisciplinary colleagues, bringing contemporary knowledge of writing issues to content-area courses. This is a strong and broadly respected movement, one that is unlikely to go away, and it provides a practical base for the ideas of the New Abolitionism that no previous such movement had.

The arguments we hear from proponents of the New Abolitionism are qualitatively different from those heard in previous avatars of the movement. New Abolitionists typically appeal first to student interests and only secondarily to the interests of teachers, departments, and colleges. Even when previous abolitionists transcended liberal-culture arguments, their calls for the end of the required course were often based in issues of self-interest—getting rid of the composition underclass, or allowing professors to teach courses they liked, or avoiding the criticism of colleagues who thought the course was ineffective. Today's abolitionists are arguing from their scholarly as well as their practical knowledge of writing issues that students are not as well served by the required freshman course as they could be by other kinds of writing instruction. They are ideologically informed in ways that even 1960s radicals such as Greenbaum were not, and they are certainly sympathetic to both students and teachers in ways that few abolitionists have ever been. Most significant, this change in the institutional base of the argument means that we may see fewer reformist claims based in the need to safeguard jobs, turf, and respectability.

Finally, and perhaps most important, the New Abolitionists are in positions to make their critique stick. Since most of them are administrators or advisors to administrators, they know the institutional situation surrounding composition programs, Writing Across the Curriculum, and literary studies. They know what is possible, and they know how to get things done—not just whether they should be done. Because they are respected scholars and teachers, they can and do counter the expectable response from traditionalists and reformists by taking a position of informed sympathy mixed with telling argumentation. And because they are composition insiders, they can make their case from within the discourse of the field rather than complaining scornfully from without, as most abolitionists have done in the past.

It may just be, then, that the New Abolitionism will come to have a real effect. It may be that after a century we will begin to see some actual abolition of the required freshman course in favor of other methods of writing instruction.

Unless. Unless any of the familiar nemeses of abolition, most of which are now quiescent, makes an appearance.

Unless we see another literacy crisis widely cried up in the media. As the literacy crises of the 1870s spawned the freshman course and the literacy crisis of the 1970s saved it from the radical critics of the 1960s, another literacy crisis could send abolitionism scurrying. There is no lack of evidence of literacy problems that can be dug up at any given time; the report in 1992 that 20 percent of American workers could not read well enough to do their jobs most effectively or the more recent news that more than 50 percent of American adults were less than functionally literate are just the two latest lightning strikes ("Workplace"; "Study"). But not every foundation report on literacy can start the sort of large-scale crisis that gets the whole country listening, and we cannot tell which of these scattered grass fires might blow up to be the Class A crown fire that the "American Boys" or "Johnny" crises were. If such a major crisis impends, count on an end to any sort of requirement change in the freshman curriculum and get ready to batten down the "back to the basics" hatches.

Unless the United States gets involved in a serious or lasting war. Twice this century, world wars have created cultural conditions that have meant the end of credible abolition movements, and even the smaller Korean War damped down the pedagogical change of the period 1945–1952. The only exception to the general rule that war is good for the required freshman course was the war in Vietnam, which created a radical backlash on campuses previously unknown in the United States. Wars seem to create a desire for tradition and stasis where they can be achieved on the home front. War does not, thankfully, look likely as of this writing, and the ending of the Cold War may indeed bode well for such curricular changes as abolitionism. But if any major war does involve the United States, kiss curricular change goodbye—if you're able.

Unless there is a serious backlash against abolition of freshman courses on the part of those who teach them. Every abolition proposal during this century has been criticized most strongly by reformists, people who believe that the freshman course is the right answer to the question, albeit one that needs more tinkering. It is difficult to know what the growing split between the scholarly members of the tenure-track composition studies community and the instructor-level teachers in the composition trenches will mean for this issue. As Crowley says, "[T]enured academics have always dictated the terms of Freshman English teaching to its staff, and it is tenured academics who fight over its curriculum" (168), but composition studies is listening to the voices of the teachers who work on the course. If the New Abolitionism comes to look like a clash between tenured academics who want to remove and ship to some unknown place employment that composition teachers have come to depend on, and those teachers who need or want that employment, we can count on many a painful tale and many a bitter fight on levels ranging from department to CCCC. The New Abolitionism may be our own small version of the jobs/trade debate over the North American Free Trade Agreement, and if it becomes such, reform rather than abolition of the required freshman course will come to seem the only possible compromise. Working people have vested interests even in jobs from which they are alienated.

None of our historical knowledge can really predict the outcome of the New Abolitionism movement. What we can learn, however, is what may promote or block such changes in entrenched curricular practices. My own position, if I have not already tipped my hand, is one of sympathy for the New Abolitionism. I still believe that we have more of a chance today than ever before to rethink in a serious and thoroughgoing way the best methods for working on student literacy issues and that we can do so without harming the best interests of either our students or our colleagues. I look forward to a continuation of the debate and even—could it be?—to real changes in our world of teaching and thinking about writing.

5 Around 1971: Current-Traditional Rhetoric and Process Models of Composing

SHARON CROWLEY

According to a popular thumbnail history of writing instruction, around 1971 composition teachers rejected product-oriented instruction, adopting process-oriented teaching in its stead.[1] This move from product to process has been proclaimed to mark a paradigm shift within the discipline of composition studies (Hairston).

I will argue here that this history and its attendant proclamation are mistaken. According to historian Thomas Kuhn, who coined the term in 1962, paradigm shifts are distinguished by adoption of a new way of seeing, that is, by adoption of a new epistemology (117–8).[2] I see no evidence that an alternative epistemology has ever succeeded in dislodging the hold of current-traditionalism on writing instruction in American colleges and universities, although one or two paradigmatic alternatives have been suggested since the 1960s.[3] But composition teachers' adoption of process-oriented pedagogies cannot have challenged the epistemological assumptions that undergird current-traditonal rhetoric for two obvious reasons: that very rhetoric is still a dominant feature of contemporary composition instruction, and process strategies fit quite comfortably within its framework.

The Continuity of Current-Traditionalism

These assertions can easily be demonstrated by examination of best-selling composition textbooks.[4] Take, for example, *The Bedford Guide for College Writers*, third edition dated 1993, written by X. J. Kennedy, Dorothy M. Kennedy, and Sylvia A. Holladay. The rhetoric portion of this huge tome, which also includes a reader and a handbook, is divided into four parts: "A Writer's Resources," "Thinking Critically," "Special Writing Situations," and "A

Writer's Strategies." The first three sections feature process-oriented exercises divided into stages called "generating ideas," "planning, drafting, and developing," and "revising and editing." The fourth part, on composing strategies, begins with a section on generating ideas that includes instruction in brainstorming, freewriting, keeping a journal, asking a reporter's questions, and seeking motives. This marvelously eclectic collection of heuristics is followed by a process-oriented discussion of drafting that easily accommodates current-traditional formalism: "planning" includes advice about stating and using a thesis and outlining; "drafting" includes advice about topic sentences and coherence; "strategies for developing" include examples, classification, analysis, definition, comparison and contrast, cause and effect. Under the heading of "revising and editing," the authors give students a short course in the detection of logical fallacies.

Since this text is representative of currently best-selling rhetorics, I conclude that composition teachers' adoption of process-oriented teaching strategies did not amount to a paradigm shift. In other words, the adoption of a process orientation did not challenge us to alter the epistemological and rhetorical assumptions we bring to our teaching. Much less did it stimulate us to rethink the huge institutional apparatus within which composition instruction is delivered. The failure of process to dislodge the universal requirement is particularly pointed because, at least as it was conceived during the 1950s, process-oriented instruction was to be adapted to the composing needs of individuals or small groups of students working in laboratory settings. Its more widespread advocacy during the 1960s and 1970s, then, presented teachers with a clear opportunity to rethink what one of its early proponents called "mass methods" of instruction (Mills 25). By 1967, however, process-oriented techniques had already been appropriated into new editions of current-traditional textbooks prepared for a mass market.

Our habit of contrasting process with product conceals their inequity. Product-centered teaching was generated within the context of a full-blown rhetoric that was itself developed from a distinct set of epistemological premises.[5] Process, on the other hand, invokes neither a rhetoric nor an epistemology; rather, it describes a set of pedagogical tactics that can apparently be comfortably deployed within epistemologies as various as the romantic expressionism that undergirds freewriting or the Burkean analysis from which Kennedy, Kennedy, and Holladay claim to have derived the tactic they call "seeking motives." Indeed, when process-oriented composing strategies were introduced during the 1970s, they were fitted to current-traditional epistemology and were used to help students produce current-traditional texts (Kytle). As *The Bedford Guide* and its ilk attest, they are still being used in this way.

Current-Traditionalism and Process

I have argued elsewhere that current-traditional rhetoric maintains its hold on writing instruction because it is fully consonant with academic assumptions about the appropriate hierarchy of authority. In what follows, I hope to show that the hegemony of current-traditionalism played an important role in the adoption and transformation of process pedagogy to business as usual.

As early as the 1950s, process tactics were recommended, not for theoretical reasons, but as antidotes to the sterility of current-traditional instruction. In 1953, Barriss Mills argued that teachers' "unwillingness or incapacity to think of writing in terms of process" resulted in failed teaching. "Too many teachers," he wrote, "still think of communication in terms that are static, atomistic, non-functional" (19). Mills attributed his insight about the centrality of process to the appearance of a vaguely defined intellectual climate whose components included semantics, linguistics, propaganda analysis, and a literary criticism that stressed "the connotative or psychological and emotional aspects of meaning in communication, often finding these more crucial in pragmatic terms than denotative, dictionary meanings" (20). But his targets were the outlines, drills, workbooks, and the "police-force" notion of usage associated with current-traditional pedagogy as well as the standardized theme assignment typical of mass instruction in writing.

Process tactics were also recommended during the 1950s as a means of stretching institutional resources. During the late 1950s, composition teachers heatedly discussed "the Oregon plan," which was intended to alleviate the work load imposed by the mass of students returning to school on the GI Bill. Charlton Laird and John C. Sherwood, who helped to develop the plan, defended their adoption of peer workshops and small-group conferencing, not on intellectual grounds, but on pragmatic ones. As Laird put it, "We assumed that if I could teach the class in seven or eight hours without worse results than I should have expected from eleven hours, we could theoretically increase an instructor's load twenty-five to thirty percent without either him or his class suffering appreciably" (132).

During the 1960s, however, a few teachers began to rethink traditional instruction in more far-reaching ways. Among these were D. Gordon Rohman and Albert O. Wlecke, whose 1964 Project English study introduced the term "pre-writing" into composition teachers' lexicon. To my mind, Rohman and Wlecke's most important contribution to composition studies lay not in their advocacy of pre-writing, which, as has often been remarked, was consonant with current-traditionalism. Indeed, Rohman's discussion of pre-writing in his 1965 *College Composition and Communication* article makes explicit his current-traditional convictions that "thinking must be distinguished from writing" and that "in terms of cause and effect, thinking precedes writing" (106).

What Rohman and Wlecke accomplished, and this is no small matter, was to establish theoretical ground on which a discipline could be erected. They relied on Jerome Bruner's work on creativity, particularly *On Knowing: Essays for the Left Hand* (1962), for the design of their project. They borrowed Bruner's distinction between two kinds of structure—that which governs subject matters such as mathematics or biology, and that which is developed by individuals as they respond to their environment. Their innovation was to assume that the structural subject of writing was what they called "the principle of Pre-writing," which they defined as "the stage of discovery in the writing process when a person assimilates his 'subject' to himself" (106). That is, pre-writing marked the point in the writing process when the structural subject of the discipline became assimilated to the structure of the individual. Although Rohman and Wlecke do not say so, this conflated area could become an object of study, as it did in their work.

Of course, I am not arguing that Rohman and Wlecke's provision of prewriting as a subject of study single-handedly created the discipline of composition studies. I will suggest, however, that moves like theirs legitimized the disciplining of composition studies in terms that academics were used to—that is, in intellectual rather than institutional terms. The pressure to disciplinize has been constant in American universities since the late 19th century. Composition studies succumbed to this pressure at a relatively late date in its history because, prior to the 1970s, its teachers had focused their attention on a course rather than on a body of research. This focus changed around 1971, partly because pre-writing (or, more globally, the composing process) gave them something to study.

In 1971, NCTE published Janet Emig's *Composing Processes of Twelfth Graders*, which historians often cite as an influential source in composition teachers' adoption of process pedagogy.[6] The documentation in Emig's monograph suggests that, like Rohman and Wlecke, her interest in composing processes stemmed from her reading of Bruner's work on cognitive development.[7] However, Emig also cited her acquaintance with artists' and scientists' accounts of their creative processes as an important stimulus to her work. Certainly, professional interest in creative processes was in the air around 1971. Though I cannot yet document this claim, I suspect that growth in the quality and number of creative writing programs throughout the 1950s may have directed composition teachers' interests toward intellectual work concerning the creative process. Surely the widespread use of workshop pedagogy in those programs could not have escaped their attention. If so, it must also have been apparent to composition teachers that creative writers got good writing from their students without the use of current-traditional strictures.

Some commerce between teachers of creative writing and composition is apparent, at least, in a 1964 issue of *College Composition and Communication*, "Composition as Art," published under the editorship of Ken Macroric. Interestingly, the issue contains an article by one Janet Emig, entitled "The Uses of the Unconscious in Composing" and sandwiched between pieces by poets Marvin Bell and William Stafford. Unlike these efforts, Emig's essay was not a pious paean to the mysteries of the creative process. It began, rather, with a decidedly unrestrained attack on contemporary composition instruction, which then featured in-class essays and the "theme-a-week assignment" (6). Commenting on contemporary textbooks, Emig states:

> It must be acknowledged that the writers of these texts do not promise more than mere competency of product: if method is surface, expectation is appropriately low.
>
> There is no wisp or scent anywhere at this time that composing is anything but a conscious and antiseptically efficient act. Nowhere in such an account is there acknowledgment that writing involves commerce with the unconscious self and that because it does, it is often a sloppy and inefficient procedure for even the most disciplined and long-writing of professional authors. Nowhere are there hints about preverbal anguishing and the hell of getting underway; of the compulsions and fetishes governing the placement of the first word or phrase on the page—the "getting black on white" of de Maupassant; of subsequent verbal anguishing; of desert places; of the necessary resorting to the id as organizer and energizer.
>
> It could be said that I am asking—primal sin—for composition textbooks to be something other than they are meant to be; and perhaps they are used chiefly for their prescriptive annexes on usage. But nonetheless, one longs for them to make at least a small obeisance in the direction of the untidy, of the convoluted, of the not-wholly-known, of a more intricate self and process. (6)

Emig's scorn for traditional pedagogy was no less marked in the 1971 monograph, where she famously characterized the five-paragraph theme as a mode "so indigenously American that it might be called the Fifty-Star Theme. In fact, the reader might imagine behind this and the next three paragraphs Kate Smith singing 'God Bless America' or the piccolo obligato from 'The Stars and Stripes Forever'" (97). In other words, Emig's disgust with current-traditional rhetoric cannot be discounted as a motivating force in her turn to process pedagogy.

During the late 1960s, students also began to express their dissatisfaction with business as usual in the freshman writing class. Sometimes this dissatisfaction was expressed compellingly: at Iowa, for example, the rhetoric building was burned down. But this measure was insufficient to dislodge Iowa's universally required rhetoric courses, in place since 1944. Responding to student pressure, a few universities did lift the requirement for introductory composition instruction during the early 1970s, but the more typical response was to keep the requirement in place while developing the sort of student-centered courses that Bruner had recommended in *The Process of Education* (his report of the 1960 Woods Hole conference) and that British scholars had defended at the Dartmouth conference in 1966. In a recent interview, Gary Tate remarked that in 1971, "There were . . . experimental courses going on around the country as teachers, under the influence of changing social, political, and educational attitudes, began trying to make the classroom more student-centered, more responsive to the rapidly changing world outside the classroom" (McDonald 37). Tate's observation is borne out by the professional literature from the period. In the February 1970 issue of *College Composition and Communication*, for instance, Harvey Stuart Irlen pointed out that traditional composition instruction was no longer suited to its students because "the operating word is 'now.' Traditional freshman-English courses are not now; and, increasingly, freshman are" (35). Irlen urged the adoption of small-group instruction in writing and reading in the name of three key terms: freedom, relevance, and responsibility. Each of these values was impossible to achieve in traditional instruction, Irlen thought, because "we have set an arcane body of knowledge between ourselves and the students" (36).

Truly "hip" teachers demanded that freshman English be turned into a "happening." In 1967, Charles Deemer urged teachers to remove their authority and to engage "students' active participation"; the goal was "a class of students actively aware and participant, a class that does not swallow the 'teacher's' remarks but considers them" (123). Deemer recommended that teachers use surprise and shock to upset students' expectations about traditional authority relations in the classroom; he suggested, among other things, that teachers "speak, not from behind a podium, but from the rear of the room or through the side window" and that they "discuss theology to Ray Charles records" (124). In 1971, William Lutz explicitly connected the happening to process, arguing that happenings focused teachers' and students' attention on the fact that "writing is creative." He defined a happening as "structure in unstructure; a random series of ordered events; order in chaos; the logical illogicality of dreams" (35). To their credit, both Deemer and Lutz realized that traditional instruction was tightly implicated with the hierarchical and authoritarian structure of the university, and, in line with that realization, they recommended restructurings of classrooms and realignments of institutional authority along with more sweeping innovations. As Lutz put it, "We need to look anew at the student, the role of the teacher, the classroom experience, the process of writing, human nature, original sin, and the structure of the universe" (154).

As these accounts suggest, the adoption of process tactics in writing instruction was closely associated with a focus on students rather than on subject matter. To put this in another way, when teachers rejected traditional instruction around 1971, they characterized this rejection as a transfer of attention from "a body of arcane knowledge" to the lives and experiences of their students. This distinction was not lost on contemporary observers, particularly those who were familiar with the proceedings of the Dartmouth conference. Robert Gorrell observed in 1972 that "this concern for what the student is rather than what he does . . . provides at least some basis for a distinction between new and old or traditional" (265). Made uncomfortable by the pedagogy of happenings wherein "making scrapbooks or collages or films" sometimes replaced instruction in writing, Gorrell argued for a more balanced perspective: "The development of the student seems to me infinitely more important than the sanctity of the topic sentence or rules for using a semicolon. But I do not believe concern for the student's growth precludes trying to give him some help, even some information" (266).

Gorrell was perceptive enough to see that, in their rush to reject current-traditional rhetoric, teachers sometimes rejected any and all discipline in the introductory course. He argued in this essay and throughout his career that "a college-level course in composition is justified only if composition can profitably be distinguished as an academic discipline" (265). What he could not anticipate was that students' writing processes, rather than his beloved rhetoric, would eventually provide the disciplinary center of composition studies.

Current-Traditionalism and Invention

One other intellectual current must be given its due in any discussion of the emergence of process pedagogy around 1971. I refer to professional interest in invention.

To avoid a confusion that was not always avoided around 1971, I want to distinguish between invention and process. Invention, as this was understood by ancient rhetoricians, is any systematic search for or generation and/or compilation of material that can be used to compose a discourse suitable for some specific rhetorical situation. Invention may go on throughout the composing process; as delinquent students know well, invention often begins anew during editing. Since invention can rely solely upon a composer's linguistic and memorial resources, it can occur at any time—when the composer is doing things other than composing, or even when he or she is asleep. Invention may or may not include writing or speaking activities; for example, medieval composers invented in memory, using writing or speaking only if they wished to publish their compositions (Carruthers). On the other hand, it is possible to devise an account of the composing process that does not include invention, and it is possible to teach writing without reference to invention, as was commonly done in current-traditional instruction through the middle years of the 20th century. In other words, invention can be conceived quite independently of composing processes.

During the 1970s, however, writing teachers assumed a close relation between invention and process. In his 1976 survey of invention, Richard Young remarked that "it is no accident that the gradual shift in attention among rhetoricians from composed product to the composing process is occurring at the same time as the reemergence of invention as a rhetorical discipline. Invention requires a process view of rhetoric" (33). Young correctly associated the renewed interest in invention with the emergence of process pedagogies. However, historically speaking, it is more accurate to say that process views of rhetoric required invention. Young's remark reflects the historical situation in which he was writing: universally, early advocates of process pedagogy challenged traditional pedagogy by giving renewed attention to invention. In other words, adding invention to writing instruction seemed to turn writing into a process. This perception was widespread around 1971, precisely because invention was not explicitly attended to in current-traditional rhetoric.

Several inventional models were circulated in the professional literature published around 1971, but I want to concentrate briefly on only one of these. During the 1960s, a distinguished group of composition theorists—Dudley Bailey, Edward P. J. Corbett, Frank D'Angelo, Robert Gorrell, Richard Weaver, and W. Ross Winterowd, among others—recommended that the inventional schemes adumbrated with ancient rhetorics be appropriated in the teaching of composition. Despite the professional authority commanded by its advocates, the use of ancient rhetorics never caught on among teachers of introductory composition. Their limited appeal is not surprising. The extant texts of ancient rhetorics are expensive and hard to obtain; they are also difficult to use without a fairly thorough grounding in ancient history and culture. Although Corbett's elegant *Classical Rhetoric for Modern Students* (1965, 2nd ed.) remains popular even today, it has largely been used in graduate rhetoric classes or in teacher training, which testifies to the perceived difficulty of its subject.

But I do not want these observations to obscure my central point, which is that ancient rhetorics have serious failings when read from a current-traditional point of view. Ancient teachers insisted that their students develop *copia*, an abundance of topics on which to elaborate. Copia, hoarded and filed in a well-trained memory, went with rhetors wherever they traveled; a copiously supplied rhetor had no need to retreat to one of the few sparsely stocked libraries that existed in ancient times. Ancient invention also drew on communal epistemologies that privilege the commonplace; that is, they began with tradition, precept, generally accepted wisdom, what everybody knew. The communal bias of ancient invention is evident, for example, in its frequent deployment of ancient Greek values such as justice, honor, and expediency. Obviously, these emphases on copiousness and communal knowledge are foreign to current-traditional rhetoric, which reveres economy, abhors evaluation, and privileges the individual author who can originate and own new ideas.

The teachers who advocated the use of ancient rhetorics during the 1960s tried either to overlook or to erase the epistemological incompatibility of ancient rhetorics with current-traditionalism, but, as Susan Miller has argued, they did not succeed. I suspect that ancient schemes of invention feel "added on" in a current-traditional milieu; that is, teachers who define writing in current-traditional terms recognize on some level that ancient rhetorics are theories of composing in their own right, theories that are not epistemologically consistent with current-traditional rhetoric. So, while it is possible that the "revival" of ancient rhetorics during the 1960s and early 1970s did provide historical authority for a renewed interest in invention as a viable part of composing, ancient rhetorics were never a serious competitor to current-traditionalism.

Disciplining Composition Studies

To give process-oriented instruction its due, teachers' adoption of it around 1971 did alter the way in which invention was conventionally taught.[8] Teachers who adopted process used new classroom strategies—freewriting, brainstorming, workshopping, peer review, and the like—to teach invention. To some extent, they also abandoned the current-traditional inventional model of select-narrow-amplify, although its vestiges remain in the ubiquitous advice still given to students regarding the composition of thesis statements.

If composition studies did not undergo a paradigm shift in the 1960s and 1970s, what did happen? What was it that felt so revolutionary then? What caused the enormous changes that have occurred in the professional lives of those of us who were lucky enough to be around at that time? What brought about the huge transformations that we have seen in the configuration, size, and status of our discipline, which now even has a name—composition studies? I will hazard that what changed was our professional identity.

Throughout the early history of composition studies, college teachers of writing were drawn together by their concern for the quality of the required freshman course. In fact, the Conference on College Composition and Communication was formed in order to monitor and improve instruction in this course. But around 1971, we discovered a subject matter for composition studies, a subject around which a discipline could be built. As I have suggested, that subject matter was the composing process of freshman students. Of course, this discovery occurred within the context of other institutional factors that exerted pressure on us to disciplinize. But we justified our adaptation to that pressure by convincing ourselves that we could erect a discipline around our study of students' writing processes. While hardly a paradigm shift, this alteration in our professional definition of ourselves was nonetheless momentous.

Notes

1. My title appropriates that of Jane Gallop's "Around 1981." As she does, I use this date to evoke the spirit of an era. I would like to thank Janice Lauer for insisting that this essay be written.

2. Kuhn refined his notion of paradigm shifts in subsequent editions of *The Structure of Scientific Revolutions*. I use the first edition here for historical reasons.

3. Paradigmatic alternatives to current-traditionalism would perhaps question and certainly reject the modernist epistemology that underlies it. William Covino's textbook, *Forms of Wondering*, does not critique traditional approaches to instruction, but it does demonstrate the possibilities opened by poststructural approaches to composing. Molefi Asante's *Afrocentric Idea* does critique the modernist paradigm and develops a rationale for an African rhetorical theory that has potential as a composing process. The feminist technique of consciousness-raising could (and ought to) be adapted to writing pedagogy, on condition that its advocates remember that the personal is also the political. That is, consciousness-raising can become a nontraditional heuristic technique only if its practitioners continually remind themselves that its function is not only to articulate self-identities but to discover cultural, social, and political critiques.

4. For this study, I reviewed currently best-selling rhetorics published by major houses: HarperCollins, Macmillan, McGraw-Hill, Prentice Hall, St. Martin's, Simon and Schuster. *The Bedford Guide* is representative of this group. I forestall the objection that textbooks may not be representative of teaching practice by pointing out that these books are best-sellers—purchased if not read in the hundreds of thousands annually. I remind readers that composition is still taught for the most part by untrained teachers whose anxious supervisors attempt to teacher-proof their hundreds of sections by using massive textbooks, and I direct skeptics to Richard Larson's recent Ford Foundation study, which found current-traditional epistemology to be operative in about half of the college writing programs surveyed.

5. For a history of current-traditionalism, see Crowley, *The Methodical Memory*.

6. James A. Berlin claims that "the effect of Emig's study was widespread and significant" and that "her effort resulted in more teachers calling upon the process model of composing" (*Rhetoric and Reality* 160–1). For additional accounts of

Emig's influence, see Faigley, "Composing Theories of Process" 532; Faigley et al. 5; Voss 279.

7. As Berlin has pointed out, Bruner's influence on the development of professional interest in process pedagogy cannot be underestimated (*Rhetoric and Reality* 122).

8. The adoption of process also foregrounded personal writing. Although I do not have space to make this argument here, it can be demonstrated that personal writing was always part of current-traditional instruction, if only implicitly in some of its historical manifestations. The romantic expressionism from which personal writing derives is the reactionary antithesis of the Enlightenment rationalism that spawned current-traditional rhetoric. Liberal humanism is the politics of both. Epistemologically speaking, then, expressionism and rationalism are siblings under the skin.

6 Prim Irony: Suzuki Method Composition in the 21st Century

RESPONSE BY C. JAN SWEARINGEN

I have a dream. It is the ultimate nightmare. Around 2000, Suzuki[1] freshman composition will be taught in all the football stadiums that are being refurbished across the land while faculty and library funding are slashed. Rush Limbaugh will stand in the center of the field with a foghorn. The epistemological fog will have become dense. Students will compose fragmentary virtual texts, copying what Limbaugh opines onto backlit plastic clipboards using electronic styluses. Everything they write will immediately be put under copyright and thereby removed from public access. Athletic departments will fill their coffers by charging students a fee to retrieve their own texts, copies of Limbaugh's copies of public opinion, which has been shaped by the newly streamlined, smooth Suzuki literacy. Too "multi" for ethnic cleansing, " 'merca" will achieve cognitive communion.

Happily, our session allowed me to deem this dream but a worst-case scenario. Depending on your epistemological denomination, you could say that our session produced, discovered, invented, or composed many alternative paths leading out of the abolitionist-reformist cycle, and the process/product epistemological abyss as well. Abundant virtual texts of possible futures resulted from our roundtables. Discussants reported back with ample questions and proposals firmly located, as one group insisted, in the realms of power and in larger contexts. Many asked for more on the epistemological and pedagogical issues developed in Sharon Crowley's thumbnail history, particularly on the relationship between epistemological process and textual product that was a central issue in Crowley's account of the alleged paradigm shift of around 1971: the much touted shift that was not. Rather, we came to understand, her contention was that a continuation of current-traditional textual structures was confounded, and confounded students and teachers alike, with a vague, unsettling cognitive blur, a fog caused by individualist and expressivist doctrines of composing process and epistemology now cohabiting in the same textbooks, classrooms, hearts, and minds with linear, Enlightenment, rationalist current-traditional text outlines. The subject of composition changed, around 1971, to the writing process, but that did not, according to Crowley, constitute a paradigm shift.

Robert J. Connors's talk drew questions concerning the abolitionist versus reformist positions that were advanced past and present and how to determine which should be advanced for the future. Equally central was the question of the vested interest we have in the current system even as we critique it. Are we pseudoreformists, engaging in hand-wringing as we cry all the way to the publication bank? Respondents called for moving beyond critique, whine, and public confessional. Several noted that many current historical models and accounts seem to be taking agency away from teachers and students alike, suggesting that somehow agency is politically or epistemologically incorrect. Hard questions were asked concerning the complicity of all of us in the production of the textbooks that feed the blur and, just as importantly, sustain the system of mass freshman composition taught largely by part-time and GTA staff. Have the vo-tech aspects of Writing Across the Curriculum diluted or decentered freshman composition in the same dumbing-down ways that the abolitionists of past eras objected to, or are these programs needed reforms that distribute responsibility for writing instruction? What alternatives to the present curriculum, such as the rhetoric of inquiry, could move composition beyond the impasse that Crowley and Connors both describe: too much introspective writing in ostensibly-but-not-really process classrooms that still require the production of current-traditional texts? Several suggested that we need not so much the either/or cycles of abolition and reform but something stronger: revolution.

Many questions and responses from our groups concerned epistemological and process nuances built into pedagogies and emphasized the rabbit-and-duck perceptual difficulty that is created by trying to look simultaneously at the epistemology attributed to—or imposed upon—students and that which is implicit in the textual products of composition. Here, in brief, is a thumbnail sketch—my virtual text—of Crowley's thumbnail sketch, highlighting and extending the questions of epistemology and pedagogy that were prominent in our groups' responses.

Crowley posits that today's process entails invention of a sort different than classical invention's *copia* and common topics; process emphasizes individualism, whereas the copia and common topics relied upon shared procedures and knowledge. Her analysis suggests that classical invention's copia was a body of already assimilated knowledge—"what everyone knows"—ready for the composer. In contrast, today's process has no content prior to the introspective hunt for unique and individual insights, only procedures and protocols. Thus, Crowley argues, the addition of the modern "inventional" concepts known as process to current-traditional textual outlines did not bring about the much acclaimed paradigm shift "around 1971." Instead, the process pedagogies that describe pre-writing and "getting started" procedures remain in most textbooks preambles to essay text outlines that are current-traditional. No epistemological shift occurred with this addition, Crowley asserts, because the process models refer not to content but to activities that students are encouraged to use to produce contents arranged, still, as current-traditional texts. She observes in recent composition textbooks a conflict of epistemologies brought about by the addition of process models to composition protocols still centered in text production. The texts produced in both current-traditional and contemporary curricula include the personal essay and the essay developing a thought or idea in belletristic style. Classical invention's common topics and copia were based on collectively held values, axioms, and knowledge, whereas both current-traditional and process models place a high priority on originality, novelty, creativity, unique insights, and personal experience—values not current in the culture that produced the common topics and copia. There was some healthy contention on this last point.

For purposes of clarification and to test the boundaries of several of Crowley's definitions, I modestly propose that we extend her thumbnail history of the paradigm shift that did not occur around 1971 all the way back to the fourth century B.C.E. when the oral equivalent of *The Bedford Guide for Writers* was being mass-marketed in the service of the Athenian empire. Then, as now, I suggest, what we have dubbed a current-traditional formalism provided by outlines of the parts or segments within a speech manifests itself within a superficially process-cloaked composing pedagogy attributed to—and proudly claimed by—the Sophists and their students. How clever of Protagoras to propound a radical new linguistic and epistemological contingency—man is the measure of all things—while helping to arm the Athenians' minds for arguments that would effect an *Anschluss*: the annexation of neighboring city-states. Protagoran contingencies saw to it that Athenian man, newly named and measured, was the measure and marauder of all things. The point is that within this extended time frame, Protagoras may be viewed as one of the founders of The Tradition (actually, there were many) that continues to be mass-marketed with the claim of paradigm-shifty process pedagogical correctness. In the current process and contingency traditions lingers none other than the outline for a speech that was already getting old when it was first parodied by Plato as mechanistic rhetoric that would foster *National Enquirer* minds.

My friendly amendment concurs with Crowley that there was no paradigm shift around 1971 and posits that, give or take a few epistemologies, there has arguably not been one since the fourth century B.C.E. if we look at the text structures that are prescribed and produced. Discussants drew from Crowley's elucidation several key discontinuities betwen 1971 and now, first and foremost her comparisons of classical rhetorical invention, current-traditional models, and process pedagogy. She explains that the product that was the apotheosis—the alleged death and the transfiguration—of current-traditional pedagogy does not readily bear comparison with process models. These are apples and oranges. Crowley further suggests that current-traditional and process cannot be construed as opposites; they are siblings under the skin, two elements in the larger whole comprised by romantic and post-Enlightenment notions of language, thought, individualism, liberal education, and liberal political humanism. As with Protagoras's epistemological and linguistic liberalism in the service of empire building, liberal humanism's focus on hyperindividualism can get caught in its own contradictions.

Both Crowley's and Connors's histories allow us to see that the Cold War classrooms of the 1950s and the liberation pedagogy classrooms of the 1960s and 1970s are siblings under the skin as well. Both pedagogies, albeit for different reasons, place high value on individualism, creativity, autonomy, and agency—or empowerment, as we have come to call it. Both current-traditional *and* process pedagogy—the process *and* the product, Crowley emphasizes— reflect institutional problems and social values that in a quirky sense have become the inventional devices and copia of the late 20th century. Many respondents' questions and comments on this issue suggested a growing, shared consciousness that there is a form of epistemological and textual colonialism going on in imposing personal essays as well as contentious argumentative and political modes upon non-Western students, a process that Crowley's presentation allows us to see as an imposition of Western copia and common topics—common topics of individualism and introspection. Crowley's discussion bears witness to the twilight of all these idols.

Questioners persisted. By making students' writing processes the subject and content of the pedagogy, have we not debased or effaced other epistemologies, ways of knowing, and voices we might have provisioned—or found in our students? Are zero-degree introspection on the one hand and prescribed guerrilla political voices on the other becoming the only, equally pre-formed options in today's writing classrooms? Is this the problem, or is it the beginning of a solution? Can the rhetoric of inquiry become an alternate subject of composition, or autobiography, or new literacy in oral cultures?

Connors was commended for tackling epistemological, pedagogical, and institutional questions alongside one another. Reformers, in his account, have always tried to get the content, or a content, back into pure process pedagogies.

Abolitionists, he notes, have often advanced the claim that composition has no content, or that its content is beneath the dignity of academia. I cannot help but think of James Murphy's comment, long ago, that if rhetoric is defined as a process or method apart from a subject, then it has no history in the Middle Ages. A similar point has been reached today with regard to composition and its ties to subjects. The either/or tension between reformism and abolitionism, Connors asserts, has recurrently surfaced in eras—like our current historical moment—when two claims are illogically combined by administrators, legislators, and the public. One, it is not the duty of universities to teach composition understood as basic writing; students should have already mastered the elements of style and grammar before being admitted. Two, English departments can, will, and should get maximum FTEs and SCHs out of writing instruction that will be staffed with part-time, adjunct, and TAs who have no faculty rank or benefits. To the required but no-credit version of this course, Crowley and Connors propose a second abolitionist alternative: elective only, and for credit. In this, Connors's discussion helpfully emphasized two different kinds of abolitionist positions: advocacy of removing writing instruction from English departments either within or outside the university and advocacy of altering the writing requirement so that it is not a universal requirement but rather an elective. Some of today's abolitionists might be styled segregationists, in the following sense. True abolitionists want to abolish freshman composition as currently taught, institutionally located, and pedagogically defined. However, they welcome a move outside of English departments, as with the recent secession of the writing programs at the University of Texas at Austin, the University of Arkansas at Little Rock, and San Diego State University. Like separatist women's studies or African American studies or multiethnic literature programs, the new segregation is something to be watched, reflected upon, considered. Is it abolition, reform, or both? Is it a welcome revolution?

I pcrorate with a selection from the provocative questions and observations that were compiled by our roundtable leaders. How are we implicated and complicit in the institutional structures and social values that keep composition in its second-class, poorly understood, and inefficient condition? What can we do about it? What of the scandal of high-profit textbooks that feed the amalgam of current-traditional/process pedagogies and textbooks, subsidized by the institutional decision to staff required freshman composition courses with an equally diverse human amalgamation? Shall we sustain an ironic detachment from all this? Kenneth Burke characterized the noblesse oblige manifest in the discreet gentlemanly irony of the ruling class in Britain and in America's South as prim irony, or comic primness: a manner by which the members of an elite class retain a certain detachment from the class system that benefits them on the grounds that they do not possess—indeed, they believe that they cannot possess—historical knowledge of its origins. Even if they did, they would be unable to act upon it given the constraints imposed upon them, too, alas, by the class structure in which they live out their lives. Thankfully, our historical knowledge has been edified by Crowley's and Connors's discussions.

How, now, can we act upon this knowledge? Transcend the endless cycles of abolitionist-reformist debate with a revolution or two. Instead of teaching the conflicts as a spectator sport, as the observation of someone else's arguments, teach students how to conflict and contend without war. Epistemology will no longer be a problem if we complement descriptions of processes with engaging examples of their use and contents in different situations. Perhaps even the subject of composition will become history: how the subject became the subject of composition, and learned, once again, to speak.

Note

1. The Suzuki method of teaching violin and piano is adapted for young children to learn basic techniques and chords in very large groups through repetition and memorization.

Part 3 Who Will Assess Composition in the 21st Century and How Will They Assess It?

7 Writing Assessment in the 21st Century: A Utopian View

PETER ELBOW

How shall we deal with what lies ahead? In his essay in this volume, Edward M. White warns us of future dangers and urges us to steer away from them. I will point to future ideals and try to get us to steer closer.

It makes me mad when people criticize me as utopian. Surely there is something misguided when the term "utopian" is used to criticize and is taken to mean "unrealistic" and "unsophisticated." We need the utopian or visionary impulse to keep from being blinded by what seems normal—to help us see that what is natural is constructed, not inevitable. When I get stuck I can often help myself by asking, "How *should* things be?" This helps me pry myself loose from the web of assumptions we live in.

What if we had a regular state college without grading? It sounds utopian, but teaching nine years at The Evergreen State College in Washington showed me it could be normal. Evergreen is a good-sized, non-elite state college. It has the same teacher/student ratio and faculty salaries as the other colleges in the state system. It has proved that students with narrative transcripts and no grades at all can get into good graduate and professional schools and get good jobs.

What if we could write without being careful, without planning, without thinking about readers, without coherence or correctness or even a topic? Sounds utopian, but freewriting is exactly this kind of writing. Freewriting is a prime utopian move: an act of breaking out of the "nature of things." Visits to the utopian "nowhere" of freewriting have concretely helpful effects on our "normal" writing under conventional constraints.

So let me suggest four utopian models for assessment in the 21st century.

Portfolios

What if we did not make any serious assessments of someone's writing unless we had multiple samples: multiple genres produced on multiple occasions and most of them produced in natural writing conditions? The point is that we cannot get a trustworthy picture of someone's writing ability or skill if we see only one piece of writing—especially if it was written in test conditions. Even if we are only testing for a narrow subskill such as sentence clarity, one sample can be completely misleading.

Since the explosion of interest in portfolios, this principle does not feel very utopian any more. After all, a significant number of massive assessments use portfolios, for example, those at Miami University and the University of Michigan. Yet notice how most writing tests are based on single samples, and parents and the news media seem to take single-sample scores with complete faith.

"What about statewide tests? They could not use portfolios." But they could. Vermont and Kentucky already do. And statewide tests could use portfolios more easily if they did not try to test every student but rather tested more selectively. Selective testing, if it were more trustworthy through the use of portfolios, would serve the goals that are reasonable for such huge tests: to identify which schools need extra resources to bring more students up to par and to provide samples of unsatisfactory and exemplary portfolios for teachers—samples they could use for more local assessment at the school or regional level in order to give some genuine feedback to every student.

An Alternative to Holistic Scoring

What if we finally admitted the problems with holistic scoring and did something about it? Holistic scoring sometimes feels to people like the normal, accepted, "default" mode for evaluation—even the desirable mode. (And historically, holistic scoring helped us push for direct rather than indirect tests of writing.) But in fact, many people have been pointing out serious problems (see my appendix of works that question holistic scoring), and there is considerable exploration of alternatives. Here is a quick summary of problems with holistic scoring.

1. Holistic scores are not fair or trustworthy. They score complex, multidimensional performances with single numbers along a single dimension. More important, readers simply do not agree on holistic or single scores. The high levels of alleged interreader reliability that testers sometimes brag of for holistic scoring are the artificial effects of "training": getting readers to ignore their actual responses and values as professional readers. Portfolios have highlighted this reliability problem because they are so rich and complex that no single-dimensional score is adequate. Thus, portfolio scorers are turning out to be more resistant to "training" and peskier about sticking to their disagreements. (For three empirical accounts of these difficulties in portfolio scoring sessions, see in my appendix Broad; Despain and Hilgers; Hamp-Lyons.)

2. Holistic scores give no feedback to the learner or teacher. A holistic score is nothing but a single point on a "yea/boo" applause meter and provides no evidence as to why readers shouted "yea" or "boo." Sometimes testers provide a "scoring guide" along with holistic scores, allegedly describing the strengths and weaknesses of papers for each score. But these platonic descriptions cannot be used for feedback to students because they so seldom fit actual papers.

3. Holistic scoring feeds the dangerous assumption that there is a "true score" for any piece of writing (or even portfolio). Ed White addresses this danger directly: "When we evaluate student writing . . . we sometimes find differences of opinion that cannot be resolved and where the concept of the true score makes no sense. . . . Some disagreements (within limits) should not be called error, since, as with the arts, we do not really have a true score, even in theory" ("Language and Reality" 192).

4. Holistic scoring fuels what is probably the biggest enemy of thoughtful evaluation: judgment based on holistic, global feelings ("I like it / I don't like it") rather than judgment that tries to describe and to discriminate strengths and weaknesses.

5. Holistic scoring similarly feeds the cultural hunger for ranking and evaluation—the feeling that evaluation is not "real" or honest unless it comes in the form of a single number. Too many students assume that everything must be evaluated—indeed, that the *point* of writing is to be evaluated.

A truly utopian impulse would prompt us to ask why we need numerical scores at all. Why not make do with readers' descriptive accounts of what they see as strengths and weaknesses? This would be the most trustworthy evaluation because it would give the most valid picture of how readers actually read and value texts.

In fact, we *could* get along with nothing but that kind of writing assessment if we made some institutional changes. But I want to back down from the full utopian impulse and give in somewhat to pragmatic and institutional pressures as they now exist. That is, I want to acknowledge that we sometimes need, given present institutional realities, a bottom-line verdict. We need to know which students to admit or refuse, which students to pass or to oblige to repeat a course, which ones to give a scholarship to or not. Nevertheless, we do not need all those holistic scores from 1 to 6. We could just as well use what I call "minimal holistic scoring" or "bottom line scoring." For example, in many situations we could give only two scores: Unsatisfactory and Satisfactory. Sometimes we might want to give a third score: Excellent or Honors. Minimal or bottom-line holistic scoring might seem theoretically odd, designed to offend both those who love holistic scoring and those who hate it. In fact, however, a version of minimal holistic scoring is being used in the writing programs at many places, for example, at SUNY at Stony Brook (Elbow and Belanoff), Pittsburgh University (W. Smith, "The Importance"), Washington State University (Haswell and Wyche-Smith), and University of South Carolina (Grego and Thompson). The theoretical principle behind it is simple, crude, skeptical, and pragmatic and could be stated as follows: single-number scores for complex performances are inherently untrustworthy (especially for things as rich and complex as portfolios), and so we should make as few as possible. Therefore, let us figure out what minimal scores we *need* and make only those judgments. If we only need to know which students should get extra help, score only that one category.[1] (Notice also how so-called real-world scoring tends to be a form of minimal or bottom-line holistic scoring: you are hired or fired; your manuscript is accepted or rejected; your grant proposal is funded or not.)

Minimal scoring is much easier and cheaper. It costs a lot of money to score every paper or portfolio from 1 to 6. Minimal scoring is also more trustworthy, if only because it produces radically fewer untrustworthy scores. Yet it still gives us what we need.

It also leads to a significant and interesting psychological benefit: an emphasis on what might be called "good enough writing." (I adapt the concept from D. W. Winnicott, an interesting British psychoanalyst who coined the term "good enough mother." He was trying to question the emphasis on a kind of ideal mother who is always active and attentive to the baby and who makes everything happen right. He showed in the most concrete way how babies and toddlers need a mother who is *there* and available but not paying too much attention or doing very much for the child—a figure whom the child can move away from on longer and longer forays and always find there on return. He showed the importance of a certain kind of wise neglect. I pass over the fact that he framed all this in terms of the mother only.)

I have found the concept "good enough writing" useful in my teaching where I use minimal grading in conjunction with a contract. Students are not sweating their precise grade or score so much because they know that I will notify them if I see their work as not satisfactory—or as excellent. Those who do genuinely poorly get pushed; those who are hung up with winning push themselves for scores of Excellent—they "write to win." Most students can rest secure that the piece of writing they turned in is, overall, "good enough" and can thus think more productively about the nonholistic or analytic feedback they get from me and their peers about what happens in readers' minds during reading and what readers see as particular strengths and weaknesses. (Formerly, students were too preoccupied with whether the grade was B or C, and I was having to gear my comments toward justifying my often dubious choice.) Most of all, this emphasis on "good enough writing" helps students begin to pay more attention to developing their own criteria for writing and to become less dependent upon teacher evaluation.

Let me emphasize that by "good enough writing," I do not mean mediocre writing with which we cannot be satisfied. But I do not mean excellent writing, either. Some people believe we must never be satisfied with anything but excellence; the notion of "good enough writing" will be offensive to them. In my view, the concept is particularly appropriate for required writing courses where many students are there under duress and are more interested in satisfying the requirement acceptably than in achieving excellence. (Can we hold that against them?) Yet in elective writing courses, "good enough writing" is also appropriate because students there are more ready to develop their own autonomous standards.

An Alternative to Basic Writing

Let us question the pervasive assumption here: that if we want to give unskilled or inexperienced writers the help they need, we must give all students a placement test in order to identify the problem students ahead of time and put them into separate "basic writing" courses where they have no contact with the rest of the students.

In the Spring 1993 issue of the *Journal of Basic Writing*, there are three essays that question basic writing itself. David Bartholomae suggests that basic writing is a cultural construct that leads to institutional structures which "reproduce existing hierarchies" in a dangerous way (14). Peter Dow Adams investigates the records at his community college and is alarmed at how few basic writing students make it through the regular 101 course. He wonders whether these basic courses might actually impede rather than help the students placed in them. William Jones argues that basic writing courses often function in a racist way.

Furthermore, in a piece of extensive research that won the 1991 Braddock Award for the best essay in *College Composition and Communication*, Glynda Hull, Mike Rose, Kay Losey Fraser, and Marisa Castellano show how easy and natural it is for teachers of basic writing to mistake difference for deficit. They give us a helpful and detailed picture of how a basic writing teacher—a good and smart and caring one—comes to perceive a basic writing student as having a serious cognitive deficit when in truth the student's problem seemed to be that she engaged in discussion and conversation in a way that the teacher found inappropriate and indeed annoying. (In fact, part of her problem seemed to be that she was "too" assertive and behaved too much like a peer—she was not sufficiently deferential. This recalls the research by Sarah Freedman on how teachers respond negatively to student writing that is not deferential.)

The authors do not paint the teacher as incompetent or prejudiced—in fact, they imply that all of us would probably be embarrassed at what would come to light if our teaching were examined and analyzed so closely. That was their point: circumstances tempt all of us into misguided behavior. For it was the student's placement in a *basic* class that tempted the teacher into seeing a cognitive deficit where there was just an odd or even annoying way of talking. If the setting had been a regular course, the teacher would have probably just seen the behavior as "behavior." And imagine if the student had been in an honors section: "Lord, aren't these smart kids *pushy*! Sometimes I just get tired of them interrupting all the time and trying to steer the conversation their way."

These critiques of basic writing are tricky and debatable—indeed inflammatory.[2] Bartholomae and Adams tread very gingerly in their doubts about whether basic writing courses are worth having. Hull, Rose, and their colleagues do not question basic writing courses per se (though I think their findings do, along with the title of their article). Therefore, I will not push a negative argument—that basic writing programs do not work or do harm. Surely they often work well, and I would like to assume for the sake of this paper that they *always* work well.

But I can still pursue a *positive* argument. I want to propose a picture or model of how things *could* be, in the belief that this picture will attract us so that we will want to move in that direction by the 21st century—even if all our present basic writing courses work well.

Let me try to give a concrete vision of how we might arrange things if we decided to skip all this placement testing and temporary tracking or segregating of basic students. All entering students would be placed into the regular first-year course. The only ones excluded would be those who cannot put down on paper in English the words they find on their lips or in their head—students who cannot blurt words on paper. They would not have to be able to spell those words well or get them into correct or even clear sentences; they would simply have to be able to put much of their speech on paper. Thus, the population of the first-year course would be very mixed indeed: very skilled writers cheek by jowl with extremely poor ones.

"What a mess! And what about poorly prepared, frightened students who need so much help to survive? You are just sending us back to the bad old days where universities accepted these students and gave them no help—so they soon flunked out." The important point here is to notice the stranglehold link in our current thinking between *helping* unskilled writers and *segregating* or quarantining them into separate basic writing courses. We need to break that stranglehold and notice that there are a multitude of ways to give these students supplementary help without identifying them ahead of time and separating them from the rest. As long as they get help, unskilled and inexperienced writers can benefit from working along with more skilled students—and the more skilled ones will benefit, too.

What I am suggesting builds on a crucial pedagogical consensus that has been developing in our field: that instruction in composition does not depend on everyone having the same knowledge or skill and that the same instruction should go on in basic classrooms as goes on in regular ones. Indeed, most of the problems with the teaching of basic writing come from too much emphasis on how basic writers are a different breed of people and on how basic courses should provide a homogeneous, lockstep kind of teaching that consists of drills or other instruction requiring all students to be at the same skill level. Staunch defenders of basic writing such as Karen Greenberg agree that the main problems in basic writing classes come from thinking too much in terms of "levels" and assuming a deficit or cognitive deficiency when the students arc just unskilled:

> Despite critical insights into basic writing gained from research in composition in cognitive psychology, and applied linguistics, too many basic writing courses are still based on a remedial model, and too many basic writers are still subjected to skills/drills content and to pedagogies that conceptualize writing as a set of subskills that must be mastered in a series of steps or stages. Finally, many programs continue to define student writers as "basic" based on their ability to identify and correct errors in someone else's sentences or texts. ("Politics" 67)

In short, the kind of instruction we want for first-year students of all abilities is exactly the kind of instruction that would be forced on us if we had classrooms with extremely mixed abilities. We would have to focus on the nitty-gritty essentials: having students write, share their writing with us and with each other, and get feedback from us and from each other.[3]

"But Peter, you are just being hopelessly utopian." Having learned to expect this criticism, I have prepared two replies.

First, think back to the problems Karen Greenberg just described as common in the teaching of basic writing courses: the tendency to teach to a deficit. Is it not just as utopian to think that we could change this tendency in the teaching of basic writing as it would be to move in the heterogeneous direction I am suggesting? Think of all the structural pressures that lead to the problems that Greenberg describes: basic writing teachers have rooms full of students culled from the general population because they are alleged to have writing problems; basic teachers often get less recognition and reward than "regular" teachers; and sometimes, unfortunately but understandably, the weakest or most inexperienced teachers are given this usually uncoveted assignment. In short, we are stuck having to work toward one utopia or another (unless we want to continue to cheat these students). Surely my utopia is as feasible and more exciting.

My second reply must begin with a confession: I have tried to play a trick on you. That is, this seemingly utopian approach is currently being used with success (Grego and Thompson). At the University of South Carolina, the first-year writing course that serves about 1,700 students is entirely heterogeneous (except for some English as a Second Language classes). They have no placement exam, though students bring a portfolio of prior writing to their regular writing class for their teacher to look at. On the basis of this portfolio and lots of additional writing during the first week, teachers identify students they think will need supplementary help, and these students join what they call the Writing Studio.

Writing Studio students meet weekly in groups of four with instructors. In these sessions, the students get practical help with the specific tasks of the regular 101 course for that week, but they also do some ongoing work on their relationship to writing (involving work on memories and feelings about writing). Students so placed are obliged to go; thus, there *is* some stigma. But they do not get any extra work—indeed, the Writing Studio gives them help with the regular work. These meetings probably get them through their regular homework a bit more quickly than if they did not attend.

After the first year of using this approach, Writing Studio students accounted for only about 6 of 75 or so students who failed 101 (and those few tended to fail many or most of their courses, so it probably was not a writing difficulty that held them back). And many Writing Studio students did well in 101.

The University of South Carolina has now completed its second year (1993–1994) of applying this program to the entire entering class, and they are even more pleased about it. None of the Writing Studio students failed the course. I have met a number of times with Rhonda Grego and Nancy Thompson, who designed and run this program (and with the director, Tom Waldrep, and with a number of teachers and tutors, some of whom teach in both the regular course and the Writing Studio). They have an interesting story to tell. When teachers worked in the previous, conventional system (using a placement exam and basic writing classes), they were accustomed to thinking in terms of this creature called a "basic writer." The goal of the placement test was to identify basic writers and put them in the basic course. That same mentality persisted somewhat into the first year of their new heterogeneous system. That is, they were still trying to identify basic writers, but this time for placement into the Writing Studio—and individual teachers were making these decisions from within the 101 classroom. But still they tended to think in terms of "basic writers," and not surprisingly, the emphasis still tended to be on problems with syntax and mechanics.

During the second year, they have found that the concept of basic writer is beginning to dissipate. The teachers are beginning to think more in terms of a wide range of *different difficulties* that students have. Individual teachers are beginning to acknowledge more clearly how each of them is better at dealing with some of these difficulties than with others. For example, some teachers are not bothered by severe problems with syntax and mechanics, and so these teachers are not tempted to place students with these problems into the Studio; they feel confident they can help them. But other teachers feel quite the opposite and do send such students to the Studio. Similarly, some teachers do not mind working with deeply tangled, incoherent thinking—but some do. Some teachers don't sweat massive blockage and fear—but others do. In short, teachers are beginning to make more nuanced judgments than they used to make about which students to send to the Writing Studio. And they are beginning to realize that they do not always use the same criteria. Thus, they do not so much think of these students as "basic writers" but simply as writers who need a kind of help that they themselves cannot give.

In short, Grego and Thompson are noticing a profound change in mentality. Members of the writing program no longer view the world of students so much through the lens of basic/nonbasic; they do not so much see a world of sheep and goats. Instead, they are beginning to see a range of students with particular locations in a complex universe of strengths and weaknesses. This is exciting to me.

By the way, they are also finding some students joining the Writing Studio voluntarily—and often good students (for example, some pre-med students who have been told that writing skills will matter for their entrance assessments).

This interesting experiment in South Carolina is not a fluke. Berea College has also set up a heterogeneous first-year reading and writing course where students whom teachers identify as needing extra help are obliged to meet in small groups with faculty tutors. Interestingly, these students can cycle in and out fairly briefly when they demonstrate they understand what they were sent to work on; that is, they are not obliged to stay for a whole semester. California State University at Chico has been experimenting on a small scale and will institute a full change in the fall of 1994 (see Rodby): all students will be placed in the regular English 1, but those judged as needing extra help will take a series of four four-week workshops. Students will meet weekly in groups of 10 with an instructor. The first workshop is an exploration of the students' literacy history and practices; for the second and third workshops, the student has a choice among various topics (for example, understanding the assignment, narrative, research, and citations); and the fourth is on preparing a port-folio (which is the final assignment for all English 1 students). Washington State University has been using a one-credit supplementary course for students who need extra help and has now gotten rid of all basic writing sections (see Haswell and Wyche-Smith). New York University has long had a one-credit tutorial that students could take as a supplement to the introductory writing course. Johnson C. Smith University, a historically black institution, reports success in getting rid of remedial or basic courses in all subjects and moving to heterogeneous courses: "In addition to retaining more students, we are increasing student achievement as indicated by both internal and external measures" (Kidda, Turner, and Parker 22). No doubt there are other examples I do not know about where schools are exploring this kind of approach.

We can also see around us examples of the larger general principle involved here: that heterogeneity is an advantage; that instruction will permit and perhaps even benefit from difference. This was Bartholomae's point in "The Tidy House," calling on the work of Mary Louise Pratt, and he could also have called on Mikhail Bakhtin. Bartholomae and Pratt argue that linguistic homogeneity is the exception rather than the rule. Many elementary and secondary schools are getting rid of tracking, even though many people thought it was impossible. Also, we see lots of "mainstreaming" that was hard to imagine before. All the peer tutoring we see in schools and colleges is built on this same principle: bringing students of different skills together rather than keeping them apart. But we must remember that this approach is not an *alternative* to giving extra help to inexperienced or poorly prepared writers; it is a different *way* to give extra help and instruction. That is—and this is crucial—we do not get to save all the money now spent on teaching basic courses: much of it is needed for a different deployment of extensive support.

Objections to This Heterogeneous Approach

1. Allies of basic writers might object and say that I am attacking basic writing programs just when they most need defense. Administrators and legislators are looking at basic writing programs with a hungry eye: "Why should we pay for learning that students should have done before they came to college? Let unprepared students go back to high school or night school and prepare!" Administrators or legislators have already taken credit away from many or perhaps even most basic writing courses. They are now threatening the next step: to take away funding itself and simply drop basic courses altogether. There is lots of money to be saved.

So am I just playing into the hands of such administrators with my suggestions? No. The real problem for unskilled writers is the present system with its emphasis on assessment and on labeling students as basic writers and putting them in separate courses. This sends a very dangerous message: "These students are not yet ready for a regular college writing course." What I am proposing is a structure to send a very different message: "These students are bona fide college students. They have been accepted by the admissions process. They *are* ready for the regular college writing course. Of course, we provide extra help for some students—as we have always done."

2. Some people may object that poorly prepared writers themselves will feel uncomfortable, intimidated, and humiliated by having to work in the same class with the regular students. The argument is that these students *want* to be held apart in a separate and protected situation. No doubt a certain number of students do feel this way, so perhaps it would make sense to have a conventional basic writing course for those who want it. But let us ask them and give them a choice instead of deciding for them. Thus, students would only be in basic writing by choice; and they probably ought to be free to drop it when they decide it is no longer helpful. (No doubt some students would take this course when we would not have placed them in it.)

This principle respecting students' own sense of what they need in order to succeed is one of the main arguments in favor of heterogeneity. One of the main products of the present basic writing system with its limited tracking is student anger and resistance. An enormous amount of the slow learning and nonlearning we see in school is really a result of resistance more than of inability. Listen to this student writing about her experience: "The first day of school when my friends and I were discussing our schedules, I found that I was the only one taking Basic Writing. . . . The day came for me to go to Basic Writing for the first time. I went to class that day thinking that maybe no one knows that this is a basic class. The word 'basic' just makes me think of dumb, and the fact that there were less than 10 of us really did not help." Is this an attitude that will maximize learning? What kind of proof do we have that students are wrong when they say, "I don't belong in this dummy class"? We have enough evidence that some so-called basic writing students can function satisfactorily or even well in a nonbasic course. Maybe others could, too, especially if we give them lots of extra help while they are there. We need more exploration.[4]

Another product of the present system is student self-blame, lack of confidence, and consequent low motivation. Think how much these attitudes slow down learning. Listen to this student in a classic statement of self-blaming: "Before closing I have to comment on my teacher. Mrs. Chamberlain is a good and caring teacher and she is teaching this course well and if we fail a test or quiz it's not because it wasn't taught to us well but because we fail to meet our potentials." (These statements were written by students to me as an outside visitor, in confidence from the teacher.)

3. The most telling argument against heterogeneous classes is this: "Our basic writing classes are *better* than our regular 101s—and these students need and deserve better writing classes." Basic writing classes *are* better at many campuses, including my own. They can be better in various ways: they can have better teachers and curricula and can provide better support, more sense of community, and a richer, more productive cultural mix. But are they really better if they insist by definition on holding the students back a semester or two, costing them time and money? If the basic course is really better, why cannot a student satisfy the writing requirement with it? In short, if we really want to treat these writers well, why cannot we explore the model they are developing in South Carolina and Cal State-Chico? That is, why cannot we continue to give these students all the advantages we currently give them (better teachers, curricula, support, and culture) but *not* give them those two dubious "advantages": being kept out of the regular course and being prohibited from satisfying the writing requirement as quickly as everyone else? (Northeastern University has a freshman program for basic writers that, though it segregates them, does not cost them more time.)

I fear I have drifted into using a more pugnacious voice because of the adversarial structure I have used (answering objections). I do not want to be dogmatic about something we understand so little. What we clearly need is more exploration and trial. We have plenty of experience with quarantining students who do poorly on placement tests. What we lack is experience with heterogeneous courses where we nevertheless give lots of special, supplemental help to those who need it.

Implications for Assessment

It is important to recognize that the present basic writing system is deeply complicit or symbiotic with large-scale testing. Placement testing for basic writing is now the most frequent kind of writing assessment in higher education. (This is the finding of three research reports—CCCC Committee on Assessment; Greenberg, Wiener, and Donovan; and Lederman, Ryzewic, and Ribaudo—cited in Greenberg, "Validity" 17.) It eats up more money than any other kind of assessment. Because it is so expensive and yet seldom trustworthy or fair (usually being based on single samples written in artificial conditions), I resent it. I am looking for ways to save that money for teaching—and also get away from the labeling and segregatory structure of most first-year writing instruction.

And really, all this basic writing assessment is part of a much larger problem: simply too much assessment, too much preoccupation with evaluation and measuring. Schools and colleges and legislators are more willing to spend money for testing than for teaching and teachers. We are dominated by a cultural assumption that our problems in education will be solved by more test-ing, more standards. We accede too often to a general tendency to mistake assessment for education, to feel that if we get the testing right, students will finally learn. The explorations I have engaged in here and the successful ex-periments at the University of South Carolina and Berea and the new program at Cal State-Chico suggest some very concrete changes we can make by the 21st century in our assessment practices.

We can avoid the large-scale assessments that basic writing programs have tended to foster—assessment detached from instruction—and get the assess-ment we need with small-scale, local assessments rooted in instruction. In South Carolina, it is the teachers themselves who make the placement deci-sions, and they make them in terms of which kinds of students they can deal with. William Smith has developed an interesting placement process at the University of Pittsburgh on this principle, as has Washington State University (Haswell and Wyche-Smith). The fact is that large-scale testing plays into the hands of administrators who want to cut programs by means of simplistic judgments about ability.

We can avoid entrance testing and use exit testing instead. That is, we are misguided if we try to decide ahead of time whether someone will benefit from regular writing instruction. We are not justified in setting up barriers to en-trance, but we are perfectly justified in setting them up at exit. If we are more open and welcoming at first, we surely have to be tougher about not giving students credit for the regular first-year course until they produce a portfolio of "good enough writing," not a shoddy minimal competency but rather some-thing of genuine substance.

The Yogurt Model

Utopian thinking does not try to be realistic; it tries to provide visions or models. But I have been toying with the utopian genre in order to show repeat-edly how something that looked utopian was in fact feasible under normal conditions. What looked like a vision was something we could see with our two eyes.

But let me turn a corner and talk about something I *have not* seen. I want to extrapolate principles from what we have already seen and push toward a utopian model that could guide our future planning. The essential principle in the yogurt model is the *mixing of cultures*: we benefit from the presence of an older, developed culture present whenever we are trying to teach a newer or inexperienced culture.

Let me describe what a first-year writing program would look like that built on the principle of mixed cultures. All students would be required to take the same three-credit writing course, but the course would be structured in a somewhat competence-based or outcomes-based way. When students produce an acceptable portfolio, they would get three credits and could leave. Thus, skilled students could get finished more quickly than unskilled ones. However, even very strong writers would have to stay at least half a semester, for the requirement would also be trying to ensure that students learn a process, such as the skills of generating, revising, and working with peers. Unskilled students would not just languish, however: they would also get lots of supplemental help—which might be obligatory for some, voluntary for others.

Because there would be no barriers to entrance and students could leave sooner or later according to their accomplishments, the stakes would be higher than usual on assessing final portfolios. Programs might want to put in some guidelines like these: portfolios would have to contain writing of different, roughly specified sorts and genres, illustrating various dimensions of the writing process. Portfolios would have to be ruled satisfactory by one other teacher in addition to the student's own teacher. To help guard against plagiarism, perhaps students would have to include a paper or exercise or two produced wholly in a classroom workshop setting over a number of sessions so that they have plenty of opportunity for reflection, conversation, feedback from peers and teachers, and revision but not opportunity for taking these particular pieces home.

Notice how this yogurt model makes us re-imagine our conception of a "course." A course would no longer be a voyage where everyone starts out on the ship together and arrives at port at the same time; not a voyage where everyone starts the first day with no sea legs and everyone is trying simultaneously to become acculturated to the sea. It would be more like the Burkean parlor (Burke 45)—or a writing center or studio—where people come together in groups and work together. Some have already been there a long time working and talking together when new ones arrive. New ones learn from playing the game with the more experienced players. Some leave before others. People continually trickle in and trickle out, but they work and talk together while they are there. Unskilled writers would be there longer, but they would often function as veterans, experts, elders, carriers of the culture. They would be better than the hotshot students at the writerly processes of sharing, cooperating, feedback, even revising. Thus, teachers would no longer have what seems to me the hardest job in teaching: starting out each course each semester with a room full of students who do not know how to function as members of a writing workshop—trying to build a culture from scratch.

At the very beginning, we would start out with only half the regular number of students, so we could work closely and pay lots of attention to them for about three or four weeks to build a strong writing culture. As we and they build the culture and get better, we would bring in new students, so that the new ones join into groups with the experienced ones and get acculturated. From that point on, there will always be veterans with the new ones, always new ones joining veterans. We would get to keep the culture over the semester breaks—even over the summer. We would always come back to the new semester with a class of two-thirds veterans who already know how to function as writers. Notice, by the way, that this is how most real-world learning groups work: there are always veterans around when new people join.

This vision of students trickling in and out rather than remaining a stable population might make us fear that everything will be chaos, impermanence, and lack of community: just a kind of "commuter culture" where students attend only to their own progress and do not connect with others. But do not lose sight of the fact that most students would be there for 14 weeks; and for every student who would get out early, others would be there for longer than 14 weeks. For this model would lead to fairly tough standards. The conventional "time-serving" model of a course often functions as a way to permit lots of students to get by with writing that is *not* "good enough." Many of us cannot bring ourselves to fail students who come to class and turn in all their assignments for 14 weeks—pieces of writing that more or less follow the assignment but are really not good enough. After all, the conventional system sends everyone in 101 the following message: "These students passed the placement test; all they need is 14 weeks of dutiful treatment. Then you can let them go." It is hard for teachers to be demanding about what they require for a passing grade.

I am influenced here by my three years on a research team looking at competence-based programs in higher education. (See Elbow, "Trying to Teach," and the essays in Grant.) A competence-based, yogurt structure creates more incentive for students to invest themselves and provide their own steam for learning—learning from their own efforts and from feedback from teachers and peers. For the sooner they learn, the sooner they are free to get credit and leave. Instead of resenting the need to revise (as so many first-year students do), they will soon see that revising will make the biggest difference to how soon they can leave. They are not stuck for a prison term of 14 weeks. (By the way, some people might think that the administration of this kind of flexible system would be impossible. But competence-based programs managed to do it— with much less time, expense, and complication than it currently takes to administer huge placement tests. Imagine if you had never heard of placement testing and someone proposed setting it up.)

Notice finally how this approach reshapes what is probably the main influence on learning—the dimensions of freedom and coercion. This approach says all must take writing. But what counts is learning and results, not putting in time. Though no one is forced to take a "baby" or "dummy" course, no one is exempted.

Given this structure, I suspect that a significant fraction of skilled students will in fact stay for longer than they have to when they see they are learning things that will help them with other courses—*and* see that they enjoy it. It will often be their smallest and most human class, the only one with a sense of community like a Burkean parlor. But, and here is the point, they would no longer be there against their wills: they would be doing it by choice. The presence in a classroom of even two or three skilled writers staying longer by choice will have a significant effect on the culture.

What is so sacred, inevitable, necessary, or natural about our default models for teaching and learning—in particular our model where we assume 20 or 25 students must stay and learn together in a room for 10 or 14 weeks? Utopian thinking helps us see that what looks natural is really a historically based construction. So while we are exploring heterogeneous grouping and variable lengths of stay in a class, let us also explore our unthinking assumptions about size. That is, we could have a similar kind of "course" where students did not meet in whole classes—only in groups of five or six. These small groups would meet once a week with an instructor for an hour or so; and then meet for two hours a week or so on their own at a time and place of their own choosing. Or perhaps one of these hours would be with an undergraduate tutor. (See Nelson for explorations of how teaching and learning can be structured around small groups rather than whole classes.)

Conclusion

My theme is that we need to honor the utopian impulse. What looks at first like unrealistic utopianism can turn out to be realistically feasible; what looks like a "nowhere" (what "utopia" literally means) can turn out to be a some-where. Fredric Jameson speaks of the difficulty of utopian thinking in our era. He speaks of modern readers whose "fantasy tolerance is . . . modified by a change in social relations: so in the windless closure of late capitalism it [has] come to seem increasingly futile and childish for people with a strong and particularly repressive reality-and-performance principle to imagine tinker-ing with what exists, let alone its thoroughgoing restructuration" (Ruppert xiii–xiv). In our culture, people tend to have a powerless feeling that no major changes are possible. When I published *Writing Without Teachers* in 1973, teacherless groups or peer feedback groups were accused of being hopelessly naive and utopian. But we have seen the practice become commonplace. Who is to say that some of the utopian visions I have described here will not become commonplace as well?

Notes

1. Someone might object, "But we need more than those minimal scores because we could never get the scorers to give us exactly the number of basic writing students that we can afford to teach. We need a range of scores so we can make the students and the dollars match each other." But this very problem should lead to a sound assessment practice: compiling one list of failing students about whom all readers agreed, and then one more list of students about whom readers disagreed.

2. Arguments against basic writing courses often talk about tracking. But in all fairness, a distinction needs to be made. In the worst form of tracking, targeted students are put on a separate track in order to ship them to different terminal stations—so the different populations never meet. In the typical university writing program, however, the tracking is less noxious: basic students are segregated on a separate track, but the goal is eventually to move them to the same station that all the others students reach—and with full integration during the last leg of their journey. In the end, I believe basic courses are a kind of tracking. Singling students out and separating them surely has an effect on their motivation and self-image. But it is not the kind of tracking we see in many schools that shunts off—"cools out"—the allegedly less skilled students so they do not have a chance to reach the desirable station. Perhaps we should call it "temporary tracking."

3. It is true that certain "instruction" depends on homogeneity or prior knowledge. In mathematics, you cannot learn Y unless you understand a particular X that precedes it. Yet look at how even mathematics has a long tradition of heterogeneous classrooms where individual students follow particular paths at different speeds working in small groups or individually and using workbooks or computer-aided instruction.

4. Let us think for a moment about all the students who fail the regular writing course who were not placed in basic writing. They take longer than one semester to reach acceptable levels of writing. Perhaps their placement test was read badly; perhaps their placement writing really did look stronger than their characteristic ability; perhaps they did not work hard enough; perhaps they drank too much. Whatever the reason, we must indubitably say about them what we indubitably say about those who fail the placement test: these students were "not ready for success in the first-year writing course." Should we give a placement exam for motivation? Such tests exist, and they are at least as trustworthy as our writing placement exams. Or should we perhaps give all students a chance to make it in one semester—with extra help for those who look as though they need it?

Appendix: Works That Question Holistic Scoring

Belanoff, Pat. "The Myths of Assessment." *Journal of Basic Writing* 10.2 (1991): 54–66.

Broad, Robert. " 'Portfolio Scoring': A Contradiction in Terms." *New Directions in Portfolio Assessment: Reflective Practice, Critical Theory, and Large-Scale Scoring*. Ed. Laurel Black, Donald A. Daiker, Jeffrey Sommers, and Gail Stygall. Portsmouth, NH: Heinemann, 1994. 263–76.

Buley-Meissner, Mary Louise. "Reading Without Seeing: The Process of Holistic Scoring." *Writing on the Edge* 4.1 (Fall 1992): 51–65.

Charney, Davida. "The Validity of Using Holistic Scoring to Evaluate Writing: A Critical Overview." *Research in the Teaching of English* 18 (Feb. 1984): 65–81.

Despain, LaRene, and Thomas L. Hilgers. "Readers' Responses to the Rating of Non-Uniform Portfolios: Are There Limits on Portfolios' Utility?" *WPA: Writing Program Administration* 16.1–2 (Fall/Winter 1992): 24–37.

Elbow, Peter. "Foreword." *Portfolios: Process and Product.* Ed. Pat Belanoff and Marcia Dickson. Portsmouth, NH: Heinemann, 1991. ix–xvi.

——. "Ranking, Evaluating, Liking: Sorting Out Three Forms of Judgment." *College English* 55 (Feb. 1993): 187–206.

——. "Will the Virtues of Portfolios Blind Us to Their Potential Dangers?" *New Directions in Portfolio Assessment: Reflective Practice, Critical Theory, and Large-Scale Scoring.* Ed. Laurel Black, Donald A. Daiker, Jeffrey Sommers, and Gail Stygall. Portsmouth, NH: Heinemann, 1994. 40–55.

Gorman, Thomas P., Alan C. Purves, and R. E. Degenhart. *The IEA Study of Written Composition I: The International Writing Tasks and Scoring Scales.* Oxford: Pergamon, 1988. Vol. 5 of *International Studies in Educational Achievement.* 5 vols.

Gould, Stephen Jay. *The Mismeasure of Man.* New York: Norton, 1981.

Hamp-Lyons, Liz. "Scoring Procedures for ESL Contexts." *Assessing Second Language Writing in Academic Contexts.* Ed. Liz Hamp-Lyons. Norwood, NJ: Ablex, 1991. 241–76.

Hamp-Lyons, Liz, and William Condon. "Questioning Assumptions about Portfolio-Based Assessment." *College Composition and Communication* 44 (May 1993): 176–90.

Hanson, F. Allan. *Testing Testing: Social Consequences of the Examined Life.* Berkeley: U of California P, 1993.

Huot, Brian. "Reliability, Validity, and Holistic Scoring: What We Know and What We Need to Know." *College Composition and Communication* 41 (1990): 201–13.

Lucas, Catharine Keech. "Toward Ecological Evaluation." *The Quarterly* 10.1 (1988): 1–3, 12–17; 10.2 (1988): 4–10.

Scharton, Maurice. "Models of Competence: Responses to a Scenario Writing Assignment." *Research in the Teaching of English* 23 (1989): 163–80.

Smith, Barbara Herrnstein. *Contingencies of Value: Alternative Perspectives for Critical Theory.* Cambridge: Harvard UP, 1988.

8 Writing Assessment Beyond the Classroom: Will Writing Teachers Play a Role?

EDWARD M. WHITE

The problem for writing assessment in the future will be to bring together the goals, instruments, and methods the most informed writing teachers use in their classrooms with those used by the assessment community to shape public policy. I am not much worried about who will assess writing in the writing classrooms of the future or how they will do it; English teachers will do it, and we will do it in ways that reflect our teaching. The creative suggestions that Peter Elbow makes in the previous chapter will no doubt become part of our continuing effort to restrict the destructive uses of assessment and increase its positive effects in our classrooms. We are accustomed to debating our teaching methods, our curriculum, and the way we assess writing, and I have seen great advances in all of them since I began teaching my first freshman composition course over 35 years ago. I am, however, very much concerned about who will assess writing beyond our classrooms and how they will go about it.

I am not suggesting that classroom assessment is unimportant; it matters immensely to our students and profoundly affects our teaching. But no one outside our classes much cares about what we do in class, how we do it, or why we do it—as long as we turn in our grades on time. Whether we use portfolios or spelling bees for measuring student progress, our classroom practices have little or no effect on the assessments going on outside our classrooms. As the increasing numbers of campus, statewide, and national assessment programs show, the rest of our colleagues do not even trust our grades to indicate minimum writing proficiency (however they may define it), and they are ever ready to put their faith in any old test rather than in our classroom assessments. We need not fear that they are eager to take over the job of teaching writing; however little they trust our practices and our standards, their terror of teaching writing will keep us employed. But we do need to realize that when we talk about classroom assessment, we are essentially talking among ourselves about teaching—a useful and important discourse for teachers. But we need to expand that discourse to include what the rest of the world means by assessment.

The assessment community is large, powerful, and of immense importance to higher education, but most of the writing community cares little and thus knows little about it, despite the fact that its measures are coming closer and closer to our budgets, our programs, and even our classrooms. Furthermore, most of the writing community regards the assessment community (if we regard it at all) as hostile to the most valuable purposes and methods of teaching writing, while the assessment community sees the writing community as largely irrelevant to serious measurement. If this division continues, writing assessment will remain as two separate activities, with no real connection between what we do in our classrooms and the crucial assessment activity that goes on outside these classrooms.

The situation is reminiscent of the old joke about power in marriage. "I make the big decisions," the husband says, proudly, "while my wife makes the little ones."

"Really?" replies the interlocutor. "Give me some examples."

"Sure," the husband continues. "I make the big decisions about how to pay for health care for the unemployed, what to do about the homeless, how to bring about peace in the Balkans, and how to end hunger in Africa. My wife takes care of the little decisions, such as where I work, where we live, how to spend our money, and how to bring up our children."

Marriages can and should produce better partnerships than this, and so should we. If we persist in holding ourselves aloof from external measurement, the assessment community will be content to leave the big decisions about classroom assessment to us, as long as they continue to make the little decisions about where the university spends its resources, which programs live and die, and what national goals for writing should be.

Assessment Beyond the Classroom

We ignore assessment beyond the classroom at our peril, as public school teachers could inform us if we listened to them. Every elementary school has a few heroic teachers working against odds to help children love reading and enjoy writing as a way to learn, to express themselves, and to gain power over their worlds. But these teachers must stop such work when assessment time comes, for most schools still use old-fashioned multiple-choice tests of standard dialect and usage as measures of performance in English. The teachers have no choice but to stop teaching reading and writing so they can drill the children in test-taking skills and workbook items. In many districts, these test results are widely published, affecting the jobs of principals and teachers and influencing the flow of education funds; often, test scores help determine such tangible matters as real estate values and such intangible ones as community pride. The teachers, overworked and fully involved with their students, usually have no influence whatsoever on the tests that measure the effectiveness of their work and that have such large ramifications for their communities. Because so much school English teaching reflects the dead hand of those tests, students come to college English classes largely unaware of the adventures of reading or the creative power of writing.

Even apparently benign assessment programs can degrade curriculum, as the Advanced Placement Program has shown. Although many AP courses have brought exciting reading and careful writing into the high school curriculum, far too many such courses limit the students' writing to practice for the AP essay tests. Such writing surely has value; the practice test questions are usually clear and interesting. But, just as surely, an English class that has no room for longer exploratory papers, revision, library work, or the writing of poetry or fiction is too narrow for the best students, or for any students.

If we imagine that in the future, college writing programs will be free from the demands of external assessment, we are ignoring all the signs around us of their increasing importance; they will have more and more effect on what we do. We have only two choices: we can ignore them in the vain hope that they will go away, or we can participate in them in an informed way to make them as good as possible. If we ignore them, they will not only *not* go away but also will intrude more and more into our daily lives, as they have in the schools.

The federal government is developing a national test for all college graduates (White, "Assessing"). This measure of accountability was first proposed by the National Education Goals Panel, set up by President George Bush with then governor Bill Clinton as a major participant. The panel envisioned a national test as a way to provide comparative information about college graduates' performance in three areas, including what they called "communication skills"—the kind of information that the National Assessment of Educational Progress has been providing for primary and high schools. I proposed instead a portfolio assessment system with many alternative models of portfolios (White, "Portfolios"), but that proposal was rejected: "The portfolio idea, strongly advocated, won little support, as people felt they were uneven, unwieldy, and perhaps not relevant to NACSL [National Assessment of College Student Learning] as presently conceived" ("Workshop Proceedings"). Amazingly, such a statement seems to be saying that actual writing is not relevant to a college education! I had expected the proposed national assessment of college graduates to die of its own inflated weight and the absurdity of the multiple-choice measures it was contemplating, but quite the reverse: it has gained momentum and is moving full-speed ahead. The *Chronicle of Higher Education* summarized its progress recently with ominous calm, reporting that the National Education Goals Panel recommended that the government "create a test to measure [college] students' critical thinking, communications, and problem-solving skills" in order to "provide some accountability measures for the state and federal resources committed to higher education, and to insure that adult-learning programs actually enhance the skills of students." Education Secretary Richard W. Riley concurred, the report continued, wishing " 'to make higher education more accountable,' but expressing some misgivings about the value of collecting data on a statewide rather than an institutional basis" (Zook).

Secretary Riley's concern for institutional comparisons is particularly disquieting; traditionally, such data are used to confound academic and social issues. If any of us are wondering if graduates of Dartmouth might get higher scores than graduates of inner-city community colleges, such data will settle our doubts and comfort our prejudices.

A request for proposals to develop such a test has gone out, and some of the most powerful assessment institutions and individuals in the country will be applying for the contract. We should not expect English faculty to be much involved, for we are not normally seen as players in these high-stakes games. For example, *Performance and Judgment: Essays on Principles and Practice in the Assessment of College Student Learning* (Adelman), an influential book on assessment recently published by the United States Department of Education, aimed to break new ground by focusing on active rather than passive assessments. It featured an essay on writing assessment by Stephen Dunbar, a psychologist at the University of Iowa. Although Dunbar is informed and responsible, he comes out of different traditions and a different discourse community than we do, yet he is the one who speaks for writing in that book.

I am feeling increasing urgency as I argue—as I have for 20 years—that we should focus as much energy as possible on improving the assessments coming from outside our classrooms. As we contemplate the future of writing assessment, we should resist the easier and more congenial topic of our classroom assessments and instead investigate the relatively unknown territory of those other assessments. If we do not make ourselves heard and respected as these external assessments develop, we will have to live with definitions and measures of what we do that have been constructed by those who do not know, understand, or, in some cases, even value what we do. We may indeed face a future in which writing will be assessed by specialists in psychology, critical thinking, education, and tests and measurements—most of whom seem to have an unbounded faith in the virtues of multiple-choice tests.

English Faculty and Assessment Beyond the Classroom

In fact, composition specialists are experienced with assessments beyond the classroom, and we have much to offer the larger assessment community. For example, most English faculty are involved in developing and scoring the written portions of the following types of tests:

Placement before entrance. Most of our universities require some kind of assessment designed to place students of different ability levels into appropriate courses. Although a number of institutions use national multiple-choice tests, many colleges now add an essay portion of their own devising, and English faculty are usually involved in creating and scoring the writing task.

Equivalency assessments. These are intended to allow students who believe that they already know what freshman composition teaches to prove it. Most colleges use national programs, such as AP or CLEP (College-Level Examination Program), sometimes supplemented by their own assessments. The California State University has used its own test, developed and scored by English faculty, for this purpose for over two decades. Miami University has developed a portfolio assessment for the same purpose.

Coursewide assessments. Everyone taking freshman composition, for example, must pass the same assessment—usually an essay test or a portfolio assessment administered by English faculty; this then becomes an important part of the instructor's course grade.

Rising junior assessments. Every student must pass this multiple-choice, essay, or portfolio assessment in order to enter upper-division courses.

Graduation writing requirements. Sometimes these are part of course distribution requirements (for example, every graduating senior must pass two courses with a "W" designation, such as History 305W—the "W" indicating a writing-intensive course), but more usually they consist of a writing test or portfolio assessment.

If we can continue to use our considerable power to influence these assessments on our home campuses and if we can develop more credibility in assessment among our colleagues in other disciplines, we will be able to affect these other assessments coming our way. To do this, we must be willing to join assessment committees and to participate in the often dreary work that leads to assessment decisions; we need to press for writing components, including portfolios as well as essay tests, on assessments at the campus, state, and national level. "The train has left the station," the test makers kept saying at a recent national assessment conference; "the important question is who is on board." As long as we think assessment beyond the classroom is someone else's business, is somehow "nonacademic," or is not worth our time and attention, we remain chatting among ourselves in the station, abandoning our discipline and our students to those on the train.

Appropriate Uses of Essay Testing

In addition to our traditional aloofness, a second reason we currently have so little influence on assessment beyond our classrooms is that we spend too much time fighting each other about which kind of writing assessment is best. This question is not only the wrong one, and thus pointless, but a destructive one; discussions of assessment make sense only in context. That is, we must ask "Best for what purpose?" before our arguments about assessment methods begin to make sense.

An assessment is a means of gathering information to answer questions. So, we should be clear about what questions we are asking, what information we need to answer them, and how we will use that information before we decide about the assessment. This way of thinking about any assessment seems obvious enough, but very few assessment programs of any kind actually follow it. In most cases, the method of testing is the first issue decided instead of the last; the answer is sought before the question has become clear. Typically, some influential campus figure or group presses for a particular test (such as a new commercial measure of general education outcomes) or a new type of assessment (such as portfolios) as a valuable device *in itself*, regardless of campus goals or context. But it is wasteful and intrusive to gather more information than we can well use, and it is pernicious to use instructional funds to gather information that has no instructional purpose. Furthermore, it is dishonest to use a test designed for one purpose as if it provided information for another just because the scores happen to be on hand, as many campuses use the SAT or ACT—aptitude tests designed to predict which entering freshmen will return for the sophomore year—for writing placement. Before we decide on any assessment method, we surely should insist that it respond to clearly defined goals within our own context.

The typical college placement test, for example, seeks information that will help students enroll in courses for which they are ready, so all students have a reasonable chance to succeed. In English composition, that usually means a rough division between those who are likely to do passing work in freshman writing courses and those who need additional instruction before (or during) the course to have much chance of doing well. I am not here concerned about the nature of the help the campus provides, whether it is a special remedial or developmental program or some kind of tutorial arrangement within the writing course; if we intend to keep college opportunities alive for the ill-prepared, we must provide some kind of help, and that means identifying those who need that help. What kind of information is actually needed to make a placement decision?

Not much, in fact. While the actual choice about this information must be made on campus, with participation by the teachers who know what is actually being required and taught, most American campuses find students ready for freshman composition if they can read pretty well and write complete sentences. Many open-enrollment schools need to extend the definition of a sentence to accommodate some oral variations. More selective schools might look for more complex matters, such as an ability to write coherent paragraphs or to analyze difficult texts. But remember, these tests address what is needed at *entrance* to freshman composition, abilities that should not be confused with what is taught in the course, which usually devotes a good bit of attention to paragraph and essay construction and more complicated reading. Most of us would be happy if our entering freshmen really knew how to predicate and read.

If this—or something like this—is all that the testing program is trying to discover, an essay test is perfectly appropriate. A test development committee can come up with questions that will allow students to demonstrate the specific abilities in question, with whatever variations may suit the local situation; 45 minutes is plenty of writing time to demonstrate sentence production and some reading comprehension. Although essay tests are under attack these days, and we should not exaggerate their value, they can indeed give us some important information we can trust.

Because we can gain this useful information about our students from impromptu essays, it is easy to understand why many portfolio programs now include one or more of them. Among other matters, we can be sure that the student writing on the scene is the author of the work to be evaluated. But beyond this, we can take advantage of the focus and concentration that impromptu essays require to see how students can perform under pressure (White, "An Apologia").

On the other hand, numbers of institutions are using impromptu essay tests to examine students for entry to junior-level courses or even as a condition for graduation—obviously inappropriate purposes. Among other matters, advanced or graduating students should be able to use sources intelligently to support, not substitute for, their own ideas; they should be able to discover and revise complex arguments, show some depth of understanding of a topic, and understand the discourse community of a particular field. Timed impromptu essay tests seldom address these matters.

I repeat, because the point is so often ignored: no assessment device is good or bad in itself but only in context. Only when we know what we are seeking to discover can we claim that a particular kind of assessment is appropriate or not. In the many situations that are appropriate for impromptu essay tests, we should use them without guilt but also without exaggerating what they are able to measure. It is not worth saying that portfolios are better than essay tests, just as it is not worth saying that the Ferrari Testarossa is a better car than a Honda Civic; of course it is. But that does not mean that every Honda owner should rush out and buy a Testarossa, whatever the budget or situation may allow—or that every writing assessment must be a portfolio assessment.

In fact, the advocates of portfolio assessment should stop attacking essay testing as a means of promoting portfolios. What they have in common—student production of text in response to some kind of assignment—is much more significant than their differences. One way to envision a portfolio is, after all, as an elaborate essay test, with lots of portions and revisions, done over an extended period of time. Conversely, we could consider an essay test with one or two questions to be an abbreviated portfolio, one that might be expanded when the resources become available. These are differences of scope, not of kind. Attacks on essay testing ignore its crucial value for the development of portfolios and its continued value in writing assessment as a direct measure of writing with proven reliability; these attacks weaken our position in relation to the assessment community, which insists, properly, that any measurement must be demonstrably fair if it is to be taken seriously.

Portfolios are a natural outgrowth of essay testing and represent a clear advance in the assessment of writing under many circumstances. It is natural for advocates of portfolio assessment to stress its advantages over the essay testing that has now become familiar, even routine, but the similarities between portfolios and essays are much more significant than their differences. One or the other of these direct methods of writing assessment may be most appropriate in a particular situation, and either is preferable to multiple-choice testing in almost all cases.

The relatively wide use and credibility of essay testing allow many of those now looking at writing assessment to ignore multiple-choice testing and its threat to writing. Nevertheless, for most faculty outside the English department and for almost all administrators, assessment still means multiple-choice testing; evaluation of actual writing, whether impromptu essay tests, term papers, or portfolios, is generally regarded as hopelessly subjective, unreliable, and arbitrary. The common parlance for multiple-choice testing is a mistaken judgment, disguised as a description: "objective testing," as if the instruments had been created by a value-free, apolitical machine without human input. True, new interest in "performance assessment" or "authentic assessment" has arisen in the assessment community, but that interest is, as it has been for generations, peripheral to most assessment practice and to the concerns of writing teachers. We must recognize that the direct measurement of writing, so widely accepted now in writing programs, remains deeply suspect by the higher education community at large.

As we look to the future, the historical perspective is particularly important, for many of the attacks on essay testing fail to take into account the way it developed as a response by writing teachers to the dominant multiple-choice testing in American education.[1] Even today, the supposed efficiency, objectivity, and economy of multiple-choice testing remain in the background of most discussions of writing assessment. In most situations, the choice is not, as the English teacher debate would suggest, between an impromptu essay and a writing portfolio but rather between a multiple-choice test and some kind of essay test or some combination of the two: a recent survey of placement practices by a CCCC committee shows that "of all assessment methods being used for this purpose, approximately 48% are multiple choice, 49% timed writing samples, and 3% portfolios" (Murphy et al. 22). Anyone with a role in writing assessment must keep in mind the multiple-choice specter that hovers just offstage; no stake has ever been driven through its heart to keep it in its coffin, however much it may be wounded.

The painfully won and documented scoring reliability of essay tests is our best defense against the draining of our curriculum by this sharp-toothed phantom. To be sure, we have bought this reliability at the expense of a bit of our treasured individuality; we have been willing, for the sake of fairness to test takers, to say that we will agree, temporarily, to score a set of papers according to a single set of test criteria. In recent years, this reliability has allowed actual student writing to influence many decisions—even so tense and litigious a decision as admission to medical school. While that reliability is not perfect, it is high enough to allow essay tests to claim some validity as a direct measure of writing ability. This validity is much more limited than many of us would like and not nearly as encompassing as many of us claimed two decades ago, when (in our passionate opposition to machine testing) we claimed that essay test writing was "real writing." But without reliability, claims for validity—such as are being made prematurely for portfolios—ring hollow.

Portfolio assessment may eventually be able to demonstrate reliability, but studies have only recently begun on ways to achieve it. The difficulties are enormous, probably many times those of single essay scoring, but some programs (such as those at Miami University of Ohio, the University of Michigan, and New Mexico State University) are coming up with encouraging statistics. Portfolios contain multiple samples of writing, which should increase overall reliability, even as they make scoring more complicated. We should not follow the lead of those who, despairing of achieving reliable scoring of portfolios, attempt to discredit the concept of reliability itself. The fact that we disagree about values in life does not mean that we cannot agree, temporarily, on values in an assessment. It is paradoxical to say that we can only achieve honest measurement by abandoning fair scoring. The future of portfolios and of their influence on external assessments depends on the development of reliable scoring procedures, which are being adapted from those now known to work for single essays. When portfolio assessments demonstrate unreliable scoring (as recently occurred in Vermont), the only way to preserve the direct assessment is to change procedures to increase the reliability of the scores.

If portfolio assessment can cope with the reliability problem—and I am hopeful that it will—it promises to bring into writing assessment some of the most creative aspects of the English curriculum. One difference between a collection of materials and a portfolio is the "reflective letter," or "self-assessment," that is becoming a standard feature. The broadened scope of the portfolio not only allows inclusion of various kinds of expository writing but also invites such reflection as well as poetry, fiction, and other imaginative forms. In contrast to the narrowing of vision typical of the multiple-choice tests, portfolios open possibilities of new evaluation, and hence valuing, of the creativity our society badly needs in the next century.

In the future, as in the past, we are likely to see steady conflict between educational assessment in the classroom and the assessments done for other purposes beyond the classroom. If we are wise, we will enter the debate and resist the simple sorting of winners and losers through the reductive tests our society loves with ignorant passion. After all, we writing teachers are committed to help those born losers become winners and to redefine those very labels so they encompass more than economic or social values. Again, if we are wise, we will find ways to join the ranks of the assessors as a way to change these assessments for the better. But history urges us to be cautious in our optimism: American academicians have not usually been wise or effectual in such matters, preferring in general to sit back and complain while powerful commercial interests dominate society and even education itself.

The next decade will test writing teachers, as we seek to wrest at least part of the definition and measurement of educational goals from those who see the world as containing one right answer amidst four wrong ones. The increasing community of energetic faculty working to make portfolios effective will have the major responsibility to promote writing; but the society as a whole must decide if education is to foster the thinking and writing process or merely to train workers for piecework. The future of assessment is bound up with the future of education, and the future of education reflects the values of the entire society. But we as a profession can affect the way our society measures and defines its goals if we elect to join and influence the assessment community, and the evaluation of writing has an important role to play in that process.

In my more optimistic moments, I see a future in which writing faculty routinely take leadership in assessment efforts, based on knowledge, enlightened self-interest, and a wide sense of social responsibility. I see them asking the right questions about context, goals, and uses before assessment devices are chosen. I see them insisting that all kinds of writing are valuable for assessment and instruction and that writing measures must require appropriate writing to be valid.

The assessment of writing in the future at its best can offer a troubled society a vision of active learning, creative thinking, and a much needed blend of skills with imagination. We cannot be confident that such a vision will be welcome in the future, but we can be absolutely certain that teachers of writing should be among those struggling to achieve it.

Note

1. I describe this history in considerable detail in Williamson and Huot (79–106) and, in a slightly different form, in the last chapter of White, *Teaching and Assessing Writing*, 2nd ed. 1994.

9 The Need for a Theory of Writing Assessment

RESPONSE BY BRIAN HUOT

In their discussion of "Who Will Assess Composition in the Future and How Will They Do It?," both Peter Elbow and Edward M. White contribute much to our understanding of what the crucial issues are and have been in writing assessment. Elbow outlines the importance of teaching and curriculum and how eliminating an assessment practice like placement can vastly affect the way our classrooms look and the way our courses are conducted. White calls for the increased involvement of composition teachers in assessment beyond the classroom to guard against the control of outsiders who, without our involvement, would assess our students and programs in ways and with criteria irrelevant and detrimental to the teaching and learning of writing. Elbow's notion of minimal holistic scoring, in which raters make limited decisions depending upon the context for the evaluation, supports research findings that indicate that raters in holistic scoring sessions for placement base decisions upon such things as the "teachability" of particular students rather than on points of a scoring guideline (Pula and Huot). William L. Smith, who developed a system in which teachers place students in the courses they teach without scoring guidelines or achieving high rates of agreement between independent readers (interrater reliability), analyzed talk-aloud protocols and found that teachers can read a single essay and "see" a student in their class. We need to heed White's contention about the importance of context in testing and the irrelevance of preferring one type of an assessment procedure over another. This is critical if we are to use appropriately the assessment options we now possess and develop others to meet future challenges.

My chief disagreement with the two papers is in terms of focus. Both papers, while well grounded in research, experience, and logic, address practice rather than theory and in this way speak more to the past than the future. It is true that before we can talk about the future of writing assessment, we must remember its past. But historically, we have either ignored or denied any theoretical basis for writing assessment (Gere, "Written Composition"). Supposedly, we have not addressed a theory for writing assessment because we have been too concerned with developing methods to assess our students and programs. Consequently, theoretical considerations have had to be put on the back burner (Faigley, Cherry, Jolliffe, and Skinner). The result has been a praxis for writing assessment. Although we have been able to move from single-sample impromptu essays to portfolios in less than 20 years, we are still primarily concerned with constructing scoring guidelines and interrater reliability. The next two decades hold the promise of bringing radical changes that will more accurately reflect the way we teach and theorize about writing and its learning. This promise will be withheld from us if we do not address the larger questions involved in articulating a theoretical basis for our assessment practices.

In his chapter, White accurately identifies the main problem for the future of writing assessment: "to bring together the goals, instruments, and methods the most informed writing teachers use in their classrooms with those used by the assessment community to shape public policy." My question is, How we will bring these changes about? In response to White's call for compositionists to "develop more credibility in assessment among our colleagues," several groups of participants at the Conference on Composition in the 21st Century responded by talking about the need to learn more about statistics and other aspects of the technology of testing. Nonetheless, increasing our knowledge of testing will have limited value to "affect these assessments coming our way" with the methods we now use in the classroom. I contend it is more important that testers learn the theories that inform the teaching and learning of writing. And, there is some evidence to suggest that they have been doing just that. In a recent chapter on the history of the relationship between the testers and teachers of writing, Roberta Camp of the Educational Testing Service (ETS) traces the evolution of writing assessment from multiple-choice tests to single samples to portfolios as evidence of the increasing influence of the growing body of composition literature on writing assessment practices. According to Camp, the inroads made in portfolios and other alternative assessments of writing are a direct result of the rapid development of composition as a field of study.

The emerging theories of alternative assessment are especially relevant for writing assessment because they are being supported by the same theoretical movements in the social construction of knowledge that are presently being used to explore and explain written communication in a postmodern age. These new theories of assessment are being fueled by shifting ideas of teaching and learning. Learning, as it is being currently defined, most always contains subjective, personal, and reflective features if it is to become relevant and appropriate for drawing inferences, making decisions, and applying concepts to real-life situations (Bruner). According to theories of alternative assessment, future methods for assessing will need to realize and include the contextual nature of the learner and his or her environment. Certainly, the importance of context and personal involvement is not new to those of us who teach and study written communication. However, traditional forms of assessment have either ignored or attempted to mask these subjective characteristics of student ability in search of outside, objective measures of student ability.

White is correct in his assertion that "new interest in 'performance assessment' or 'authentic assessment' . . . as it has been for generations [is] peripheral to most assessment practice" (like single essays 20 years ago or portfolios 10 years ago). However, it is a mistake to ignore the theoretical movement in assessment or to fail to align ourselves with it. The theoretical basis of educational assessment has been undergoing a radical series of changes. Lee J. Cronbach and Samuel Messick, two of the most important validity scholars in testing theory, have been revising their theories for the last decade. (For a good review of the continuing development of validity in educational assessment, see Moss). For both of them, the validity of a test is now inextricably bound to its use and effects. In other words, a test that has a negative influence on teaching and learning can no longer be considered valid, a far cry from traditional views of validity that center on the degree to which a test measures what it purports to measure. These positions on validity are rather conservative compared to some who would devalue or eliminate validity altogether. For example, Evon G. Guba and Yvonna S. Lincoln, in their book *Fourth Generation Evaluation*, posit a theory of evaluation based on the tenets of social construction in which validity is seen as just another social construct. Peter Johnston argues "that the term validity, as it is used in psychometrics, needs to be taken off life support" (510). And, Howard Berlak contends that "validity as a technical concept is superfluous" (186). These shifts in testing theory can strengthen our position with testers and our ability to devise new and more appropriate measures for the evaluation of literate activity.

As Elbow asks us to experiment with the way we assess our students' ability for entrance or exit from individual courses or White urges us as a profession to become more active in assessment matters outside the classroom, I find little to disagree with. However, I also find few answers here about the future, about what will drive these practices in the classroom or allow us to stand on equal footing with a measurement community that has a rich history and vast literature. The future of writing assessment needs to move beyond practice to formulate a theoretical basis for addressing important issues. These new theories will then need to support the creation of new and innovative ways to assess how well our students write and how effective our pedagogies and programs are.

The chief challenges for a theory of writing assessment will be to construct assessment programs accountable to the outside forces and public agencies that fund education while helping to ensure that these same programs are true to our philosophies of education, our theories of language, and our pedagogy for productive classrooms. We will need to reconcile the drive for objectivity, which in writing assessment takes the form of agreement of individual raters, with the inherent variability of the readings given by individual judges. Our theories need to recognize that just as writers need contexts within which to write, raters need contexts within which to read. The biggest challenge, perhaps, is to recognize that we do, indeed, lack and need a theoretical base for the assessment of writing. Certainly the present time, with the compatible and emergent theories in alternative assessment, should provide us with the opportunities to begin the formulation of theories for writing assessment that can guide our efforts in assessing our students and establish assessment practices on a sound basis, consistent with our developing pedagogies for the teaching of writing.

Part 4   What Issues Will Writing Program Administrators Confront in the 21st Century?

10 The Long Revolution in Composition

ANNE RUGGLES GERE

> The long revolution, which is now at the centre of our history, is not for democracy as a political system alone, nor for the equitable distribution of more products, nor for general access to the means of learning and communication. Such changes, difficult enough in themselves, derive meaning and direction, finally, from new conceptions of man and society which many have worked to describe and interpret. Perhaps these conceptions can only be given in experience. The metaphors of creativity and growth seek to enact them, but the pressure, now, must be towards particulars, for here or nowhere they are confirmed.
>
> —Raymond Williams, *The Long Revolution*

More than 30 years ago, Raymond Williams identified as "the long revolution" the historical process by which individuals interact with changing government, industry, and culture to participate in the creation of and negotiation with new realities. Fueled by the conviction that persons "can direct their own lives, by breaking through the pressures and restrictions of older forms of society, and by discovering new common institutions" (347), the long revolution embodies "contradictions between different parts of the general process of change" (294). Although Williams focuses his discussion on Great Britain through 1960, his delineation of the long revolution offers a method of analysis that can, I believe, be usefully applied to composition studies. During the 30 years since Williams first wrote about the long revolution, we who work in composition studies have helped to create and negotiate with new realities, and looking at where our own long revolution has taken us can provide ways of looking toward the future.

The methodology Williams proposes does not look at a single pattern of change but considers the contradictions within multiple patterns. It assumes that change does not occur uniformly but contains oppositions and resistance throughout its uneven action. This analysis can provide, according to Williams, "the ratifying sense of movement, and the necessary sense of direction" (355). I propose, then, to look at some of the contradictions within the evolution of composition studies, point to areas of opposition and resistance, and, finally, to suggest directions we might pursue, particularly as we find ourselves filling the role of Writing Program Administrators (WPAs).

Among the sites of composition that embrace contradictions are the subject position of students, the baccalaureate, writing itself, the field of composition, and composition instructors. While these sites lack symmetry among themselves, they all represent the kinds of particulars through which, in Williams's view, new conceptions of humans and of society ultimately take form. Our shifting ideas about students, the baccalaureate, writing, the field of composition, and instructors embody oppositions and contradictions that have shaped and been shaped by the uneven processes of change that have marked composition studies over the past three decades.

One set of oppositions contained within the subject position we assign to students centers on the relative stability and/or unity of their identities. Susan Miller, for example, has argued that we tend to conceptualize our students as presexual, preeconomic, and prepolitical, and, in her view, assigning this identity to students has direct implications for the status of composition studies and those who work in it: "So long as these identities are maintained for composition students and their courses, it is unlikely that requirements on Practitioners of whatever rank will change. These expectations invite them to be irresponsible about making 'knowledge' in the sense that scholars and researchers do, despite their possible commitments to 'practice as inquiry' " (Textual Carnivals 192–3). This argument and its sequel, that changing the subjectivity we attribute to students is essential to changing our own marginal and service-oriented status, assign to students rather stable and unified identities. In arguing that terms such as "economic" or "sexual" can be applied to entire groups of students, Miller underplays the enormous diversity of students' racial, ethnic, and socioeconomic backgrounds as well as the personal and work identities they construct for themselves. (I anticipate Shirley Brice Heath's contribution to this volume in pointing to these identities.) Miller is not, of course, alone in this view. Theorists who embrace the so-called expressive view of writing predicate a stable and unified identity from which the "authentic" voice emerges in writing.

Those who operate from a postmodern perspective take a different view and describe students in terms of multiple subjectivities. Rather than conceptualizing students in terms of the dialectic between political and prepolitical or economic and preeconomic, these theorists describe students in multiple and conflicting terms. As Lester Faigley, for instance, observes, "Postmodern theory understands subjectivity as heterogeneous and constantly in flux" (*Fragments* 227). Drawing upon the example of the electronic classroom, Faigley demonstrates how students construct and interact with multiple identities and asserts that "the illusion that students form a coherent group is shattered when what would seem to be facile points of interpretation produce divergent responses" (230). For Faigley, this multiplicity, because it fosters creativity, does not represent a liability, but it "does require theorizing and, if teaching practices are to be involved, new metaphors for the subject" (230). Such theorizing and metaphors begin from the premise that student identities cannot be defined as stable or unified.

The contests and oppositions evident in these varying ways of thinking about student identities only suggest the many new concepts of humans that have emerged in composition studies during the past couple of decades. These concepts have contributed to and been shaped by continuing changes in our field. Another area of contest and opposition is the baccalaureate itself. Even though our nation has, from its earliest days, promoted education as a means to social equity, cultural attitudes toward education—particularly college education—remain complex. This complexity manifests itself in the status assigned to the baccalaureate degree.

None of us can claim ignorance of the recent virulent attacks on higher education. The media has cited, among other things, curriculum debates about including non-Western literature in undergraduate education, partial (and often inaccurate) representations of complicated theories such as deconstruction, and the supposedly luxurious working conditions of professors as evidence of the decadence of higher education. This attack has been strengthened by the recent economic downturn and the subsequent "jobless recovery," a phenomenon that points to large and complex shifts in employment patterns in our society. Since the mid-19th century and the rise of the professional class, higher education has provided credentials for those who wish to enter professions. As Burton J. Bledstein and Magali Sarfatti Larson have explained, higher education created a symbiotic relationship with the professions, simultaneously providing and receiving credibility. Higher education also guaranteed its graduates a larger share of the economic pie than those who completed only high school. In recent years, much of this difference resulted because the wages for high school graduates have been declining, but between 1987 and 1991, real salaries for the college-educated also declined (S. Kirsch 65). As the economic value of a college degree declines and layoffs and/or shrinking employment opportunities reach into white collar and professional positions, the worth of the baccalaureate is called into question, and attacks on higher education become more vicious. One recent attack focused on scholarly approaches to Shakespeare. The author began by asking such questions as, "Was

Shakespeare a misogynist? A bourgeois hegemonist? An apologist for imperialism? If you, gentle reader, don't have an opinion on any of these questions, never fear: A whole raft of academics have plenty. Together they have created a publishing mini-industry that has lately been labeled the Bardbiz." The author goes on to explain more about Bardbiz and concludes, "Let the academics prattle. They're a bunch of myopic spoilsports who miss the point entirely. Shakespeare stretches gracefully from the Globe to Portland, picking up new converts every hour. He needs no further defense." This was not written by Dinesh D'Souza, or Jonathan Yardley, or Allan Bloom. It is not excerpted from *Profscam* or *Illiberal Education*. It is from the editorial page of the *New York Times*—not the op-ed page but the editorial page. Behind this attack on professors lies a profound doubt about the worth of the baccalaureate in our culture. If our institutional role of credentialing young people for employment cannot be fulfilled because there are not enough jobs in the economy for them, then our societal function and the bachelor's degree we offer remains open to attack. Not surprisingly, higher education has responded to this questioning of its worth with increased attempts to demonstrate the value it adds to students' lives. In some cases, these demonstrations have been mandated by state legislatures, and in other cases, they have been developed voluntarily, but no matter how they have developed, one of the chief means by which higher education justifies itself to the larger society is by showing how it enhances the literacy skills of future citizens and workers. In other words, displays of student writing competency play a major role in assuring an ever more wary public of the value of higher education and of the baccalaureate. The pressure for additional evidence of enhanced student writing abilities is complicated by the increasingly diverse student population in many first-year writing courses. The combination of affirmative action programs and changing demography has brought students who represent a wide range of racial and ethnic backgrounds into higher education. This group of students faces stringent gatekeeping in the writing assessments mandated by those who question the value of the baccalaureate. Students whose families have no prior experience with higher education often number among those judged deficient in writing assessments. Thus, the opposition between the egalitarian credentialing function and the value-affirming gatekeeping function of higher education contend within writing programs. This contradiction between equity and gatekeeping is further complicated by the fact that these increasingly diverse students are taught by a relatively homogeneous faculty. While student populations in writing courses have changed significantly, faculty have remained largely white.

The complicated status of writing in our culture poses another set of contradictions for composition. Whether we look at the history of literacy instruction in this country or probe our own experiences as literacy learners, we see considerable asymmetry between reading and writing. As E. Jennifer Monoghan and others have noted, reading and writing instruction were separate, gendered, and unequal during the colonial period. Reading was taught to both girls and boys, often in dame schools—the preschools of that era—while parents retained writing masters to teach their sons to write. The expense of pens, ink, and paper along with the technical skills needed to make quill pens created difficulties for those outside the writing master's realm to learn to write. Although writing instruction is offered to all in today's society and although writing materials are generally available, the nature of the composition course varies with the perceived ability of the learners. Students in upper tracks in high school and in the "regular" college composition classes receive instruction designed to foster abstract thinking and critical analysis while students in lower tracks or remedial composition courses focus on isolated skills. Jeannie Oakes, who asked high- and low-track students about the most important things they learned, reports that high-track students said things such as, "I have learned to form my own opinions on situations," "How to express myself through writing and being able to compose the different thoughts in a logical manner," and "I've learned to look in depth at certain things and express my thoughts on paper" (67–9). Low-track students, in contrast, said they learned how to "write and get my homework done," "to spell words you don't know," and "to listen and follow the directions of the teacher" (87–9).

In addition, considerable asymmetry still haunts the reading-writing relationship. Most of us can recall very positive experiences with reading. Snuggling with a loved adult, transcending our physical environment, learning new things—these are the sorts of associations most of us have with reading, and the larger culture reinforces this positive view. Books displayed on coffee tables, books given as gifts, public service announcements about the value of reading, and school programs of Sustained Silent Reading or Drop Everything and Read all signify the high cultural value assigned to reading.

Writing, by contrast, frequently arouses negative associations. We can recall being punished FOR writing (on the wall or in library books) and we can recall being punished WITH writing (inscribing "I will not talk out in class" 100 times). For some of us, the quality of our penmanship was and is a source of embarrassment, and the many negative injunctions of composition teachers— do not end a sentence with a preposition, do not use the first person singular, do not split infinitives—eliminate much of the pleasure associated with writing. When students recount their development as writers, many of them report experiences of humiliation, pain, and frustration, especially with regard to their experiences in school. As individuals and as a culture, we are far more penurious with funds for writing. Few of us purchase high-quality paper and pens as easily as we buy books, we hesitate to ask students to invest as much in writing materials as they do in textbooks, and funding agencies still support much more research in reading than in writing.

At the same time that our culture reveres writing ability as a major form of evidence for the success of higher education, it harbors ambivalent attitudes toward writing. These contradictory attitudes can be expressed in oppositional statements: writing can provide great pleasure, particularly in the area of self-development versus writing can inflict great pain, especially as it is taught in schools; education should ensure that everyone in our society learns to write effectively versus education should not expect sufficient funding to develop writing skills among all students; writing serves as a vehicle for social mobility and entrance into professional work versus writing functions to limit access, thereby preventing those marked as different or other from entering highly prized employment areas of our culture.

Composition, wherein writing is both taught and theorized about, shapes and is shaped by the multiple oppositions surrounding writing. One manifestation of this appears in the conflicted views of composition itself. "Discipline," "mixed discipline," "field," and "postdiscipline" number among the terms contending to describe composition. Often used interchangeably, these terms also function as sites of conflict, with one theorist discrediting the term "discipline" and offering an alternative such as "field" or "mixed discipline." Robert J. Connors, for example, calls composition's coherence into question and designates it a mixed discipline ("Textbooks"). Stephen M. North applies the term "field" to composition as a way of acknowledging its "loosely construed" nature (364), while I employ the same term to mean a "complex of forces . . . , the [charged] space in which the reconceptualizations attendant to the restructuring of composition" can occur (*Into the Field* 4). Frequently, the appendage "studies" (for example, composition studies) provides a compromise because it retains sufficient vagueness and at the same time implies a separation from composition teaching. This attempt to define composition as more than a pedagogical enterprise emerged concurrent with efforts to improve the conditions under which teaching is carried out.

Anxious discussions about the working conditions of composition instructors coalesced in the Wyoming Resolution, a statement endorsed by the Conference on College Composition and Communication in 1987 that called for a definition of the minimum standards under which postsecondary writing teachers should be employed and for methods to implement and enforce these standards. This, in turn, led to the CCCC statement of Principles and Standards for Writing Instruction, a document that described the circumstances necessary for good writing instruction. Yet the numbers of part-time, nontenure-track positions in writing programs multiply every year, and the working conditions of persons in these marginalized positions contrast sharply with those of their full-time, tenure-track counterparts. Crowded into inadequate office space, often without a desk to call their own, many part-time composition instructors teach more classes than full-time faculty. Since the CCCC statement was issued, the evils it deplores have only increased. WPAs lament their complicity in exploiting this largely female group of workers, but WPAs themselves are also frequently an exploited group. Many universities hire assistant professors as WPAs, often with assurances or even contracts stipulating that administrative service will count toward tenure. Then after six or seven years, when these assurances and contracts have proved valueless, the assistant professor is fired and another hired to become the new WPA. Whether tenured or not, WPAs claim, and I believe rightly, that they work harder than most of their colleagues. In exchange for relief from teaching one course, many are expected to train and supervise new TAs, handle scheduling, and design courses and/or syllabi.

This increased exploitation of writing instructors has developed concurrent with an expanded scholarship within composition. We can point with justifiable pride to the graduate programs that train the next generation of composition scholars, to the increased number of journals that publish work in composition, and to the number of tenured and tenure-track positions in composition. At the same time, however, we need to acknowledge the growing number of part-time and nontenure-track positions in our field. The radically different positions occupied by tenure-track and nontenure-track composition instructors suggest another contradiction in the long revolution of composition.

Even though we have achieved professional status for some of our members, it has coincided with (and may have actually caused) an increased exploitation of other members of the field. Williams suggests one way of looking at this contradiction by pointing to common forms of opposition to the long revolution. As he explains it, privileged groups, in this case our colleagues who specialize in literature, always resist any actions that would affect their exceptional status. As most of us know from our own experiences as well as from the observations of theorists, literature actually depends upon composition to provide the "other" against which it can stand. Not surprisingly, those in literature resist any moves from composition colleagues that might change this hierarchical relationship. Although the MLA has been advertising positions in composition for over 20 years, many English departments, including my own, resist recognizing composition as a genuine area of intellectual inquiry. Housed, both literally and figuratively, in the basements of many English departments, composition still occupies an uncertain position in the academy. Recent debates within English studies have in many ways complicated composition's relationship to English departments. While factions have developed around issues of feminism, critical theory, and the canon, composition has often found itself caught in the crossfire of the debates. Where writing programs have separated from English departments, the problems take different form, but low status numbers among them chiefly because of the continued resistance of literary scholars in English departments to any enhanced status for composition.

While it would be comforting to cite the resistance of colleagues in literature as the source of all opposition to the long revolution of composition, it would not be accurate. As Williams reminds us, another equally compelling source of opposition comes from leaders in the revolution who identify with the existing order, and WPAs most frequently take this role. The hierarchical relationship between composition and literature is frequently replicated by the hierarchical relationship between tenured and relatively well paid WPAs and the nontenure-track instructors whom they supervise. By taking on the rights of tenure and an advantaged position on the academic pay scale, WPAs can be co-opted into identifying with the same administration that locates composition at the bottom of the English studies hierarchy. Even as we acknowledge that WPAs are often themselves exploited, we must also recognize that they simultaneously participate in the exploitation of others because they identify with the existing order of the academy.

These contradictions and complexities surrounding the status of students, the baccalaureate, writing, the field of composition studies, and composition instruction carry enormous implications for WPAs. None of these issues is new. Going back at least as far as the Harvard Reports of the 1890s, we find that writing instructors have been charged with cleansing students of their writing flaws and training them for college writing. Both cultural and personal ambivalence about writing, especially when compared with reading, date to the colonial period. Composition instructors have been exploited with heavy work loads and low pay since writing instruction was introduced into the academy. From its earliest appearance in the academy nearly a century ago, composition has been marginalized as a field. The present form of attack on higher education may be new, but the differences and hostilities between colleges and the communities around them have a long history, as the phrase "town-gown" suggests. I see no reason to think that any of these conditions will change soon, and indeed several of them—such as the status of writing instructors and the attack on the baccalaureate—may get worse. From this perspective, the title of this book seems particularly apt: composition, and WPAs in particular, appear to face a set of crises that will last well into the 21st century.

Crisis does, however, offer both danger and opportunity. We can easily enumerate the dangers that these crises contain: composition might shrink to a marginal service operation and lose whatever institutional standing it has gained; the new graduate programs in composition might disappear under the assault of other constituencies in English studies; journals that publish work in composition might be starved out of existence; and writing programs might assume even larger gatekeeping and certifying functions, thereby excluding all but the most privileged students from higher education. But these crises also offer opportunities. In particular, the crises surrounding WPAs may open the way for a new model of WPA, one more in keeping with the long revolution of composition. Having recognized the multiple oppositions and contradictions in composition and having acknowledged that change occurs in irregular spurts rather than in a smooth, unbroken stream, we can look at the position of WPA from a new perspective. Specifically, we can see that compared with the complexities surrounding students, the baccalaureate, writing, the field of composition studies, and composition instruction, our thinking about WPAs remains remarkably static. The word "administrator" signals the totalizing unity that most often defines WPAs. I propose that we reconceptualize WPAs in terms of multiple subject positions, positions that are more collaborative and research-oriented and offer the possibility of forward motion in the long revolution of composition.

Collaboration has figured prominently in composition for some time. Collaborative learning in the form of peer response groups or writing groups has been employed in writing classes for over a century, although its real flowering occurred during the past three decades, and it has proved a remarkably effective pedagogy for motivating students to revise their prose, for enhancing their sense of audience, for broadening their stylistic repertoires, and for heightening their awareness of syntactic structures. Research and scholarship in composition has demonstrated the inherently collaborative nature of writing. Karen Burke LeFevre's study of the social nature of invention (*Invention*), Andrea Lunsford and Lisa Ede's examination of collaborations among authors (*Singular Texts*), John Trimbur's exploration of consensus and dissensus, and Kenneth A. Bruffee's pioneering work on peer response to writing (see for example "On Not Listening") have established collaboration's place in composition.

Most of the work on collaboration has focused on teaching and has been represented in scholarship, but I believe it has implications for administration as well. As I have already observed, WPAs obstruct the long revolution when they identify with the existing order by accepting a position in the hierarchy. Conceiving of the WPA as a single individual responsible for diverse components of hiring, training, and supervising instructors, scheduling courses, developing and monitoring entrance and exit exams or other forms of assessment, handling ongoing curriculum development, and fielding the full range of complaints raised by students, colleagues, and members of the larger community plays into the hierarchy. Alternatively, WPAs might insist on a collaborative view of the position. This is not, of course, a novel idea. At a number of universities, several individuals share WPA duties. Sometimes, in these configurations, there is still one individual designated as the "official" WPA, but even that designation rotates among the participants. By insisting on a collaborative role for WPAs, we can resist the hierarchical model that reinforces the status quo.

In addition to reducing the contradictions of the WPA position, a collaborative model can help transform the position from a purely administrative site to one where knowledge is generated, where research is carried out. When the Harvard Committees of the 1890s made their reports on the quality of student writing, they also shaped the nature of composition studies. Composed of alumni from the business community, the Harvard Committees did not have any expertise in composition. Accordingly, they concentrated on the most obvious mechanical features of writing, ignoring more complex rhetorical considerations such as audience and invention. These committees, with their excessive attention to surface features of writing, helped instantiate a nonprofessional status for composition. In the academy where departments were established and grew because of expertise based on specialized training, composition was not, until recently, viewed as an area of intellectual inquiry. Because it was often equated with identifying errors of usage, and most competent writers could assume this task, composition took on the status of common rather than specialized knowledge. Even as composition has been granted some professional status as graduate programs and graduate seminars have been introduced, its teaching and administration frequently retain an amateur status. The teaching of composition is often entrusted to graduate students with little classroom experience or to literature specialists with no training in composition, and some departments still appoint as WPAs persons who have no expertise in composition. As long as writing programs are perceived as merely administrative units, they cannot claim the power accorded to scholarship, and nonspecialists will continue to be appointed to direct them. If, however, WPAs insist on conceiving of writing programs as research sites, it would be impossible to continue this tradition of amateurism, and writing programs could integrate theory and practice. The model of research that seems most appropriate is action research.

As described by Sharon Nodie Oja and Lisa Smulyan, action research combines investigation with attempts to effect change. Its twin goals include learning more about a phenomenon and working to change it. As S. Kreisberg explains it, action research embodies transformative power. When enacted by a practitioner such as a WPA or an instructor, action research requires praxis or reflective action. The reflective practitioner takes on multiple subject positions by simultaneously carrying out and thoughtfully examining courses of action. For a WPA, this means amplifying the administrator role with a reflective quality and a willingness to examine actions and speech acts closely.

Our colleagues in elementary and secondary schools have taken the lead in action research, and we can learn from them about some of the changes that emerge from doing this kind of work. Operating under the name of teacher research or reflective practice as well as action research, K–12 teachers have developed new ways of talking about their work. Susan Lytle and Marilyn Cochran-Smith, for example, describe two kinds of talk that emerge among action researchers. The first can be characterized as what Clifford Geertz calls thick description. When action researchers talk about their work, they draw upon their reflections and their journals to create detailed portraits of what they have experienced. Not satisfied with elliptical sentences about an amusing event, they tell stories rich with complex interactions. The second type of talk that emerges among action researchers can be described as critical. These practitioners call assumptions into question; they probe categories and interrogate values because they do not accept the usual givens. Methods of diagnosing student writing ability, the length of classes, the sequence of courses, terms such as "ability" and "disability," training programs for new instructors, and a variety of other things usually taken for granted could come under the scrutiny of WPAs who participate in action research.

Another kind of change that emerges from action research centers on the use of time. Practitioners who reflect on their work and write in their journals begin to look at their time differently. They reconsider their schedules, adjusting them in ways that provide space for thoughtful reflection. This usually means being more intentional about how time is used and insisting on more control over one's own time. It also means making time for meeting with other teacher researchers to discuss observations, insights, and work in progress. In other words, it is not simply a matter of adding research to an already overloaded schedule. Action research means rethinking time.

Still another change effected by action research centers on the use of texts. Action researchers create discursive communities that are networks of citations and allusions. The texts that create these networks include researchers' own notes, written records of deliberations, transcripts of interviews, drafts of work in progress, student texts, institutional forms and documents, and curriculum materials as well as selections from publications dealing with relevant issues. Action researchers examine the interrelationship of these and other texts, not aiming to find consensus or agreement but to reflect critically on their various discourses.

Finally, action research changes the tasks of teaching. Because they call the givens into question, reallocate time, and look at texts differently, action researchers call their own work into question. Many times, the information they generate leads action researchers to make changes both in their own lives and those of their students. Their investigations cause action researchers to see teaching and learning differently, and they frequently become reformers. Specifically, they often see learning as constructed, meaning-centered, and social, and they change their practices accordingly. Action research suggests possibilities for WPAs. In addition to offering methodologies compatible with the practitioner role of administration, action research offers multiple subject positions for WPAs. Shifts in the uses of talk, time, texts, and teaching that accompany action research can render the construct of WPAs less static and simultaneously engender the production of new knowledge about writing programs. This new knowledge can answer such questions as What do students bring with them to the writing program? As the average age of first-year students continues to rise, what can we learn about the experiences and backgrounds of these returning students? What about students who are identified as having special needs? What, for example, can students identified as learning-disabled tell us about their experiences with writing outside the academy? What kinds of successes or failures have these students experienced outside school? What economic gain or enhanced power have they achieved through writing?

Although the first-year composition course is often the central undergraduate experience during the first two years of college, the one class where students are known by name rather than number, we do not know very much about the rest of the undergraduate experience, particularly where writing is concerned. Although we frequently hear complaints from colleagues about the quality of student writing, we have little information about what kind of writing is done in classes to which our students go after the first-year course. To be sure, we know something about writing-intensive courses on campuses that have Writing Across the Curriculum programs, but in general we have little information about the kinds of assignments, the guiding assumptions about writing, and the nature of the response to students' writing in courses outside the writing program. Questions about the kinds of writing assignments given in disciplines outside composition, the way our colleagues in other fields describe writing, and the types of evaluation they use can enrich our understanding of the varying academic contexts in which our students work.

Of course, our students do a good deal of writing after they leave college. While there have been a few studies of writing in the workplace, we know virtually nothing about how, in the view of our students or their colleagues, their composition courses serve them as they take on writing tasks outside the academy. What are the continuities and discontinuities between academic writing instruction and the writing practices of our students when they leave school?

One of my current research interests is what I call the extracurriculum of composition, the many forms in which persons outside the academy develop their capacities as writers. The extracurriculum is as old as the Junto that Benjamin Franklin organized during the colonial period so he and his friends could improve their skills by submitting their compositions for group critique. The extracurriculum is as new as the Ridge Writers, a group that meets to respond to works in progress at the community center in my hometown of Farmington Hills. We can ask questions about how our students participate in the extracurriculum and the relationship between it and our composition programs. Our former students can tell us about what leads them to join with others to improve their writing, what motivates them to write when neither teachers nor employers require it, what benefits—social, material, psychological—writing confers on their lives.

We can also ask questions abut the discourses of writing programs themselves. Close reading of departmental memos, curriculum reports, committee minutes, and course descriptions can provide very useful information about the writing program and about composition more generally. It can help answer such questions as How does writing program discourse compare with that of other areas of the department? How does the identity of the speaker/writer shape discourse about the writing program? What nascent theories about composition are articulated in this kind of public discourse? As Terry Caesar's recent book demonstrates, texts of the academic bureaucracy reward close readings.

These questions will vary from one campus to another because, like political change, they are finally local and derive from what Raymond Williams calls "particulars." The audiences for reports of action research can be both local and national. While I do not want to minimize the importance of national dissemination for the action research WPAs might do, we should not overlook opportunities for more local dissemination. Bill Clinton's 1992 presidential campaign strategy demonstrated that it is possible to work around the three networks of "Big Media" by employing technology and focusing on regional/local audiences. As Sidney Blumenthal puts it, "After Clinton's victory, the national press began to suffer, at least a bit, the painful process known in the business world as disintermediation. . . . What the President seeks is unmediated communication" (47). Admittedly, a comparison between Clinton and WPAs cannot be sustained, but both inhabit a postmodern world of fragmentation, and both enjoy access to technologies not previously available. The proliferation of journals in composition has created multiple discourse communities in the field, and WPAs can add to these. Desktop publishing and electronic communication systems such as Internet offer new vehicles for reaching audiences, and WPAs can use them to develop and address new populations. Deans' offices, research centers, student groups, and campus publications issued by central administration, to say nothing of community media, can disseminate accounts of action research. Effecting local political change requires sharing ideas and projects with local audiences.

Answering the sorts of questions listed above and dispersing the answers both locally and nationally accomplishes the knowledge production part of action research, but action research combines investigation with attempts to effect change. Certainly, rethinking the uses of talk, time, texts, and teaching will lead to change, but the real change will be epistemological. WPAs cannot shape opportunities from the crises of the 21st century just by asking new questions and adopting new methods. As Sharon Crowley's contribution to this volume explains, it is entirely possible to adopt new methods such as process approaches to writing without embracing the epistemologies from which they spring. Effective action research by WPAs requires an epistemological shift toward seeing teaching and administrating as ways of producing knowledge. Patricia Harkin offers ways of thinking about lore—the teacher's accumulated body of traditions, practices, and beliefs —as producing knowledge. Placing herself in a rhetorical (rather than empirical) tradition to claim that knowledge is made "by persuading an audience rather than 'found' in nature" ("Bringing" 58), Harkin goes on to argue that lore, which does not attend to disciplinary procedures, develops cognitive maps that enable practitioners to deal with the overdetermined situations of classrooms. She asserts that the academy needs to "change its understanding of knowledge production" to include lore ("Postdisciplinary" 135).

This argument for seeing lore as producing knowledge can be extended to include administration as well as teaching. Like teachers, WPAs operate in overdetermined situations and, like teachers, draw upon multiple disciplines to address the daily problems they face. By effecting an epistemological shift that enables the academy to see WPA lore as producing knowledge, WPAs will legitimize their own action research. Accomplishing such a shift will, of course, not be easy, but, as James A. Berlin has observed, the survival of action research depends upon its practitioners assuming the role of transformative intellectuals ("Teacher" 4). Like all aspects of the long revolution, change in the academy's epistemology will not occur smoothly or all at once; it will be marked by contradictions within multiple patterns. It will, however, emerge because action research will shape new conceptions of humans and society within writing programs, conceptions fueled by the conviction that WPAs, like other persons, can "direct their own lives."

11 Writing Instruction and the Politics of Professionalization

JOHN TRIMBUR

One of the issues historians of writing instruction keep returning to is why teaching composition has been held in such low regard by English departments and the academy at large. S. Michael Halloran, Richard Ohmann, James A. Berlin, Susan Miller, Robert J. Connors, and others have pointed to the decline of rhetoric, the emergence of the modern research university, the rise of corporate capitalism, the institutionalization of literary studies, and the feminization of teaching writing as possible causes of the meager status of writing teachers. But if the historians have figured causation in various ways, the story we tell ourselves about the low status of our field seems nonetheless to follow a predictable and unified pattern, a master narrative that recounts the tragic fall of rhetoric from its preeminent position in the oratorical culture of the 19th-century college to its current unpretentious position as a service function in the multiversity.

As the story goes, in the late 19th and early 20th centuries, with the consolidation of the research model of higher learning and the departmental system that gives it organizational form, the mission of rhetoric shifted from preparing citizens to participate in public life to training a newly emerging professional-managerial class in composition—not to go into the public sphere to shape democratic opinion but into corporate America to administer as rationally as possible the everyday workings of capitalism and the cultural forms that reproduce capitalist social relations. This is a story I believe to be true in its general outlines.

But the fact is that stories tend to supply, by the narrativity of telling, their own conclusions, and the master plot of the history of writing instruction is no different: it comes equipped with its own lessons. We understand this master plot to indicate the need to professionalize our activities of studying and teaching writing in both theory and practice. We believe, that is, in the need, revealed to us through our narrative, to transform rhetoric and composition studies from a service function located at the periphery of academic life into a viable discipline. Various guidelines issued on professional standards, the Wyoming Resolution, the proliferation of scholarly research and publications, the appearance of new journals and book series, the creation of endowed chairs, and the unprecedented growth of graduate programs have all contributed to this climate of opinion. If anything, at this point in our collective history, rhetoric and composition has become a booming enterprise, increasingly self-confident, even feisty, about its standing in the academy and its claims to legitimacy and respectability.

The issue I want to raise addresses something that I fear gets neglected in the way we talk about and enact the growing professionalization of our field. I worry that we are in the thrall of the stories we tell and that our master narrative points to professionalization and discipline formation as the inevitable outcome of the plot. Such an outcome certainly makes for a satisfying ending because it relies on a dramatic reversal of fortune: the lowly and illegitimate have risen up to take their fate into their own hands and to secure the rightful position that was lost but is now within grasp again. It is the sense of closure and narrative satisfaction we derive from Victorian novels that I am referring to here, when the orphaned child, after years of virtuous hard labor and despite the various temptations of the world and the cruel designs of treacherous relatives, finally is restored by happy marriage to his or her legitimate birthright. As comforting as this story must have been to Victorian readers and for all the charm it still possesses, I want to make this narrative into a cautionary tale. And I think there is good reason to do so, for the processes of professionalization and discipline formation, not unlike the patriarchal bourgeois family in the Victorian novel, are deeply contradictory phenomena. To stretch my analogy, perhaps beyond its breaking point, I want to suggest that before we succumb to the nuptial bliss of middle-class respectability, we ought to consider how the politics of professionalization affects writing teachers, writing programs, and writing scholarship in unequal and contradictory ways.

Ambivalence about Professionalization

Thus far, we have tended to describe the professionalization of our field and our bid for the legitimacy of disciplinary status largely in intellectual terms. There are rhetorics of inquiry that treat composition studies as a discursive formation and unpack the intellectual affiliations, logics, and tropes that constitute the study and teaching of writing. We are becoming self-conscious about our work as a disciplinary and disciplined project, devoted to questions that matter, and we appeal therefore to the volume and quality of research and scholarship produced under the aegis of rhetoric and composition studies to demonstrate how serious we are and how well organized we have become to address the burning issues in our field. Moreover, we have attempted to expand what it means to do scholarship by arguing why and how teaching composition, administering programs, and writing textbooks can and should be counted as scholarly activities, at least when done properly—that is, professionally, as disciplined applications of theory and research. As Anne Ruggles Gere suggests in her contribution to this volume, the acts of teaching and administering, conceived as reflexive practice, can in fact become important forms of research and scholarship.

I do not want to quarrel with these developments, which I consider useful to our self-definition as a field. But I also want to point out that they are the normal moves to establish codes of practice, bodies of scholarship, and general professional standards that disciplines invariably rely upon to draw their boundaries, to determine what counts as a contribution, and to regulate their members' activities according to the best knowledges available. At the same time, it is fair to say that despite the celebratory tone in many discussions of the heightened visibility of rhetoric and composition as an academic field, there are nonetheless traces of ambivalence that, to my mind, are revealing about the contradictory character of the professions and academic disciplines.

I remember, for example, when Patricia Bizzell and Bruce Herzberg spoke at the Conference on College Composition and Communication about their work on canon formation (before they published *The Rhetorical Tradition*), and there was considerable resistance to their project. This resistance was based in part on a nostalgia for the good old bad days, when writing teachers formed a kind of underground or affinity group of like-minded individuals circulating mimeographed reading lists and giving each other much needed professional and personal support. And in part, the resistance was based on the fear that institutionalizing our field as an academic discipline would turn CCCC into another version of MLA, with its typically agonistic style of discourse, its privileging of publishing over teaching, its trendiness, and the self-deception of its academic leftists "striking great blows against capitalism in the realm of theory" (as one well-known theorist put it). It was not simply status anxiety or legitimate anger about how literary studies had devalued the study and teaching of writing that was at work in villainizing MLA. In a more telling sense, MLA was taken to represent the occupational hazard of academics' removing the subject of their inquiry—in this case, literature—from the world of ordinary people and making it instead into a matter upon which to build individual careers.

This felt sense of the limits and pressures of discipline formation is revealing because it suggests how writing teachers had cast themselves as a kind of religion of the oppressed, small islands of the saved, where the legitimacy of success seemed to threaten their very identities as the humble and unauthorized professors of a truth our literature counterparts cannot bear: namely, that we care about students precisely because we have invested ourselves, both intellectually and affectively, in their personal growth and well-being instead of in turf warfare over who is qualified to interpret a body of texts. This sentiment, I believe, is a flawed but not altogether unreasonable one. It is flawed because it makes suffering—professional and personal—redemptive. But it is also reasonable in that it points to some very real problems in discipline formation—normalizing of intellectual work, subjugation of counterknowledges, overemphasis on specialization, monopolies of expertise.

These problems have been addressed, though I believe inadequately, in recent efforts to define rhetoric and composition as a postmodern field that by virtue of its interdisciplinarity transcends the limits of the conventional academic fields of study. Andrea Lunsford ("Composing Ourselves"), Louise Wetherbee Phelps, and others have argued that composition studies emerges on the scene as a postmodern moment in academic life that resists the positivist certainties and foundational accounts that shaped the older disciplines. By this postmodern version, composition studies situates itself in a nondisciplinary or postdisciplinary place where multiple, heterogeneous, and polyvalent discourses, projects, and interests intersect. Composition studies proceeds, that is, in accord with the cultural logic of postmodernism to compose itself as a kind of pastiche, appropriating disparate and incongruous theoretical elements into a unity of difference. As a mobile and decentered intellectual project, composition studies refuses the emphasis on instrumental control and the proliferation of specialized knowledges that, as Kurt Spellmeyer puts it, have fragmented reason into many incommensurable ways of reasoning and thereby make it exceedingly difficult for laypersons and experts to speak in a common public language (*Common Ground*).

I share Spellmeyer's concern about the disciplining of knowledge that produces monopolies of expertise, on the one hand, and deference to the authority of specialists and public ignorance, on the other. The point I want to make, however, is that the professions and academic disciplines are not simply *intellectual* formations that favor specialization and expertise in ways that inhibit popular participation and democratic discussion. They are also *social* formations. To put it another way, the problem is not specialization per se but the particular forms of social organization that authorize and reproduce specialized expertise. Specialization and expertise are coextensive with the cultural life of the human species. There have always been individuals who have developed personal talents and predispositions in healing, music, art, dance, storytelling, athletics, political leadership, and so on. What distinguishes the professions and academic disciplines is that they are a relatively recent kind of social formation that organizes and regulates the specialized work of experts.

Professional Formations

Let me sketch briefly the history and sociology of these professional formations. According to historian of professionalism Burton J. Bledstein, academic specialization and discipline formation "came into existence to serve and promote professional authority in society" (290). Public debates about disease, poverty, education, and crime in the late 19th and early 20th centuries offer striking examples of how the culture of professionalism took hold in the U.S. These debates, in Bledstein's words, uncovered "abnormality and perversity everywhere" (102). Threats of illness, illiteracy, and violence seemed to call up the services of enlightened, dispassionate, and disinterested civil servants and professionals, independent of both popular prejudices and market forces. After the Civil War, the centralizing impulses of state formation redefined the relation between the state and civil society by creating a layer of bureaucratic institutions devoted to public health, social work, schooling, and corrections that displaced the familial, local, and voluntary associations of an earlier era. As Ohmann suggests, the emergence of the modern corporation and scientific models of management further amplified the movement toward professionalism, and the university increasingly became the "supplier and certifier of . . . professionals and managers" (32). Even popular entertainment, recreation, and sports were becoming more professionalized around the turn of the century.

As industrial capitalism, class struggle, urbanization, and immigration reshaped American society in the late 19th century, Americans confronted massive, far reaching, and bewildering social changes. Without traditional authorities to fall back on, Americans invested faith in science, progress, and professional expertise. As Bledstein suggests, part of the success of the culture of professionalism is that it cast professional values in a peculiarly American idiom, invoking the image of independent and democratic-minded individuals whose training and special expertise prepared them to act on behalf of society as a whole—to stand in for the public interest by controlling natural and social forces. In turn, professional expertise defined itself in contrast to the ineptitude of nonprofessionals, who were judged to be incapable of either understanding the skilled practices of professionals or evaluating the results of professional work.

Professionalism, by this account, is all about the cultural authorization of expertise and how the newly emerging social formations organized in professional associations such as the American Bar Association and the American Medical Association and in academic disciplines began to claim, in the name of the public interest, the autonomy of professional work and its self-regulating procedures. Through devices we now take for granted, such as accreditation, certification, peer review, standards of practice, codes of ethics, and so on, the professions and academic disciplines constituted themselves as servants of the common good, above popular debate and beyond public criticism. And by doing so, the professions and academic disciplines articulated processes of subject formation by which professionals and academics learn to recognize themselves and to enact identities as the subjects of disciplined discourses and practices precisely to the extent that they assume the rhetorical authority to speak as experts, in an asymmetrical relationship, on behalf of a client population of laypersons who need or want their services.

This portrait of the professions and academic disciplines does not, of course, correspond to their public self-images of rational and efficient bodies of experts responding disinterestedly to pressing social and intellectual needs, as the standard Weberian account might have it. Rather, the professions seek a monopoly of the services they provide, to keep authorized practice independent of other practitioners and other markets and at the same time autonomous and self-regulated in relation to their client populations. In this sense, the professions, as Pierre Bourdieu suggests, are social formations to allot recognition and to determine who may speak, about what, and on whose behalf. Professionalization, as Bourdieu sees it, deals in the currency of credentials—or symbolic capital—as the primary means of exchange, not simply as personal fame or name recognition but as the power, distributed differentially, to act on the world, to achieve practical effects by determining how the world is represented.

Stratification

Bourdieu's sense of the way professions and academic disciplines allot recognition brings me back to the problem of professionalization in rhetoric and composition. My point, to put it as bluntly as I can, is that the production, distribution, exchange, and consumption of symbolic capital follow the same laws that govern the cycles of circulation for industrial capital, favoring monopoly and concentration and leading to internal differentiation—or a stratified class system—even within the professions and academic disciplines. Let us face it: it is monopoly capital and not just Reaganomics that makes for the rich getting richer and the poor getting poorer. This is the law that Robert Merton, the sociologist of science, found operating in academic science and that applies as well to rhetoric and composition. It is what Merton calls the "Matthew effect," after the biblical passage "he who hath shall receive"—that status and prestige accrue to those who already have it.

The Wyoming Resolution, of course, was an attempt to deal with the problem of equity in the teaching of writing, but it defined the issue largely in terms of the differences between full- and part-time faculty, between tenured or tenure-track teachers and those on short-term contracts, arguing that part-time and nontenure-stream faculty should have the same conditions, rights, privileges, and prorated pay as full-time tenured and tenure-track faculty. This has been an important initiative, but focusing on the differences between full- and part-time faculty ignores internal differentiation within the tenured and tenure-track faculty and differences in the material conditions that enable and constrain the study and teaching of writing. These differences organize the social and intellectual structure of our field. Let me cite three major differences that we need to know more about to understand the stratification of the profession.

Differences in the provision of writing instruction based on type of educational institution. Here we would need to look at differences in salaries, teaching loads, class size, faculty development, secretarial support, photocopying budget, and so on. My sense is that the provision of writing instruction follows the same stratified patterns of class reproduction that Samuel Bowles and Herbert Gintis identified in American postsecondary education, from community colleges to low-prestige state colleges to high-prestige liberal arts colleges and research universities, with teaching loads and class sizes larger and salaries and institutional support smaller in community and state colleges. The fact that elite colleges and universities often value scholarship over teaching in tenure and promotion decisions should not obscure the fact that the conditions of teaching are better in the high-prestige schools. Faculty typically teach fewer courses (two or three a term instead of four or five) and thereby have more preparation time to devote to their classes, even if you figure in the pressures to do research and publish. While some faculty in elite schools are certainly more concerned with released time than with teaching, there is nonetheless a greater investment of resources in teachers and students in high-prestige colleges and universities than in low-prestige ones. I do not want to suggest here that writing teachers at community and state colleges are not providing for their students. My point is a structural, not a personal, one that concerns the unequal distribution of material resources in the political economy of writing instruction.

Differences in access to opportunities for research and professional development. Here we would need to take into account differences in availability of travel funds, speakers programs, library resources, expectations about tenure and promotion, released-time policies, and sabbatical guidelines. And I think we would find consequential and stratifying differences in the political economy of research. But it is not simply that the time to do research is unevenly distributed, depending on type of institution. This uneven distribution of research opportunities also affects the lived experience of writing teachers by determining their nearness to or distance from the social and intellectual networks of the discipline. The relative positioning of individuals within a field of study begins early on in graduate education and continues in mentoring relationships between senior and junior faculty and in the blurred personal/professional relationships among peers that articulate the social networks of a discipline. In the professions, where a good deal of knowledge and skills are not quantifiable or readily communicable in the form of rules, a practitioner's nearness to or distance from the "cutting edge" of a professional field may appear to be mysterious, a matter of personal talents that cannot be taught but rather are enacted through the exercise of individual charisma. What I want to suggest is that the expression—and recognition—of individual talents is mediated by both the material conditions that enable and constrain research and the social relationships and sense of connectedness to the intellectual life of a discipline that sustain the labor required to pursue scholarly projects.

Differences in the production of scholarship. Here the forces in the political economies of writing instruction and research converge, producing marked differences in who publishes, about what, and in what journals. As Theresa Enos and Sue Ellen Holbrook have indicated, there are significant gender differences in publication patterns in rhetoric and composition, with more female authors publishing pedagogical articles in journals devoted to teaching writing while a greater percentage of "theoretical" articles in high-prestige journals are written by men. Though I do not have any hard figures, my guess is that rhetoric and composition resembles other academic fields, in which a fairly small percentage of professionals—10 percent or so—produces around half of the publications. Such stratification is further amplified by the fact that not all publications are equal in influence and prestige. Citation indices that count which articles and books are cited in subsequent publications would reveal, I believe, even greater stratification of the field.

"Insiders" and "Outsiders"

The picture of rhetoric and composition that emerges from these differences prohibits any easy celebration of disciplinary status and professionalization. While the ethos of the profession is certainly more egalitarian and democratic than that of most other academic disciplines, there is nonetheless a growing felt sense that the field is composed of "insiders" and "outsiders." Two notable documents that appeared in *Rhetoric Review* in 1988 and 1989, "CCCC: Voices in the Parlor, and Responses" and "The Conversation Continues: *Voices in the Parlor,"* present a "chorus" of voices charging that CCCC meetings are now characterized by a "star" system of big-name celebrities who have sold their idealism for fame and by the grandstanding use of a theoretical (and implicitly impenetrable and exclusionary) discourse that seems far removed from the practical realities of teaching. For a field such as rhetoric and composition, which is committed so self-consciously to democratic practices and values, these are troubling charges. On the one hand, of course, the "insider/outsider" dichotomy that the "chorus" notes seems a predictable outcome of the meritocratic organization of academic work: the best will rise to the top and a "natural" and justifiable stratification of talents will inevitably occur. But on the other hand, as I have just tried to suggest, an analysis of the material conditions and social relationships that govern teaching and scholarship challenges such meritocratic premises of equal opportunity and the structural results of stratification within the profession.

The unsigned (but initialled) contributions to "Voices in the Parlor" did not do much to clarify the consequences of professional stratification. Rather, they reproduce some of the differences I have already mentioned: the "outsiders" feel excluded, constituted as spectators at someone else's show, and the "insiders" say, "Murmuring discontentedly won't cut it," that in fact there is plenty of room in the conversation as long as you produce "serious" "quality work" (RJC 213), and besides, we (the "insiders") "do this work . . . for love, not money" (LZB 408). In other words, both the "insiders" and the "outsiders" reproduce the logic of professionalization by assuming that "entering the conversation" depends on personal acts of will, individual enterprise, and career building.

In one sense, this should not be surprising. As Magali Sarfatti Larson argues, "Most professions produce intangible goods: their product, in other words, . . . is inextricably bound to the person and the personality of the producer" (14). The relative autonomy of professional work, in which individuals experience their everyday work lives as a series of independent decisions and acts of judgment, all too easily disguises the structural constraints within which professionals operate and often leads to attributing success and failure to personal effort and talent. What this misses, of course, as Larson goes on to say, is that for a profession to corner the market on a distinct service, it relies on a fictitious commodity: "the producers themselves have to be produced" (14). From this perspective, the "serious" "quality work" RJC invokes may be seen not only as the result of personal effort and talents but also as structurally determined by differences in the production of producers—by the social networks that begin in graduate school and extend through professional life and by the material conditions that shape the formation of careers in rhetoric and composition. Moreover, to see professional subject formation as a structural phenomenon calls into question the adequacy of self-representations such as LZB's that figure professional work as a vocation or personal call to service, an expression of the individual personality—"work . . . for love, not money"— outside and beyond the market forces and the circuits of symbolic capital that organize the political economy of the professions.

The Contradictions of Professional Life

I have been trying to suggest that professionalization is an uneven and contradictory process. At this point in history, the provision of professional services and the distribution of professional opportunities are stratified and highly variable. As Richard Johnson points out, professional work is also caught up in the fiscal crisis of the state, which has led to budget cuts, withdrawal of faculty lines, and overall lack of support to writing programs that are making it more and more difficult to provide services according to even the most minimal professional standards. This is also true for the legal and medical professions. Lawyers, who need to generate billable hours, and doctors, who need to report to health management agencies, as well as writing teachers and writing program administrators, are finding their work experience defined as much by accountability measures of productivity and cost-efficiency as by the provision of professional services, and increasingly, professional life is characterized by a tension between the desire to perform services well and the material constraints and undemocratic organization of work.

It would be too doctrinaire and pessimistically deterministic simply to lay the blame on the system, though I certainly believe capitalism deserves it. The contradictions I have pointed to play themselves out in the lives of actual men and women, teachers and students, lawyers and clients, doctors and patients, who, despite the debilitating constraints of their situations, are often trying to do the best they can. So the issue, to my way of thinking, is, how do we *read* the contradictory situations within which professionals must operate? How, in other words, can we take into account the contradictions of professionalization without abandoning the hard-won accumulative experience of professional expertise in the study and teaching of writing, but without defending the outcomes of composition's meritocracy as the natural selection of the best and the brightest, either?

The contradictory politics of professionalization are enacted not only ritually at CCCC but at the point of production, in the everyday workings of writing programs, and therefore it may be useful to describe how these politics shape the living experience of writing program administrators. By a Foucauldian account of professionalization, WPAs, precisely because of their professional knowledges, are invariably implicated in acts of surveillance that constitute both staff and students as "docile bodies." Through course design, textbook selection, testing, placement, grading sessions, and classroom observations, WPAs oversee the work of teaching and learning that takes place in writing programs and classrooms. The WPA's professional identity in this regard is inseparable from the micropolitics of discipline—differentiating, measuring, hierarchizing its subjects. In fact, Michel Foucault's description of how discipline works sounds remarkably like a description of a WPA doing course scheduling at the beginning of a term. Discipline, Foucault says, operates "on the principle of elementary location or partitioning. Each individual has his own place; and each place its individual. . . . Disciplinary space tends to be divided into as many sections as there are bodies . . . to be distributed" (*Discipline* 143).

By this account, knowing means mastering, using, and controlling bodies, and the apparently prosaic task of course scheduling reveals that knowledge is invariably a means of discipline and the WPA its human agent. This, I realize, is a rather bleak portrait of the WPA, and one that appears to be without contradictions, a seamless and largely unacknowledged system of power that operates behind the back of its actors. But Foucault also provides a critical opening into the contradictions in the micropolitics of discipline when he calls for an "insurrection of subjugated knowledges" (*Power/Knowledge* 81).

By "subjugated knowledges," Foucault means both the conflicts and struggles suppressed or disguised by the systematization and functional coherence of disciplinary ways of knowing (what I have been referring to as professionalization) and the popular knowledges (*savoir des gens*) of patients, delinquents, students, and so on that have been disqualified as naive and unscientific from the prevailing cognitive hierarchy. I want to emphasize the connection between these two forms of subjugated knowledge: how, that is, the professionalization and cultural authorization of expertise filter and "purify" the professional subject in such a way that makes it difficult to hear, much less listen to, countervoices and counterknowledges that do not fit readily with existing professional practice. And yet, at the same time, the knowledges subjugated in the formation of the professional subject are not eliminated but rather are driven underground, where they exert a residual tug at the margins of professional experience.

To articulate the knowledges that have been subjugated in the processes of professionalization and the technologies of power that constitute experts and laypersons will require a new look at our discipline and how it has disciplined us. Studies of professionalization, such as Carol Berkenkotter, Thomas N. Huckin, and John Ackerman's analysis of the socialization of a graduate student in rhetoric and composition, too often rely on an expert-novice model that treats alternative forms of knowledge as interference in the acquisition of mastery, white noise that needs to be eliminated or silenced. On the other hand, in her recent study of women writing in the academy, Gesa Kirsch gives a much more prominent and problematical place to the desires and knowledges women have had to keep under wraps in their struggles to acquire authority and credibility in their disciplines. One of the striking refrains from Kirsch's informants is the urge to use their professional training to produce not only individual careers but also socially useful knowledge by linking their expertise to social movements and publics outside the academy.

It is not simply that Kirsch's subjects want to write in popular genres, speaking as experts in a language more accessible to laypersons; rather, they want to popularize knowledge by redefining the relationship between professionals and their publics. Nor is it simply a matter of divided loyalties pulling Kirsch's subjects between the need to gain recognition and establish professional identities on the one hand and their desire to articulate professional work to forces seeking social change on the other. As Larson points out, conflicts such as these grow out of a structural contradiction in the political economy of the professions—the contradiction between the exchange value of professional work and the use value of its services. This contradiction, of course, is not peculiar to professionalization. Marx pointed out over a century ago the contradiction between the social nature of production and the private appropriation of its products that haunts capitalism as a mode of production. And for this reason, the contradiction between exchange value and use value is not likely to go away or to be resolved easily in the practice of professional life. But this contradiction does offer a way to understand the everyday struggles of professionals to define themselves and their work.

To return to the WPA, we can see the contradiction between exchange value and use value operating, among other places, in the design and practice of Writing Across the Curriculum programs. From one perspective, the goal of any profession is to achieve a perfect monopoly of its services. After all, professional claims to a corner on expertise make little sense if anyone can be an expert or perform a particular service. In fact, one of the key struggles of rhetoric and composition has been to counter the idea that anyone can teach writing, that no particular training or professional knowledge is required. To claim that writing instruction requires professional training based on a standardized body of knowledge and an institutional infrastructure of entry into the profession seeks to enhance not only the academic legitimacy of the field but also the exchange value of studying and teaching writing by keeping it distinct from other services, such as teaching Shakespeare or doing research on the 18th-century novel. In Writing Across the Curriculum programs, however, the contradiction between the exchange value of writing instruction and its use value arises to the extent that such programs attempt to make professional knowledge about teaching writing more widely accessible in the academy, to popularize it as socially useful knowledge that non-experts can draw on and enact. In this regard, Writing Across the Curriculum programs seem to me exemplary instances of WPAs working from within the contradictions of professional life by producing new producers of knowledge outside existing monopolies of expertise.

This rearticulation of expertise reveals, I believe, that we do not need either to abandon professionalization as an obstacle to socially useful knowledge or to embrace it uncritically as the necessary outcome of our collective history. We need, rather, to develop new ways to read the contradictions of professional life, to grapple daily with the persistent conflicts between building individual careers and popularizing expertise for broader social purposes.

12 Seeking a Disciplinary Reformation

RESPONSE BY CHARLES I. SCHUSTER

Let us imagine a more perfect world, at least a more perfect academic world as it relates to English departments, composition, and Writing Program Administrators. The world I envision reestablishes the centrality of English as a subject of study by articulating the fundamental importance of reading, writing, speaking, and listening. That conception gets played out in classrooms, not in the schizoid fashion we see now with composition taught at eight and literature at noon, but rather through a reconceptualization of our fields of study. In this new English, faculty conceive of verbal activities as mutually reinforcing; they hold that writers must read, that to teach even the seemingly passive activities of reading and listening (which are not passive at all), students and teachers must engage in a whole array of work from journal writing to performance, from minute textual analysis to etymology, reading aloud, and hermeneutic inquiry. In this highly idealized world, the WPA disappears—or at least the WPA's role shifts dramatically—for there are no more composition courses, no separate (and unequal) domains of writing and reading, production and consumption (Scholes 6–17). Instead, it becomes impossible to distinguish the dancer from the dance, writing from reading, speaking from listening, practice from theory, rhetoric from aesthetic.

This vision is parallel to the one articulated by the participants in the 1987 English Coalition Conference. In his account of that conference, Peter Elbow paraphrases Shirley Brice Heath's view that the central business of English studies has three main parts:

- *Using language* actively in a diversity of ways and settings . . .
- *Reflecting on language use* . . . [and]
- Trying to ensure that this using and reflecting go on in *conditions of both nourishment and challenge.* (*What is English?* 17–8)

Elbow makes clear that Heath provided "a set of terms that united people from elementary school through college" (18), a fact that should give hope for reform. Unfortunately, prospects for this utopian view of English studies remain dim. They require massive revaluation, an acknowledgment about shared work and responsibilities, a considerable shift in the ways English departments recruit, train, hire, tenure, promote, and reward doctoral students and faculty. That our efforts would, I think, be appreciated by legislatures, parents, and students is beside the point; few faculty in any discipline are willing to overthrow the established professional conventions that produced them in the first place. English studies, for all its deconstruction and Marxism, its gender and cultural studies, is conservative—and one of its primary missions is to conserve its current privileges and procedures exactly as they are.

WPAs, like the field of composition studies that they reflect, represent, and recreate, find themselves mostly on the outside of English studies as it is currently practiced, particularly in research universities and large English departments. "Marginalization" is the key word, voiced by most compositionists, WPAs and otherwise. How else can we explain the willingness of English departments to assign an academic staff person to oversee an instructional program that includes scores of instructors, thousands of students, and half a million dollars? What justifies the willingness of English departments to give its most difficult and consequential job to first-year assistant professors or even advanced doctoral students? Would English faculty elect themselves a department head from the ranks of academic staff? Yet many WPAs are exactly that, the justification being that their work is administrative and not scholarly, a false binary that serves primarily to insulate many English faculty from the work of composition programs.

The position of Writing Program Administrator is thus almost certainly the most conflicted within the academy. Although many university administrators serve multiple constituencies (faculty, students, departments, divisions, parents, legislators, and businesses), WPAs are situated within a tangle of contradictory loyalties. A typical composition director engages in disciplinary research and curricular reform; works with undergraduates; upholds collegiate standards; serves on college and university committees; tries to please department head, dean, and provost; negotiates intellectual and pedagogical issues with teaching assistants, part-timers, and full-time temporary instructors; and creates a programmatic identity that is equal parts model teacher, arbitrator, leader, facilitator, scheduler, budget officer, impresario, cheerleader, psychologist, confessor, disciplinarian, and standard-bearer. More important than any of these, however, the WPA builds respect, esteem, and goodwill among departmental colleagues, all the while fighting for resources and recognition.

Anne Ruggles Gere and John Trimbur, and the conference participants who responded to their essays, reflect this conflictual identity of the WPA and of composition studies itself. Both Gere and Trimbur seek models of empowerment. Gere argues for a redeployment of composition studies through collaborative models, action research, and sustained critique of ourselves, our students, technologies, and the production of knowledge. Trimbur resists the professionalization of our discipline, noting that as we gain in disciplinary power and prestige, our originary vision of a democratic, literate, socially responsible academic practice is attenuated. Just as Gere finds hope in the consolidation of composition studies through the academic research model, Trimbur suggests that WPAs tolerate a bit of professional disintegration in order to redeploy those principles of social idealism that (re)launched the discipline some 30 years ago.

Conference participants mapped out similar tensions. In their responses to Gere and Trimbur, discussion groups offered metaphors of WPA as overseer on a Southern plantation, as tectonic plate, as Velcro ball toward whom every odd job and unsolvable problem is thrown. While they searched for the positive and productive, they worried about the uneasy relationship between composition and literature, the dwindling of financial resources, the fear that WPAs (and compositionists) would replicate the very patterns of professional abuse that we deplore among our literary and theoretical colleagues. They recognized the value of marginality, its strength as a position of otherness. They worried about part-timers, about the inequities of pay and privilege that seem an inescapable part of administering writing programs. They argued for a view of writing as productive of socially useful knowledge resulting in meaningful dialogues among professionals, laypersons, and the academy. Perhaps most of all, they sought change; they sought a disciplinary reformation.

Part of the problem results from substantially differing perspectives about who we are and what we do. Faculty in composition hold different responsibilities from those in literature, a distinction that could be characterized as holding either private or public office. Literature faculty hold private office. For the most part, they are accountable to themselves; their responsibility is to teach and publish in their specialty. They work alone, largely away from the public. Their habitat is the library carrel; their tool of the trade, the *PMLA Bibliography*. Their expertise is slotted within genres, critical approaches, or centuries; their primary commitment as defined by departmental mandate is to improve appreciation and understanding of the literary aesthetic and to further scholarship, both extremely worthy goals.

Composition faculty, on the other hand, hold public office. Most are hired with a departmental eye cocked toward eventual administration. As needs arise, they are asked—or are volunteered—to create programs, develop alliances, teach in-service workshops, serve on local, regional, and national task forces. Their commitment to composition instruction concentrates their teaching at the undergraduate level where every hour of class time expands into four to six hours of intense response time to student writing and where the aesthetic disappears in the face of communicating "the psychology of information," to use Kenneth Burke's term. Compositionists visit high schools, create and staff writing centers, develop Writing Across the Curriculum programs, participate in NCTE state councils, develop K–12/college partnerships, create grass-roots networks.

Few of my literary colleagues are known by any of the regional or state high schools and colleges; most of my composition colleagues work actively at this local level. Of course, few of my literary colleagues have either the interest or the expertise to engage in such work; instead, they teach and publish—and it is hard for them, as it is hard for me, to assess the one kind of work in relation to the other. The criteria are simply not the same. Unfortunately, the private officeholder's value system is dominant; thus, the accomplishments of a public officeholder are often viewed by department faculty as simultaneously valuable and negligible—valuable for others, negligible for the department.

The powerful and differing critiques of Anne Ruggles Gere and John Trimbur offer signposts for change. My response is that the tensions between these two essays can be resolved only through a major reformulation of academic English, a reformation that would erase the divisive differences among CCCC, MLA, and NCTE; that would reemphasize undergraduate education; that would create a dialogic discipline in which every verbal activity shaded into all the others. Naive idealist that I am, it is toward these sets of practices that I hope we commit our professional energies.

Part 5 Who Should Teach Composition and What Should They Know?

13 Disciplining Students: Whom Should Composition Teach and What Should They Know?

JAMES F. SLEVIN

> Therefore it is right to say that the beginning and the end, indeed the total sum of man's happiness, are founded upon a good upbringing and education. . . . Education is that special task that has been entrusted to us.
> —Erasmus, "De Pueris Instituendis"

> He enters the school-room for the first time, he sees them crouching at the desks, indiscriminately flung together, . . . like the presence of the created universe. The glance of the educator accepts and receives them all.
> —Martin Buber, "Education"

I am concerned in this essay with how to understand the place and the cultural representation of students in academic disciplines, particularly the discipline of composition. I therefore question certain powerful ideas of disciplinarity in order to restore the intellectual work of students, and teachers with them, to the center of our discipline and its representation. I consider it equally crucial to extend the possibilities of such a representation to other disciplines as well. To that end, composition, as a discipline, should endeavor to gain and exercise "academic leadership," by which I mean the ability (specifically, the authority and the power) to change institutions so that they do a better job of educating students. I will argue that this process of reform is one that composition as a field can lead, giving direction and being an example. I would therefore suggest that it is time to go on the offensive, or at least to stop being so defensive, about what we do as teachers and what we and our students do as workers in the discipline of composition.[1]

Questioning hegemonic conceptions of disciplinarity entails addressing the gap between research and teaching in colleges and universities. It is relevant, in that regard, to comment on the very occasion of these remarks. This essay was given as a talk at the "Who Should Teach Composition and What Should They Know?" session held at the Conference on Composition in the 21st Century. Our session ran concurrently with "What Direction Will Research in Composition Take and How Will Research Affect Teaching?" That conference participants had to choose between these two sessions in some ways defines the situation of postsecondary educators in our time, even those of us in composition. The choice reflects the contradictions in our own ways of conceiving of our discipline, uniting and yet at the same time separating research and teaching. This paper tries to address, perhaps even redress, this state of affairs by taking up, and taking on, the idea of disciplinarity that underlies it.

To do this, I want to interrogate the original title of this session, "Who Should Teach Composition and What Should They Know?" I want to avoid, first of all, any temptation to try to answer it apart from considering the circumstances of particular institutions and, within any given institution, the circumstances of those students one is going to be teaching. So, what teachers of writing need to know—and what they are in fact learning in the best training our field provides—must include something about students, and I do not mean the "generic" student. There is, as there should be, a good deal of attention devoted, in graduate training and beyond, to the different ways students learn, to the differences among student populations and their needs, and to the different levels on which one might be asked to assume teaching duties. Prospective teachers of writing need to learn something about research in cognitive science, with particular attention to learning styles and the gender, class, and cultural issues that these considerations entail. Graduate education needs to provide graduate students with more information about and greater insight into changing demographic patterns in higher education and about changing institutional expectations for these students. And new faculty members need to learn how to become critical readers of curricula, discerning the aims of both the programs they teach in and the programs their students will encounter as they move toward their degree. Unlike nearly all other graduate programs, composition programs pay close attention to these matters in ways that should be the envy of other disciplines.[2] That we are not so envied is the problem, partly for us, but primarily for students.

We have already begun to take greater control over questions about the constitution and training of composition faculty members. These questions now arise from our own desire to assess our practices in responsible ways and not just in response to invasive scrutiny by others who address us with skepticism about the nature and aims of our work. But such incursions still happen, and we tend on such occasions to respond defensively. In trying to deal with this defensiveness, I find that I have written a paper, not with the title "Who

Should Teach Composition and What Should They Know?" but rather with the title "Whom Should Composition Teach and What Should They Know?" In other words, this paper has turned out to be about what composition as a discipline has to teach other disciplines, and so it is about what all the disciplines in higher education need to know if we are going to have *education* in higher education—this is not a given.

That primary attention to student learning is not a given in many other disciplines is a serious problem for higher education. For example, it is hard to imagine a group of chemists sitting around wondering, as we regularly wonder for our field, "Who should teach chemistry and what should they know?" If such a question were asked, there would be no hesitation in responding: *chemists*, by which is meant those who have advanced degrees in chemistry and who have thereby been certified to know it. In other words, chemistry should be taught by those who know "the discipline of chemistry."

That is a reasonable answer, at least to the extent that circular reasoning is still a kind of reasoning. In evoking the authority of the discipline and disciplinary knowledge, such a response from chemists reveals a perfectly legitimate and in some ways enviable respect for themselves and for the discipline of chemistry and a determination to insist upon their authority to establish and implement their own professional standards. The appeal to the authority of the discipline—and the more general authority of disciplines as legitimating practices—governs the operations of higher education in our time. "Discipline," with all its authority and authorizing power, is the key word.

I want to argue that the privileged term in our professional discussions, the term we are likely to hear over and over again, is the term "discipline." It has come to govern how we think about the good and so is at the center of what passes for professional ethics in the academy. Composition wants to become a discipline; those of us who study writers and how they learn want to be recognized as a distinct discipline of research. And we want the teaching of our discipline, because it is a recognized discipline and so among the ranks of the privileged, to be taken seriously and rewarded appropriately.

These are entirely reasonable things to want to be and to gain. Unfortunately, given the way we now understand disciplines and disciplinarity, it will never happen. A discipline is currently understood as the knowledge of a given field of study, the intellectual skill and labor required for the making of that knowledge, and the disciplinary community in conversation with one another about it. It is conceptualized as a spatial object, with perimeters that contain a specialized knowledge, method, and dialogue. Disciplines are thus defined by their boundaries, and distinguished membership in the discipline, not to mention tenure and promotion, can be gained only by extending these boundaries, almost always in an agonistic relationship to others engaged in similar work. This boundary-breaking *agon* happens well apart from those excluded, those who are not—or not yet—so engaged.

The question "Who should teach composition and what should they know?" might be construed as perpetuating that exclusion. That is, the common answer—the normal way of proceeding to answer this question, as exemplified by our chemistry colleagues discussed above—would be to define what needs to be known (the discipline) and then conclude that those who know this and who know how to talk with one another about it should go on to teach it. Teaching is configured as outside the definition of the discipline, though related to it. So it is inevitable, for example, that Teaching Centers will always be outside departments and disciplines. That separation is essential to prevailing configurations of disciplinarity.

But if we come at the notion of discipline as a system of instruction—a discipline not as the knowledge of a particular area of inquiry and not as the professional conversation about that knowledge but rather a discipline as the act of inviting and enabling others to join that conversation—then we upend this normal, common(sense) way of talking about it and undermine the categories currently deployed to privilege and despise. What I wish to argue is that the activity of passing on important knowledge and nurturing in a new generation the powers that enable such knowledge may in and of itself reasonably constitute what the term "discipline" means. If so, we can restore teaching—and the academic/intellectual work that sustains teaching—to its rightful place in our representation of disciplines and disciplinary boundaries. We can thereby forward our claim for disciplinary status on our own terms, which will be a different set of terms from those now in place.

Establishing this different set of terms requires a historical recuperation, which is more than just etymological retrieval; it is also a recuperation of a different way of imagining the place of knowledge in a culture. It imagines this knowledge historically—not situated (fixedly) but transmitted and transformative generationally. A discipline, understood in this way, has essentially to do with transmission and transformation, and it includes all the agents, students as well as teachers, who engage in this activity.

Such a view is not as odd as it may at first seem.

In its original form, "discipline" derives from the Latin word *discipulus*, "learner," which itself derived from *discere*, "to learn." The first and primary meaning of discipline involved "instruction imparted to disciples or scholars; teaching; learning; education, schooling," a meaning the *Oxford English Dictionary* now declares "obsolete." In contrast to the knowledge imparted (called "doctrine," which comes from *docere*, which also gives us, among other words, "doctor"), discipline entailed the activities of imparting and learning.

In English, the word "disciple" came to mean primarily (almost exclusively) a follower of Jesus, and so one schooled in but also subordinated to doctrine. It implied a kind of unquestioning subservience. Discipleship retains that force today. But in Latin, *discipulus* meant simply a pupil or student or learner. And a discipline involved learning, studying, and the process and structure of imparting knowledge; it included centrally the work of teachers and students together. The body of knowledge that was passed on, and debates about that body of knowledge, fell under the category of doctrine.[3] At the heart of the real work in a discipline was not the scholar (or doctor, concerned with doctrine) but the learner and the teacher who helped that learning.

The meaning of discipline, as related primarily to learners and learning, and contrasted with (though not technically opposed to) teachers and doctors and doctrines, retained its force for centuries, well through the Renaissance and into the 19th century. When Puttenham (in 1589) notes that "Christians [are] better disciplined, and do acknowledge but one God" (28), he is referring not to Christians' constrained moral conduct but to their favored, and superior, instruction in the truths of the universe. When a Renaissance educator speaks of "sending such [students] to be disciplined by Erasmus," he is referring to Erasmus's power as a teacher and the humanistic learning his students would receive, not to Erasmus as an enforcer of right conduct.

From this early meaning of discipline as a course of instruction and learning, many of the more familiar metaphorical extensions emerged. For example, the course of instruction in military and religious areas came to be associated with the right order, controlled behavior, and subjection to authority that marked these fields of social and cultural activity. And so forms of military discipline and ecclesiastical discipline (stressing order, obedience, unquestioning acceptance) came to have dominance. This meaning was in turn transferred back to educational practices. But this meaning, as applied to students, seems to appear only in the 19th century.

How the original meaning of discipline—knowing what you know, teaching it, and establishing structures, like schools, by means of which learning and learners can flourish—came to mean a body of knowledge makes for a very interesting story. Keith Hoskin reminds us that "*discipline* itself in its own long history is an essentially educational term. . . . [I]ts etymology reveals that the word is a collapsed form of *discipulina*, which means to get 'learning' (the *disci* part) into 'the child' (the *puer* here represented in the *pu-* syllable in -pulina)" (297). He relates the change from this meaning to our more contemporary understanding of discipline to developments in educational practices during the late 18th century, elaborating and refining Michel Foucault's tracing of a major epistemic shift (*The Order of Things*). This change in meaning is well in place by the 19th century, at first with regard to scientific fields, but gradually—by extension—to humanistic fields as well. By the 20th century, a discipline came to mean a body of knowledge, a field of scholarly investigation, with little or no reference to teaching or educational institutions.

In any event, by the midpoint in our own century, and beginning even in the late 19th century (or around the time the Modern Language Association and other learned societies were founded), the meaning shifted dramatically, and with very significant consequences for how we understand not just education, to be sure, but even knowledge and culture. If, in the Renaissance, Erasmus's "discipline" means not only a field he studies but also his capacity to educate and disciplines generally refer to courses of learning and instruction, by our own time the meaning has nothing to do with that and rather everything to do with the subject matter and tasks of research.

I suppose it may be futile to insist upon a meaning of the term that has passed away and that has been encumbered by associations with authoritarianism and physical and psychological abuse. But evoking its earliest meanings, and attending to the process of change, may have some value in any event. For one thing, it can help us set in a historical context the "naturalized" meaning of disciplines right now—naturalized by institutional forces such as professional associations, learned societies, and academic institutions. That naturalized meaning, which sees disciplines in terms of the content, methodology, and insider-trading of researchers, if left unchallenged, places those of us interested in teaching in a permanently defensive position.

Defensively, we are trying to work within this naturalized definition, accepting a discipline as involving only two areas: first, a discipline is an area of study, defined by its content and methodology; second, a discipline is a conversation among those researchers (usually "doctors") who pursue advanced, boundary-extending work in this area of study. This contemporary naturalization of the term underwrites nearly all work on writing in the disciplines or learning in the disciplines. And that is the problem. Because once one utters the phrase "learning the discipline," one reifies discipline as something other than learning, whereas in its earlier uses, the term *meant* learning. Discipline did not refer only to *what* learners learned; it meant teachers teaching and learners learning. Once, the discipline was the course of instruction and learning; now, we are placed—and we have accepted our place—in an utterly inverted position. So we struggle to develop courses of instruction that introduce students to the discipline, that enable them to participate in disciplinary conversations. We thus buy into a conceptual framework that makes every effort to change things—even just to see things clearly—impossible.

In other words, this conceptual framework places those of us interested in teaching at a serious disadvantage. Because a discipline once was a course of instruction and learning, teaching was central to a discipline, not peripheral. What we now call "research" was in a certain sense somewhat outside the understanding of discipline, a matter of doctrine that was obviously related to the work of the discipline but not at the heart of it. From an educator's point of view, participating in a discipline entailed, essentially, knowing how to teach, knowing how to set up a course of instruction that students could learn from, and knowing how to create and sustain other institutional practices that promoted that learning. It is no coincidence that the most highly regarded men of "learning" in the Renaissance, northern and southern, were vitally concerned with educational issues. Indeed, Erasmus's writings on education are among the most enduring, and were then among the most influential, of his works. Then, discipline entailed, as we might term these matters, teaching and service. Now, it excludes, or trivializes, teaching and service.

These changes in meaning are not without consequence. The prevailing view of disciplinary work underpins the idea not only of research as the defining disciplinary activity but also of the research university as our "idea of the university." But it is not impossible to reconceive centers and margins, primary and derivative activities here. We could, for example, look to the model of the liberal arts college and find there an understanding of disciplinarity that saw teaching and intimate intellectual conversations with students and colleagues as the center of life in that discipline. It would be possible (though let me stress, too, very hard) to imagine this work as primary, with research and publication valuable as they nourish the education of students and extend the collegial conversation to a larger audience. Let me say again that it is hard to think these thoughts—they seem generically pastoral or idyllic, an escapism set against the harsh urbanity and metropolitanism of today's academy. They seem fond wishes rather than empowering conceptual frameworks.

We can hardly think these thoughts about ourselves, even though—in my view—this is precisely what the discipline of composition does. Composition is a discipline, an educational practice in the older sense I have sketched, that cannot know itself because we have lost our power to name what we do. Our discipline is about the encounter of ordinary people with different ways of reading and writing; our discipline exists in acts of instruction and discussion, not as a bounded field of knowledge expanded by research. When *we* discuss expanding the canon, we usually discuss a process originating in encounters with new student populations and new ways of reading and thinking and persuading brought into our classrooms by our students. The research we do in part arises from that encounter; the encounter does not simply follow from and get defined by the research, as it might in other fields. Our discipline arises from the need and the desirability of promoting and enriching a dialogue already underway.

It is also a dialogue changing dramatically. So we need to reconceptualize "disciplinarity" to accommodate the wide range of work in literacy that Shirley Brice Heath describes in her essay in this volume. She calls our attention to the changing role of postsecondary institutions as they respond to students' efforts to prepare for their futures in work and communities. She also calls our attention to the range of work outside of "educational" institutions to which those of us interested in composition might connect. In a future in which reading and writing will be differently conceived and in which schooling, working, and community building will be integrated within educational institutions in significantly different ways, the prevailing notion of an "academic discipline" will clearly not suffice. Or it will suffice only to obstruct important changes in educational practice, an obstruction that is not necessary and that is anything but sufficient to the needs of students.

At the heart of the educational practice I propose is a reconceptualizing of disciplinarity so that its intellectual work is located in encounters with students and in the projects that arise from these encounters. What we need is a sense of disciplinary work that supports and even makes possible these developments, a sense of "discipline" that allows literacy workers (teachers *and* students) in various institutional sites (academic *and* nonacademic) to feel the importance of what they do and to recognize their connections with one another.

I do not need to catalog the powerful institutions that discourage such developments. From learned societies to research universities to funding agencies to university presses and even some commercial presses, there is an established economic structure that virtually ensures that we will remain not only marginal but alienated from ourselves. So we retreat to our conventions and journals and classrooms, and we tolerate our marginal careers.

What postsecondary teachers of writing need to know is how to change that. We need to understand the operations of the university and the ways of claiming and exercising power there, even if we have to go outside the university to get it. What we need to forget is the fiction that our duties as educators occur solely in classrooms, in the isolated space and class and course. It is a hard lesson, and a harder forgetting. But I think it is crucial to insist on it, not because undergraduate teaching does not matter but because it does, and the fiction of the classroom as its only site undermines its quality. I do not mean here to sentimentalize rap sessions in the dorm, dinners at avuncular Professor Grundy's home, or other equally dangerous figurations of learning. What I mean to say is that the site of teaching is a site created and perpetuated, defined and made to mean what it means, by institutional structures, policies, and practices that operate often invisibly but always very powerfully in and on the work that we do.

These policies and practices inimical to a renewed conception of the work of an academic discipline are entrenched, and they need to be removed. The different conception of disciplinarity I have discussed should make the possibility and desirability of reform more apparent. I will focus on just one example, having to do with the institutionalized policies, structures, and practices in which our teaching is necessarily embedded and out of which its meaning is institutionally constructed. My concern is with the measures that are used to determine the quality of teaching and how these measures affect those interested in different kinds of teaching practices. How we can think about teaching is in many ways constrained by how we are *thought* (or thought about), as teachers, within the prevailing idea of a discipline and the codes of assessment that derive from that idea.

To the extent that it is valued at all, teaching is more measured than assisted. As we all know, to measure teaching, colleges and universities have developed elaborate systems of classroom visitations and computerized student evaluation forms. Unfortunately, these measures cannot reliably register what goes on in many classes; thus, many effective teaching practices are missed or misunderstood. This is perhaps not inadvertent. Faculty visitors tend to expect, because they have a discourse of evaluation that shapes these expectations, a class in which the teacher exhibits a strong intellectual presence (through lecture or controlled discussion) and so shapes the students' learning in immediately visible ways. Student evaluation forms do much the same, geared often toward the lecture as the standard way of "conducting" a class and so establishing "conducting" as a synonym for teaching. These forms are based on implicit norms that overvalue the teacher's performance in the classroom and devalue the students' performance and so misevaluate the teachers who enable students to perform well. This happens essentially because learners are now configured as outside the discipline (at best as apprentices or catechumens), so what *they* do does not really count. In significant ways, these norms work against the best work that goes on in many courses. Decentered classrooms, workshop and peer-group activities, open-ended discussions, continuing exchanges among students in their talk and writing, and lots of individual conferences are simply not "seen" through the current mechanisms of evaluation. This is less a conscious conspiracy than an entrenched apparatus, dependent on categories of analysis and procedures of measurement and reward that seem almost natural, and so invisible.

The current order of teaching and assessment seems to be natural, just as the prevailing notion of discipline, a very recent invention, seems to be natural. Indeed, the two naturalizations are causally related. Because of the way disciplinarity is now understood, it seems natural to celebrate powerful teaching and powerful teachers as the agents of education; it seems natural to see the classroom as the scene, and the "professor's" performance as the action, of a good education; it seems natural to hold the single course as the unit, or unity, of the story of learning; and it seems natural, too, to see other kinds of student and teacher work—work outside this particular configuration of education's agency, scene, action, and story—as not itself a part of disciplined activity. All this is self-evident, taken for granted. The dominant discourse of educational quality, apparent in the documents of assessment and reward, leads us to think, in short, within the categories of outstanding teachers, great professorial performances, and good individual courses. And so we miss, and thereby discourage, even penalize, much of what is most exciting about teaching now—collaborative, multidisciplinary, student-centered, community-oriented practices. This prevailing system of evaluation is inextricably linked to research-dominated conceptions of disciplinarity. Only a radically reconceived sense of what a discipline is, one that returns the learner to the center of the discipline's intellectual work, will make the desirable practices flourish and enable significant institutional reform.

What if we imagined a discipline—not just composition but every discipline represented in the academy—as including, necessarily and fully, every learner? I have to admit that it is hard for me to get my mind around this thought; it is so at odds with how we ordinarily think about these things. But, what if we were to say that we would understand academic disciplines in a more Erasmian way, so that by the very nature of an academic discipline, the moment a student walks into our classroom, the first day of class, that student would be seen, and see himself or herself, as a full participant in the work of the discipline—*just for showing up*. The student would not have to negotiate entry, would not have to earn the right to speak and participate. That student has already entered and by definition has that right. The discipline includes him or her as a given, and the intellectual work of the discipline includes that student's work and our work with that student.

This *is* the work of the discipline of composition; it is not the work of "teaching the discipline," because that phrase is, in this framework, a redundancy. It is in itself the intellectual work of the discipline. Alas, it is not really, at this time, considered disciplinary work at all—often not considered as such by us.

The first thing we need to do, then, is make this consideration more fully a part of who we are and how we define ourselves. The next thing we need to do—for the sake of higher education and more specifically for the sake of our students—is to make the discipline of composition not just a model but *the* model for other academic disciplines. The graduate programs that nurture teachers and scholars in our field, with their attention to pedagogy and the wide range of institutional responsibilities that dedicated teachers must assume, epitomize what disciplines might be and what faculty members might be as participants in a discipline. It is in this sense that I have tried to recast the question of this essay: not Who should teach composition? but rather Whom should composition teach and what should *they* know? Educating other disciplines, redefining the nature of what a discipline is, is the project.

I do not know of any easy ways to undertake these institutional reforms. But I do think that we have a better chance of succeeding by trying to influence new faculty members (perhaps on the model of Head Start programs). I want to conclude by telling you about one specific and tentative effort to do that.[4] In a project that I helped to direct, sponsored by the Association of American Colleges, we sought to address some of the problems in graduate education across many humanities departments. The program was in part modeled on, or rather derived from, the work of composition as that discipline that could provide for all other disciplines a new conception of the pleasures and responsibilities of educators.

The project brought together graduate faculty and students at research universities and faculty and students at liberal arts colleges. The aim was to undermine the hegemony of research in graduate education and to expose students to a wider range of their responsibilities as college teachers, focusing particularly on the centrality of teaching. Through their participation in seminars on teaching and through a series of visits to the liberal arts college (to teach classes, meet with faculty and students, attend faculty meetings, and so on), the graduate students encountered a very different academic culture from the one with which they were at that time most familiar. It is a culture where the older, learner centered notion of the work of a discipline still has some force.

This project clearly had an agenda. One of its underlying assumptions was that liberal arts colleges—and all colleges with a primary commitment to undergraduate teaching—have motive to intervene in the "disciplinary" preparation of their future colleagues. Indeed, they have more than motive; they have a right and perhaps even an obligation. But, given the way the work of disciplines is now understood, it is difficult even to imagine such an effort. It seems arrogant for teaching institutions even to volunteer, much less to demand, a voice and a role in the forming of graduate students' preparations. It would be comparable, for example, to hospitals asking to shape medical education, or law firms demanding and facilitating changes in legal education, or businesses insisting that MBA programs listen and respond to their declared needs and requirements. Of course, this is precisely what hospitals, law firms, and businesses *do*, and they do it for a very good reason: it serves their interests and makes their work better. Behind the project, then, rested the assumption that colleges and universities committed to liberal education, and faculty members at all institutions committed to undergraduate teaching, should take the same kind of initiative with regard to graduate programs. This project—and the larger project that has emerged from it—has to do with relocating the sites of graduate training and relocating the "authorities" that provide it.

The metaphor at work during this project was the notion of a college or university as a discernible and explainable "culture." The teaching fellows were cast as anthropologists, studying the campus as a complex system of overt and hidden rules, means of exchange, taboos, and often mystifying rituals of contact and avoidance. They learned of a broad range of responsibilities, including not simply classroom performance (though effective ways of being in a classroom are certainly important) but also the complex intersection of the faculty member's scholarly/professional life, collegiality, commitment to his or her department's and institution's governance, and nurturing relationship to students that goes far beyond the experience of the classroom or the single course. The project offered an introduction to all that goes on in the life of a college teacher. It provided a sense of their disciplines in which teaching and learning and students occupied a central and honored place.

That many graduate students, given a sense of alternative possibilities for a life in their disciplines, given in effect a different idea of "discipline," were so responsive to this project makes me hopeful. One participant characterized graduate school as a "culture of silence" when it comes to teaching. And graduate students are alienated from that culture; it has not yet entirely taken hold of them. Though they do not often have occasion to give voice to this view, the graduate students participating in this project entered their degree programs to become themselves some version of their best undergraduate teachers. They did not know at the time quite what such a life was like, for so much of it is concealed from students, at every level. But they knew and felt the importance of that life—its value to them and its value to their teachers—and they wanted it. One graduate student expressed her experience in the program this way: "I found it extremely valuable to sit in on classes and a faculty meeting at Guilford. It brought to mind my own undergraduate experience . . . and reminded me of why I went to graduate school in the first place (i.e., to learn to teach as well as my undergraduate professors had). The negative attitude among Duke faculty about teaching was notably absent at Guilford."

The literary device that governed most of their narratives of their experiences is what I would call the "dramatic-recovery-from-amnesia" trope. In this figuration, graduate education had induced a deep forgetfulness, and this program constituted the rescuing blow to the head that magically restored the hero's or heroine's memory and so saved the day and the movie's happy ending. What we had asked them to learn as "new" they in fact experienced as a remembering, a recovery of original motives and a recognition of what, and who, had gotten them interested in all this in the first place. We thought that they were anthropologists going to a foreign country; they felt that they had come home.

This happy ending is no doubt, in part, a fiction. But it is a useful one that bears on the need to enlarge the site of graduate education and encourage in graduate students greater autonomy in defining their own agendas for their graduate education and a stronger sense of their own authority to realize those agendas. I think these students, ranging across many departments, would feel quite at home in our discipline; they are looking for something like what we do, a discipline in the form that we and our students live out every day, something that their graduate programs currently do not provide. The effort to make these provisions may only have just begun, but it has begun, and so there is reason to hope.

Notes

1. This essay began as a series of notes, developed as I prepared for an English studies graduate seminar I offer—a seminar that devotes particular attention to the field of composition studies. I am concerned with the need we already face, and will face with increasing urgency in the coming years, to address two audiences who are not customarily thought of as primary readers of the work of our discipline. The first is new graduate students and even undergraduate students, whose commitment to our field will depend in large measure on how their elders account for it. The second set of readers is outside the academy—let me call them "ordinary people"—who are concerned right now in very particular and often passionate ways about what is going on inside the academy. In questioning the idea of disciplinarity that now governs higher education, I am trying to envision how we might talk with these audiences about our work, and particularly about the perceived gap between research and teaching in colleges and universities. It will come as no surprise that I consider the success of the reforms I propose to depend in large measure on the success of our appeals to these "outsiders."

2. Evidence for this claim is available in the Spring 1994 issue of *Rhetoric Review*, which provides a survey of graduate programs in rhetoric and composition. The program descriptions published there make clear that our field is deeply—and, I would argue, uniquely—committed to a comprehensive training of college teachers.

3. It is my basic point that much of our current talk about disciplines is really talk about doctrines and doctrinal methodology; but I will not press that point beyond reason.

4. A full description of this project can be found in Slevin, *The Next Generation*.

14 National Standards and College Composition: Are They Kissing Cousins or Natural Siblings?

MIRIAM T. CHAPLIN

American schools have always been crisis-ridden, but at no time in the history of American education has there been such a fierce sense of urgency for education reform as there is today. The publication of *A Nation at Risk* in 1983 placed education on the national agenda, and politicians ever since have rushed to make education reform an important part of their reelection platforms. The threat of America losing its competitive edge in the global marketplace because of the failure of its students to compete with those in other industrialized countries was sufficient to stir the interests of many people who otherwise would have been content to leave education to the overworked and underpaid educators.

The increased public concern spurred by *A Nation at Risk* and the widely held conclusion that American schools had failed moved President George Bush to convene his now famous Education Summit in Charlottesville, Virginia, in 1989, to which he invited the governors of all 50 states. The governors identified six education goals that would lead America into the 21st century and wrote the rationale for the America 2000 Plan—six specific objectives including the development of voluntary world-class standards and American achievement tests for students. In the April 1993 issue of *Phi Delta Kappan*, Evans Clinchy writes an interesting commentary in which he claims that, rather than failing its mission, the public school system in America has done exactly what it was designed to do. It was not designed, he explains, to educate all students. It was designed to be the "Great American Sorting Factory," and its mission was "to select, shape, fashion, and build a few students (the academically successful winners in the competitive school race) to become the leaders of society while the great masses of children—the losers of the academic race—would be shaped to occupy lesser roles" (606).

One has only to visit schools regularly to discover that Clinchy is accurate. The schools have done and continue to do an excellent job of educating the privileged students from high- and middle-socioeconomic families, while they provide lockstep schooling for the masses of children at lower socioeconomic levels. The problem today, however, as Clinchy points out, is that the few privileged are dwindling while the masses are growing. The bell-shaped curve has flattened out, and the results are no longer either acceptable or effective. Since the end of the Second World War, those left out of the academic game have demanded to enter. Their demands escalated in the 1960s, 1970s, and 1980s and now are matched with the realities of changing demographics. To allow such a situation to continue is to mortgage the future of America in a more serious way than the national debt has mortgaged it. Clinchy joins the call for massive changes in education.

The global economic landscape has also changed. The players in the world economic game represent cultures unfamiliar to Americans. Thus, the rules of the game are different. In addition, the change of the American economy from production to service necessitates specialized training for the labor force. Alvin Toffler describes today's economy as one whose primary resources are educated brainpower, innovative creativity, rapidly learned and unlearned skills, organizational transience, and postbureaucratic forms of authority. It is an economy dependent on phone and fax; on computerization and computer data bases; on a vast, fast globe-girdling infrastructure; and above all on new attitudes and newer and ever changing skills (14).

Students taught in schools that require rote memorization of facts and concepts or the following of simple directions are not prepared to participate in the workplace Toffler describes, and there are few options open to those unprepared to participate. Monocultural curriculums and pedagogical stagnation in the schools have led to the graduation of an unemployable, multicultural generation that America can ill afford.

Thus, it is not surprising that President Bill Clinton, Democrat though he is, was so willing to embrace Bush's education agenda. Real change is viewed as a bipartisan imperative, and national standards are the government's response to the problem.

Professional organizations in the content disciplines were encouraged by the government to submit proposals for standards development. It was reasoned, I am sure, that the involvement of educators who were on the cutting edge of research and pedagogy in their respective fields would add credibility to the standards and ensure that they were grounded in best practice. In addition, the organizations these educators represented would help to stimulate a national conversation about what students should know and be able to do. The proposing groups were charged with the responsibility of developing content standards that would stress both equity and excellence and that would "demystify" what was to be learned (Ravitz 769).

A joint proposal was submitted by the National Council of Teachers of English, the International Reading Association, and the University of Illinois Center for the Study of Reading. The involvement of the English profession in standards setting does not proceed, however, without opposition.

The opponents have stated their concerns and hesitations. First, they believe that the field already has standards that are expressed in public statements, organizational resolutions, and numerous publications. Second, they fear that involvement in a project commissioned by the U.S. Department of Education gives the government too much control over the sound theoretical and pedagogical approaches that scholars have developed through careful research. Third, there is concern that the compromises that the English and reading professions will have to make in order to reach consensus could pose a serious threat to the professional integrity of the English profession. Fourth, and most importantly, opponents are concerned that the standards we develop could be used to develop standardized objective tests. The profession has vehemently opposed standardized testing for many years.

I share some of the concerns of my colleagues who oppose standards, but I do not share their skepticism. I believe that the English profession cannot be of the world and not in the world. National standards in English language arts will be written with or without our involvement. We should write them because we have the experience, the knowledge, and the commitment to the field. Even though they are voluntary, it is highly likely that national standards in English language arts will be used in classrooms all over the United States. We have an obligation to the students of America to lend our expertise to their education.

I firmly believe that the time has come for scholars and educators, including those of us in the English profession, to go beyond our own organizations where we speak primarily to ourselves and instead speak to the world. We should not delude ourselves into believing that those outside our organizations, including thousands of English language arts teachers, know what we believe English language arts to be or the methodology that we believe is necessary to teach students how to use language to discover their thoughts and to make them meaningful. We must find ways to inform more teachers, and, more importantly, we must find ways to reach parents who do not know what we expect of their children. National standards offer an opportunity for us to enlarge our circle to the point that the bounds that separate us from the world beyond are broken, never to exist again.

The dialogue that standards setting portends can be a healthy experience for the profession. On two other occasions in the last 30 years, English teachers have convened for the purpose of identifying common threads in the profession, for affirming our beliefs, and for charting future directions—the Dartmouth conference in 1966 and the English Coalition conference at Wye Plantation in Maryland in 1987. Both of these meetings are important landmarks, and they provide guiding principles. We have found no systematic way, however, to turn those principles into an action agenda on a broad scale so that classroom teachers who never heard of Dartmouth or Wye can benefit from our work. National standards can help to activate such an agenda.

As a profession, we have proclaimed the wholeness of language: reading, writing, speaking, and listening. A powerful coalition of English educators and reading educators working together toward common goals will cement our beliefs. Draft standards documents evolving from the major subject matter disciplines are being shared with teachers, and feedback is being solicited. The conversation is sure to intensify as the standards near completion. This kind of collaboration may finally lead to a unified curriculum instead of the current one that separates knowledge into artificial compartments. For all of these reasons, I believe that we cannot afford to stay away from the standards process. We belong there for our own sake and for the sake of all the children in America that we represent.

While the standards are being developed only for students in grades K–12, they will have a profound impact on the colleges as well. There is a widespread belief that public demand for content standards in the colleges may be soon to come. Whether that belief is well founded or not, it is important for the colleges to begin to seriously consider what they expect of students and what they are prepared to offer in return. Nowhere is this definition more needed than in college composition.

Speaking to the Conference on College Composition and Communication, Richard Lloyd-Jones described composition as the "center of the problems in higher education." He referred to the changing student population in higher education and warned the CCCC that "we had better get our thoughts together now for how we will adapt in order to serve our students and the language" (492).

College composition is known as the gatekeeper in higher education. It performs the sorting operation that is called tracking in public schools. This is a traditional function for composition, but it increased in importance during the last three decades as more diversified populations were admitted and as remedial and developmental courses were instituted.

The English Placement Test or a state-imposed minimum competency test is the first standard that students meet subsequent to college admission. The essay scores on these tests determine where students will be placed and, accordingly, what kinds of instruction they will receive. In spite of all the advancements that have been made in the teaching of composition, the emphasis on actual writing is still sparse in noncredit-bearing composition courses. The building-block approach of sentence analysis before proceeding to paragraphs and longer pieces of writing remains with us.

Many students enrolled in composition classes have no idea of why they are succeeding or failing, because the standards are known only by those who grade the papers. Students are told only what they did not do in their writing. Those who perform excellently are the ones who have the ability to figure out the rules for themselves and/or those who have a natural aptitude for writing. In too many instances, however, the standards of excellence in composition are the possession of an interpretive community that excludes students and their parents (when they are involved), though these two groups are the ones most affected by the standards.

In an interesting article in the *Chronicle of Higher Education*, Mike Rose addressed composition standards, using vignettes from two situations. One involved a single student who survived the college experience and went on to earn a Ph.D.; the other concerned a group of remedial English students of varied ethnic backgrounds.

In the first vignette, the student had learned to write grammatically correct English prior to entering college but then met with extreme frustration when his composition teacher demanded argumentative prose. "The teacher seemed very distant and cold. I'd get my papers back graded with a C or lower and with red marks about my style all over them. . . . I kept trying but I kept getting the same grades. I went through this routine for four or five weeks becoming more withdrawn. Finally, I said 'forget this,' and stopped going to class." The student took the class again two quarters later and passed because the second teacher gave him feedback on his work and tried to understand his problem. The students in the second vignette were angry because their teachers failed to "hold high expectations for them, didn't explain the criteria for competence and hold students to them, [and] didn't help their students master the conventions of written English" ("Education Standards").

I remember vividly a young Hispanic woman enrolled in a Florida community college who spoke passionately on a student panel during a workshop devoted to the College Level Academic Skills Test (a test with an essay portion that all students in public colleges in Florida must take and pass). She said that she had been trying for four years to pass the test. She made high scores on all other parts but could not figure out what she needed to know and do in order to write an acceptable essay.

These examples can be corroborated many times over. They point to a need for some uniformity in the profession, especially in the evaluation of student writing. Not only do students need to know what composition teachers consider to be excellent writing, but teachers in the content disciplines need to know as well. High school English teachers could also benefit greatly if college composition standards were widely known.

However, proposing common standards for college teachers comes dangerously close to intruding on what college teachers consider to be their academic freedom to teach according to their own preferences. While I have no desire to deprive college teachers of their freedom, I am concerned when the teachers' academic freedom interferes with students' freedom to learn. We should teach what composition students need to learn.

Whether we are referring to national standards for public schools or common standards for college composition, there are three questions that should frame our discussion:

1. Can standards reform the teaching of English language arts without revolutionizing the profession?
2. Can there be national or common standards without standardization?
3. Can national or common standards promote equity in educational opportunity in the present climate of unequal resources?

These questions point to several underlying issues that continuously engage the attention of educators in both public schools and the colleges. Unless we can provide responses to these three questions, the debate about standards and the process of developing them will be fruitless and unworthy of our time and energy.

Can standards reform the teaching of English language arts without revolutionizing the profession? Recently, I asked this question of Miles Myers, executive director of the National Council of Teachers of English. He replied, "If the standards we write can do no more than reform present practices, then I believe we are writing the wrong standards."

What we know from the history of American education makes it clear that education reform never resolves issues. Reforms may buy time but at the expense of allowing the same concerns to fester below the surface until they erupt later—in different guises, perhaps, but always as the same unresolved problems.

The reform of science teaching in America when the Russian Sputnik was launched is an example of a short-lived movement. There was no systematic change in science education, and the low performances of students in science remain a serious problem. Student-centered classroom instruction is another issue that is persistent. The idea of planning instruction to fit the learners for whom it is intended was embodied in the open classroom movement of the 1960s. The proponents of whole language espouse many of the same ideas today.

The argument over skills versus content in language teaching is another example of a persistent reform. Skills were a central focus of the minimum standards movement in the 1970s. With the dawn of the 1980s, basic skills proved to be insufficient for real writing development to occur; content was considered to be equally important. This caused the issue to become more specific as educators attempted to define which skills and which content they should be emphasizing. In composition, the old argument over the teaching of grammar in isolation and grammar in context gained renewed popularity and was joined by a call for the teaching of higher-order thinking skills. Can one learn to employ critical thought by mastering certain thinking skills that can be taught, or are thoughts the result of particular views of reality?

Similar questions arose about which content should be included in composition courses or, more fundamentally, whether there should be content at all. The well-known discussion over the inclusion of social issues in composition courses emanated from the skills versus content issue. The discussion raised the question of whether composition is merely a sterile skills course or whether it should contain content that is current and meaningful to every American regardless of the individual's political stance. Are students to be taught to write by writing about writing, or should they learn to use writing as a means by which they can make sense and take control of the realities they experience living in this society? In reference to the English course (focusing on court cases related to individual rights) at the University of Texas, Maxine Hairston writes, "Multicultural issues are too complex and diverse to be dealt with fully and responsibly in an English course, much less a course in which the focus should be on writing and not reading." Hairston states further that "students need to write to find out how much they know and to gain confidence in their ability to express themselves effectively. . . . The writing of others except for that of their fellow students should be supplementary, used to illustrate or reinforce" ("Diversity" 190).

The issue is not new to education. The inclusion of social concerns in language and literature courses was a central issue in John Dewey's work as far back as the 1930s. Kenneth A. Bruffee, a more contemporary theorist, insists that language should not be placed on the margins of knowledge as a mere medium or conduit—a set of skills by which ideas are communicated or transmitted from one individual mind to another. Bruffee urges the consideration of language and knowledge as inseparable and believes that we should place language at the center of our understanding of knowledge and the authority of knowledge. This will place reading and writing at the center of the liberal arts curriculum ("Social Construction" 784).

In the English profession described by John Dixon as "mobile, living and elusive" (1), reform is often more short-lived than in any other field. Reform will not bring the kinds of changes that are needed in the English profession. We need substantive changes that are more than what Asa Hilliard calls a "rearranging of the deck chairs on the Titanic." "If excellence is our goal, then we must not only change from the slow lane into the fast lane; we must literally change highways. . . . Perhaps we must take flight because the highest goals that we can imagine are well within our reach for those who have the will to excellence" (36).

Can there be national or common standards without standardization? Our population diversity is an important social value. At the same time, we face social problems of a magnitude that staggers the imagination. The old problems of racism, classism, and homophobia are still with us, but they are often dwarfed by drug dependency, homelessness, poverty, violence, teenage pregnancies, and a variety of family life-styles. We can point to no standard form of life. Thus, it is unwise to attempt to standardize education. Yet, in some of our larger urban school districts, a standardized curriculum is exactly what teachers are forced to use. In the name of educational equity, these districts insist that every teacher use the same materials and cover the same subject matter at the same time in the same way. This ensures, they believe, that the lower socioeconomic students will be offered what the students in more privileged circumstances are offered. The aim may be lofty, but it is definitely misguided.

Many educators oppose such practices to standardize education. One of the more vociferous voices is that of Linda Darling-Hammond, who says that the schools must abandon the prescriptive policies that they have institutionalized. Darling-Hammond describes a new mission for education that includes the assurance that all students will learn at high levels. This can be accomplished, she asserts, by allowing students to construct their own knowledge and by allowing teachers to be responsible for student learning and responsive to student and community needs, interests, and concerns. She challenges teachers to try to understand how their students think as well as what they know. This kind of teaching cannot be standardized (754).

Integrity in the College Curriculum, a report from the Association of American Colleges dealing with college teaching, issues a similar call for less traditional teaching and more creativity. This publication even proposes that college teachers should be given training in methodology.

It is difficult to change college curricula, but it is even more difficult to effect change in the approaches used by college teachers because most college teachers do not perceive of themselves as teachers. They believe they are scholars, and they are rewarded by their institutions for their scholarship. The colleges draw a distinct line between scholarship and teaching. For as long as most of us can remember, the college lecture has been the primary mode of instruction in college classes. As I walk the halls of my institution, I see little deviance from this traditional approach. College professors continue to employ what Peter Elbow calls "a method of allowing input to precede output" (*What Is English?* 183).

In these classes, college students are forced to use the receptive language arts of reading and listening before they are allowed to use the expressive language arts of responding through talking and writing. One-directional talk is reduced to questions raised by students and responses by the teacher. This does not encourage students to think; the teacher thinks and the students react to his or her thoughts and those of the authors of the selected materials for the course. The selections, of course, are made by the teacher.

Elbow says that when input precedes output, "we reinforce the wrong idea that learning means functioning like a camera or mirror. The reversal, output precedes input, reinforces the idea that the making of meaning is the central event in learning and thinking and schooling" (183).

The nature of composition teaching leads to more classroom collaboration than in other college courses; classroom practices resemble methods used in lower levels of schooling. In some cases, the most innovative teachers of composition can be found within the ranks of part-time teachers, often graduate students who may have public school teaching experience. These part-time teachers, however, have no voice in what should be taught to students or how it should be taught because curriculum decisions are made by senior faculty who may do no composition teaching at all. Tenured faculty are also the ones designated to train teaching assistants and part-time teachers, though they may have no genuine interest in pedagogy.

There can be high standards of excellence without standardization of instruction. Excellence as a goal for all students necessitates a clear understanding of difference—difference that flows from culture, ability, interest, and aspiration. Every student should be expected to perform at the highest possible level. However, there should be alternate routes available for reaching those levels. If the standards are high and there is only one route to achieve them, many students will lose their way. If, however, the expectations are the same and teachers use their professional skill and their knowledge of the terrain to assist students in reaching their destinations, it will not be an endless journey. The getting there as well as the going will be good.

Can national or common standards promote equity in educational opportunity in the present climate of unequal resources? Noticeably missing from the calls of Presidents Bush and Clinton for high standards are the financial resources needed for students to attain them. Richard Jaeger refers to a 1991

Philadelphia Inquirer article in which President Bush was quoted as saying, "Dollars don't educate students" (125). It is a popular refrain that is heard from politicians and taxpayers. Almost always the statement is made when equalizing the funding for wealthy suburban and poor urban schools becomes the issue. It has been determined through court cases that the use of property taxes to finance public schools ensures inequities in education, including discrimination based on place of residence—discrimination that is no less damaging than any other.

When states have attempted to even funding by providing more resources to urban districts and less to suburban districts, the results have been massive revolts, often joined by teachers who teach in urban schools but whose children attend suburban schools. If, however, money does not matter, why are suburban schools bothered by the shifting of resources? After all, following their line of reasoning, it is not money that guarantees high performances for their students.

In spite of our accumulated debt, our per capita gross domestic product is more than $21,000; Germany's is $18,000, Japan's $17,000. Yet, our per capita expenditure for education is only $853. According to Jaeger, we rank ninth among the world's industrialized nations in our per student expenditure for K–12 education. Do our economic competitors benefit from their added investment in public education (125)?

John I. Goodlad recalls that President Bush, when he announced his reform agenda, named it a nine-year crusade. Goodlad comments that "a crusade invokes a mission. But there cannot be a successful mission without the moral imperative of putting in place the conditions necessary to its advancement." Goodlad calls for a "massive obstacle-clearing campaign far outreaching Desert Storm in complexity, difficulty and cost" (234). There is no indication, however, that America is willing to engage in such a campaign. How, then, can standards promote equity?

In spite of the bleak economic outlook for education, national standards may be the last and best hope of bringing equity to American education. If we can write standards that are more than performance objectives designed to elicit specific behaviors from students; and if we can write standards that are not static, but are conducive to change as society changes; and if we can write standards that will challenge students regardless of who they are or where they will go at the end of the day; and if we can write standards that the profession is willing to embrace and promulgate, we can revolutionize American education from the inside out. This is a way of focusing attention on the center instead of the periphery.

If we write the right standards, they will speak to America in a loud voice and say that these are the highest values of those who know best how to teach language education. If we write the right standards, they will forcefully relay the message that all students come to school filled to the brim with informal knowledge and a language for expressing that knowledge in powerful ways. It is the school's responsibility to take that knowledge and that language and use it to offer alternatives for broadening the students' horizons. If we write the right standards, they will not offer loopholes for educators to slip in their old agendas of separating students who clearly attain the standards early from those who need not just time but different ways of presentation to attain them. If we write the right standards, they will ask the right questions; Goodlad says that one of the right questions is "not whether the child is ready for the school but what the school must do to get ready for the child" (234).

If we write the right standards, they will do all of the above. Then, we can get on with the task of providing for all children the education they deserve.

I realize that the task does not end with the writing. As professionals, we must be willing to do all we can to see that they are implemented, and that means that we must be proactive in and outside of the schools and colleges. We must develop school-college collaborations, because education is continuous. English departments must join with education departments and solicit the support of all other departments. Composition programs must be extremely visible in this movement because of the expertise that composition teachers bring to the teaching of reading and writing. We must be concerned about students who will go on to college, but we must be even more concerned about those who will never complete high school and for whom college is an impossible dream. For these students, we must be models, but more importantly, we must be the people who understand persistence because writing demands persistence.

There is little difference between what is excellent in the schools and what is excellent in the colleges. Excellence is a quality of mind, and all students can achieve it in their own way and in their own time. Composition teachers know this to be true, and they must share that knowledge with students below the college level. College composition is not a kissing cousin to national standards of excellence. It is a natural sibling, for writing is learning of the highest caliber. No student at any level will attain excellence without it.

Note

Subsequent to the writing of this article, the U.S. Department of Education made a decision not to provide additional funding to the University of Illinois Center for the Study of Reading, which served as the principal investigator for the standards project in English language arts. Almost immediately, the International Reading Association and the National Council of Teachers of English voted to complete the project, using their own resources. The organizations' decision was based on their commitment to the development of standards in English language arts and to the improved education of American students.

15 Enlarging the Community

RESPONSE BY ERIKA LINDEMANN

Participants responding to Miriam T. Chaplin's talk expressed misgivings about who would develop national standards and how they would be used. Despite reassurances to the contrary, many believed that developing standards for the content of English language arts courses will lead to standardization and gatekeeping, to mandated curricula that discourage individual instruction and disrespect student diversity. Some participants also saw the National Standards project inevitably resulting in expensive national assessment programs and top-down management practices that exclude teachers from decisions affecting them and their students. Chaplin responded to these reservations by encouraging participants to involve themselves in the project, which attempts to communicate a consensus about what teachers value.

Participants responding to James F. Slevin's talk admitted that composition teachers have not always assumed leadership roles in promoting good teaching. Because our status in English departments is not always respected, we find ourselves polarized within our own departments by discussions that pit composition against literature, full-time against part-time and temporary faculty, and traditional against more recent perspectives shaping the discipline. Other participants rejected the polarization of teachers within and outside composition programs. They argued that excellent teaching takes place in many departments across campuses and urged composition teachers to join forces with those colleagues already committed to teaching well. When pressed to define who should teach composition, Slevin affirmed the "Statement of Principles and Standards for the Postsecondary Teaching of Writing," which he helped to write and which appeared in the October 1989 issue of *College Composition and Communication* (CCCC Executive Committee).

Both presentations can be regarded as companion pieces, each arguing for academic leadership in the reform of teaching but doing so in different ways.

Slevin asks us to remember our name and reminds us that composition teachers have always found close connections between theory and practice. We are, first and foremost, teachers. Since the 1960s, we have met challenges to reconceive our teaching for new populations of students, among them basic writers, students of diverse cultures and first languages, and undergraduates who seek advanced training in writing for the professions. We have responded with new courses and new formats for classroom instruction, with programs in Writing Across the Curriculum, with writing centers and computer laboratories. Composition teachers have little reason to doubt their abilities to adapt theory and practice to the needs of their students.

Slevin's chapter defines two new constituencies for us to teach: those graduate students who will take our places in the classrooms of the 21st century and those who make institutions of higher education places where effective teaching matters. He asks us to assert the importance of teaching within our institutions, to stand for excellence in teacher preparation regardless of which department pays the teacher's salary. Though the distinction between teaching and research will become more, not less, evident in the 21st century, good teachers will still have favorable reputations on our campuses. Composition teachers will be among them. When colleagues seek our help in preparing their graduate students to become effective teachers, we should respond promptly.

Most graduate students want to teach well, but many M. A. candidates have few opportunities to teach, and doctoral students often draw assignments—leading discussion sections or grading papers for a professor—that do not prepare them adequately for the responsibilities of full-fledged faculty members. The 21st century will also distinguish more sharply than is true now between institutions that offer master's and doctoral degrees. Many universities have begun starving their master's programs and promoting their doctoral programs in ways that, before too long, will define them as Ph.D.-only institutions. Most graduate students, 10 or 20 years from now, will pursue their master's degrees at small liberal arts colleges or regional campuses of state universities, then enroll in doctoral programs at large graduate research institutions. Because the primary mission of graduate research institutions is to train scholars, researchers, and university faculty, who will prepare the next generation of teachers for undergraduate programs, especially in liberal arts and two-year colleges?

We can. But, as Slevin urges, the effort will require coalitions among university faculty members and faculty in liberal arts colleges, two-year colleges, and public schools, who do more teaching than university faculty members do and have expertise that university faculty members do not have. Those sites of instruction promote cultures of teaching we no longer find in many universities. Smaller institutions often respond more quickly than universities do to changing demographics and new populations of students. Those teachers are not always represented at our meetings, in our journals, or in the places where we gather daily to discuss our work; yet they have important lessons to share with us. Unless we encourage the kind of collaboration Slevin describes, we will surely deprive ourselves and our students of the contributions these fine teachers outside the university make to our discipline.

Whereas Slevin argues for leadership in reforming teaching within and across institutions, Chaplin describes reforms that are taking place in the public arena. We cannot postpone our participation in this conversation. Standard setting has been part of American education from the beginning, and composition teachers have always been involved in these public debates about literacy—in establishing reading lists, in requiring composition courses of college students, in developing exit examinations and competency tests. When legislators instituted statewide testing of students in public schools in the 1970s, many college teachers kept silent. Could national standards and national assessments have been far behind? Will we wait to have our say until college students and their teachers become fodder for the assessment industry?

Writing teachers at all levels have an important role in shaping the public conversation about standards. The discussion is not happening "over there," in grades K–12; it is "here." With Slevin, Chaplin argues that we have a new constituency to teach, those who do not know our students as well as we do, those who, battered by their own experiences in schools or only generally aware of changes in our society that schooling must now address, would reform our discipline in Slevin's sense of the term. We can promote good standards for teaching reading and writing if we will become persuasive writers and speakers ourselves, if we will remember that effective rhetoricians anticipate the needs of their audiences and translate their arguments from personal preference into claims that have force in larger public arenas.

Both Slevin and Chaplin define good teaching in ways I have increasingly come to value. Success in teaching can no longer be a matter of personal war stories or warm, fuzzy feelings. It cannot be defined by the romantic individualism of such statements as "Student conferences work well for me," "My students can't do group work," or "I do the best I can." Such statements, stories, and feelings may please us; they may even motivate us individually to teach well tomorrow and the day after. But ultimately, we cannot define good teaching by private criteria. What good teaching is and what good teachers know and do depend on the larger consensus of a community that includes other teachers, students, parents, administrators, and taxpayers, all of whom have a legitimate interest in what we do. The community enables us to teach well because it invites us to new knowledge, new pedagogies, and new ways of understanding students. Though we teach reading and writing in classrooms, writing centers, computer laboratories, and offices spread across the United States, the success of our enterprise depends on gaining broad support for our efforts. The empowering concept in both presentations is that we must enlarge the community. By including all those who teach reading and writing as well as those graduate students who want to join us and those public groups who have an interest in our work, we enrich ourselves. We permit ourselves to re-member what good teaching is and learn new ways to do it better.

Part 6 What Direction Will Research in Composition Take and How Will Research Affect Teaching?

16 Moving Writing Research into the 21st Century

SARAH WARSHAUER FREEDMAN

> [T]he challenge that has always faced American education, that it has some-
> times denied and sometimes doggedly pursued, is how to create both the
> social and cognitive means to enable a diverse citizenry to develop their
> ability. It is an astounding challenge: the complex and wrenching struggle
> to actualize the potential not only of the privileged but, too, of those who
> have lived here for a long time generating a culture outside the mainstream
> and those who . . . immigrated with cultural traditions of their own. This
> painful but generative mix of language and story can result in clash and dis-
> location in our communities, but it also gives rise to new speech, new sto-
> ries, and once we appreciate the richness of it, new invitations to literacy.
>
> —Mike Rose, *Lives on the Boundary*

The challenge that Mike Rose poses for American education in his *Lives on the Boundary* is that we "enable a diverse citizenry to develop their ability" through issuing "new invitations to literacy." This is the same challenge that drives the research program of the National Center for the Study of Writing and Literacy and the challenge that I predict will remain with us into the 21st century. To begin to meet this challenge, we at the Center have assumed that, given the scope and complexity of the issues, new knowledge about learning to write and read has to be generated from many sources—from formal university-based research studies, from classroom-based teacher research, from university-school and workplace collaborations. We also have assumed that we would need the insights and expertise of our diverse citizens—looking through the eyes of learners as well as educators and community members—all representing the mix of cultures that make up our populace. And we have assumed that we would need the insights and expertise of university-based researchers across disciplines who themselves represent the diversity of our citizenry. We believe strongly that maximal progress will be made through gathering, synthesizing, and constructing new knowledge from varied sources, taking varied methodological approaches and using varied research paradigms. Overall, our research program aims to be inclusive rather than exclusive. To move composition research forward into the 21st century, I believe that our research will benefit by continuing to be inclusive—of a diverse population of learners, taught by a diverse population of teachers, using approaches that allow for a diversity of ways of learning—with new knowledge gathered from diverse sources and with diverse methods. Along with Carol Berkenkotter, Deborah Brandt, Stuart Greene, and Stephen Witte, we at the Center worry about arguments that divide the field into camps and that we think ultimately serve to keep thoughtful and committed people from finding common ground (see Flower, "Cognition").

The theory that frames current Center research helps us examine issues of diversity. I will begin by presenting the initial theoretical frame for the Center's research and will show how my own research on learning to write in inner-city schools in the United States and in Great Britain was guided by that theory. In the process, I will show how specific research on the learning of diverse populations pushes us to elaborate existing theories to account more specifically for how writing is learned across varied populations. Finally, I will explain the influence of such theory-building on my continuing research on inner-city secondary students in the United States.

We set forth the initial theory underlying the Center's research program in 1985 as part of our mission statement. At that time, we suggested a "social-cognitive theory of writing" (Freedman, Dyson, Flower, and Chafe). Consistent with our desire to be inclusive of varied research approaches, of varied paradigms, our goal was to bring together two strands of research on writing—studies of individual cognitive processes that dominated the research of the 1970s and studies of the immediate social contexts surrounding those processes that emerged in the 1980s. In her 1989 article in *College Composition and Communication*, Linda Flower argued that this integrated theory "can explain how context cues cognition, which in its turn mediates and interprets the particular world that context provides" ("Cognition" 282). Pushing further still, Center research has gone on to examine specifically how writers, from early childhood through adulthood, form social relationships with teachers and peers in ways that shape their learning and become part of their individual thinking, their cognition. This social-cognitive theory is based on Lev S. Vygotsky's notion that "human learning presupposes a specific social nature and a process by which children grow into the intellectual life of those around them" (88). To explain this process of learning and development, Vygotsky uses the metaphor of "buds" or "flowers" that, with assistance, will "fruit" into independent accomplishments (86). It is these "buds" or "flowers" that Vygotsky claims need to be nourished in the classroom. Vygotsky's theory of learning and development explains that these interactions occur within "the zone of proximal development: *the distance between the actual developmental level as determined by independent problem solving and the level of potential development as determined through problem solving under adult guidance or in collaboration with more capable peers*" (86). The implication of Vygotsky's theory is that in order to learn to write, students need to be engaged in social interactions that center around aspects of the task of writing that they cannot accomplish alone but that they can accomplish with assistance. Vygotsky's theory, explaining the intimate relationship between social interaction and learning, guided our studies of the socially interactive nature of the learning process and helped us begin to tie our findings to the learner's intellectual processes.

For example, using this Vygotskian theoretical frame, in 1985 I designed a study with Alex McLeod at the University of London's Institute of Education. We worked in collaboration with British and U.S. secondary teachers. Our goal, which took seriously the Center's focus on diversity, was to compare learning to write in inner-city schools in the U.S. and Great Britain. The schools enrolled students from multiple cultural groups, but most were working-class. In both countries, the study began with national surveys completed by teachers across grade levels and their students at the secondary level. Then, to get a closer look inside classrooms, McLeod and I worked with the collaborating teachers to develop a year-long curriculum that would involve students in a cross national writing exchange. In all there were eight classes, four in the San Francisco Bay Area paired with four in the greater London area. The classes included grades six through nine, the equivalent of what was then called Forms 1 through 4 in Britain.

For the exchanges, the two teachers in each pair worked together to coordinate their curricula so that their students were doing roughly the same kinds of writing at the same time. Although students sent personal letters back and forth, the main focus of these exchanges was on major and substantive pieces—autobiographies, books about school and community life, opinion essays, essays about literature.

The exchange activity promoted a great deal of Vygotskian social interaction, both across countries as the students, teachers, and researchers became involved in the exchanges, and within the classrooms in each country among students and between the teacher and the students. The teachers in each country also interacted with each other and with the research teams. This rich field for social interaction provided many opportunities for students to learn literacy skills and for teachers, students, and researchers to learn about the other country. The oral nature of much of the social interaction made it possible to observe and study learning.

We chose eight teachers whose classroom practices seemed consistent with Vygotsky's theories, but we found striking differences across the classrooms. One major difference surfaced first in the national surveys. When asked what made them successful, the British teachers focused their attention on understanding their students' development. They talked about nurturing their students' creativity, focusing on their meaning making, and helping them write in a variety of ways. The following comment is typical: "I'm interested in and responsive to the individuality of pupils' creative work. I'm excited by language and I'm reasonably fertile in suggestions which can open new directions from what pupils spontaneously produce without making them feel that their work is being taken over by an alien sensibility." By contrast, the U.S. teachers were more inclined to focus on creating innovative activities for the curriculum. A typical U.S. secondary teacher wrote: "I think of myself as a writer. I emphasize the writing process rather than the product. I write with my students when we write in journals. We use peer writing groups when students are competent enough to be successful with them."

The writing exchanges highlighted these contrasts and showed other differences as well. The British teachers, unless they were preparing students for national examinations, had a consistent theoretical orientation that guided their teaching. Their theory was built to accommodate mixed-ability, multiethnic classes. Specifically, a major part of social interaction in their classrooms involved the teachers in negotiating the curriculum with their students inside their classrooms. The teachers and students worked together to decide on writing activities. The British teachers set motivating contexts for their students while understanding that not all of them would be motivated by the same activity. However, the teachers believed that if they were successful in collaborating with the class on topic selection and on motivating the activity, the unmotivated students would be in the minority. When a student was not motivated, these British teachers took it as their responsibility to help that student find something more motivating to do. Students experienced no stigma if they chose a different activity.

Just before the exchange year, British teacher Peter Ross took a study leave to attend the Summer Invitational Program of the Bay Area Writing Project (BAWP) and meet with U.S. teachers. During this time, he felt a marked difference between his sense of curriculum creation and what he observed in the

United States. His sense of difference was confirmed through his experiences with his exchange partner, Nancy Hughes, and her class. During his study leave, Ross was surprised by the BAWP teachers' focus on their successful classroom practices as models: "They all seemed to be program models as to 'how you take it from me and use it in your classroom.' I couldn't do that 'cause I don't offer a program." Rather, Ross's goal was to get to know the needs of his community of students and set motivating contexts, not to create program models. Ross did not even keep files of teaching activities from one year to the next because the particular group of students shaped the activities and how they unfolded.

Ross explained that his curriculum arose out of the interaction of students with each other and with him. He said that he depended on the force of the classroom community to formulate the curriculum and to motivate the students. His curriculum was not the same as a "learner-centered" curriculum, which he associated with the 1960s; Ross found that philosophy inadequate because to him it carries the implication that teachers concern themselves only with individuals and not with the community as a whole. From his point of view, the learner-centered curriculum does not incorporate the way teachers should provide for discussions, activities, and frequent writing that needs to emerge from interpersonal exchanges that are integral to the classroom culture.

In the end, these British teachers expected all of their students to master a variety of types of writing and to practice writing to a variety of audiences. If students did not practice and master certain types of writing, the teachers considered it their own failure in setting motivating contexts. This British approach provided a frame that allowed the students flexibility and gave the teachers important responsibilities. The approach also suggests a reason why the British teachers, in their surveys, focused on knowing their students. To set up their classrooms to accommodate this negotiated curriculum, the teachers had to know what would motivate each student, and they had to be able to track each student's progress. British teacher Fiona Rodgers explains that the teacher plays a directive role to ensure that students learn as well as are interested:

> It's not like within that negotiation there's complete anarchy. There's a certain level of negotiation which is between them and myself about choosing something which, yes, is interesting, but also sometimes it's choosing something which will stretch them as learners. And so you're working together to develop and push them to higher standards and to produce better material and more interesting work.

This sense of negotiation that Rogers and the other British teachers promote is related to what Flower describes when she discusses how student mentors negotiate meaning. However, the British teachers negotiate a curriculum with their students while Flower's mentors are mentally working out their ideas, dealing with conflicts in their reading and in their experiences. When one person negotiates with another, as Flower points out, the parties in the negotiation could be arbitrating a conflict or navigating a path. In the case of the British teachers, the metaphor of navigation seems most dominant. The teacher and students work together, collaboratively, and often with little conflict, to find "a best path." They acknowledge one another's varied values. The eventual path they navigate will reflect trade-offs and will result from a wrestling with varied priorities, but in the end, it will honor the teachers' and students' judgments of what is best. These studies, then, are probing the nature of the social interaction that leads to learning.

The U.S. exchange teachers did not adhere to a consistent approach but rather exhibited substantial variety in their interpretations of how theory enters practice. In two cases, the U.S. teachers expected everyone in the class to engage in the same teacher-assigned activities (or to choose from a set of activities). In another case, the teacher attempted to move toward a completely individualized classroom in which she expected that each student would have a separate curriculum. In a final case, the U.S. teacher followed a theory that involved negotiations with her students, similar to the British model. All of the U.S. teachers were involved in some negotiations with their students, but for some the degree was greater than for others. For example, when the focus was on teaching the whole class, there was little room for individual variation. When the goal was to move to a situation in which individual variation was the expected norm and in which the individual rather than the group was the focus, there was much room for individual variation but less of a sense of the role of community. In the final case, which was most like the British version, the teacher involved the whole class, and the force of the community was expected to serve as a motivator. Also, the expectation was present that individuals might, at times, need to reshape their own activities but that this would not be the norm.

When I began to study the dynamics in the exchange classrooms, I found that the application of Vygotsky's theory of social interaction for learning to write was subject to such varied interpretations that different theories seemed to underlie the practice of particular classrooms. Since Vygotsky's theoretical concepts provide the point of departure for many suggestions for practice in the professional literature, it became critical to understand the permutations of the application of the theory so that it would be possible to provide a clearer definition of the theory itself. In the end, Vygotsky's concept of social interaction proved much too general to account fully for the teaching and learning of writing, especially when the needs of diverse and mixed-ability learners had to be met. In the exchanges, most students were interacting and learning, but the depth of their involvement in pedagogical interactions varied, and correspondingly, the extent of their learning varied. The exchanges point out that social interaction is more than a binary feature, more than a yes/no proposition (either there is interaction or there is not). Rather, the participants in any social interaction perch themselves at some point along a continuum of involvement, from highly involved to relatively uninvolved. In these writing exchanges, learners were at varied points on the continuum. For the same student, the perch sometimes shifted from one activity to the next. But the nature of the social space within the classroom also seemed to have general effects on the level of involvement of the group of students. Some classroom spaces led to highly involved interactions for large numbers of students, whereas other spaces either promoted or allowed more room for surface interactions. In this study, the classrooms that led to the most highly involved interactions were those in which students participated most fully in curriculum making and in which they felt that they were an integral part of a healthy and close-knit community. To create comfortable spaces for involvement in multiethnic classrooms, the teachers understood and paid explicit attention to the sociocultural mix of their students. (For more detail on this project see S. Freedman, *Exchanging Writing, Exchanging Cultures.*)

By 1990, my research, as well as the findings of a number of other Center projects, led us at the Center to expand our notions of social processes and social interaction. We began giving greater consideration to the cultural meaning of the students' experiences —cultural meanings related to the learner's social class, ethnicity, language background, family, neighborhood, gender. In addition, following the lead of Mikhail Bakhtin, we began thinking of writing as participating in dialogues, with each voice shaped by particular social and cultural histories. By considering the intertwining of social and cultural processes in these ways, we developed a sociocultural frame that has provided a way to understand and analyze the diversity of resources students bring to the act of writing, the diversity of resources they encounter as they write, and their interactions with those resources, which include the writer's and readers' knowledge, expectations, and motivations; the discourse communities to which they belong; and the practices they control. Stephen Witte similarly argues for the importance of this cultural dimension in his discussion of the theoretical importance of joining the "textual, cognitive, and social dimensions of writing" (248).

With this theoretical frame in mind, Center researchers, as a group, now are focused on answering the following questions:

1. *About writing*: What writing demands are made upon students in key educational, family, community, and workplace settings?

    - What relationships exist between the writing practices of schools as compared to families, communities, and workplaces?
    - How do these writing practices both support and require higher-order thinking and learning across the curriculum and across the grades?

2. *About learning*: How do students meet these demands?

    - What variation exists in students' ways of writing? How is this variation related to familial and community experiences? to language background?
    - How do students' ways of writing—their strategies—change over time? How do students adapt what they know and negotiate new literacy practices?
    - How does students' writing figure into the language life of these settings, that is, what is its interrelationship with students' ways of speaking? with their ways of reading? How do these interrelationships change over time?

3. *About instruction*: How do teachers help students meet these demands? How can student progress be measured?

    - What challenges do teachers in varied settings face as they work amidst the diversity of literacy practices, of learners, and of technological tools? What is the nature of helpful teacher behavior in writing instruction across settings? What institutional supports are needed to support important instructional changes?
    - What instructional strategies promote both writing and learning across the curriculum and across the grades?
    - What purposes does writing assessment serve—at the level of the classroom, school, district, state, and nation? What is involved in creating assessments designed to fulfill varied purposes?
    - How does assessment influence instruction, both in terms of how and what students are taught and in terms of how the results affect the school site? How does writing assessment relate to the assessment of reading and oral language development? (Dyson and Freedman xx)

With this sociocognitive theory and its sociocultural framework in place, Elizabeth Simons and I currently are working with 24 teachers to explore explicitly the dynamics of learning to write and writing to learn in urban multicultural classrooms. The project involves a national collaboration with teachers who work with us to conduct research in their own classrooms. The teacher researchers teach social studies and English in grades 8, 9, and 10. They come from four urban sites, representing different regions of the country: Boston, Chicago, New Orleans, and San Francisco. At each site, there are six teacher-researchers who are themselves multiethnic. This project builds on the U.S./U.K. study. With a focus now on multiple U.S. cities and with the collaboration of 24 teacher researchers, our goal is to deepen our understanding of teachers' theories and students' learning, from the teachers' points of view, as well as to explore the tensions teachers confront in their classrooms. Ultimately, we hope to move toward specific implications for practice.

This model for the coordination of teacher research and university research is designed to pull together knowledge from inside classrooms in ways that shed light on a pressing national problem—writing to learn and learning to write for urban youth in multicultural settings. The goal is to provide a national portrait of possibilities for Rose's "new invitations to literacy" in multicultural classrooms.

In the research on teaching writing in the United States and Great Britain, teachers collaborated in the design of the curriculum for the writing exchanges, but I designed the questionnaires and wrote the book about the project. This new project attempts another way of knowledge making. Research questions focusing on teaching and learning in multicultural settings beg for insights from a mix of researchers with the capacity to understand the complexities of varied multicultural communities of learners. We designed a collaboration in which the university team based at the University of California, Berkeley, and the participating teachers presented a multicultural mix. The multicultural university team, with the help of local site coordinators, provided support for a multicultural group of teacher researchers throughout a year-long research process. The teachers, for the most part, were inexperienced in teacher research but were known for their thoughtfulness in the classroom and interest in issues surrounding multiculturalism and literacy. The university team provided a forum for the teachers to meet and reflect on these interests in some depth as well as to learn about teacher research. The teachers decided on their own research questions; the university team helped them refine them. The university team also helped the teachers decide on what data to collect to answer their questions and aided them in devising ways to analyze their data. The teachers are now answering their questions and writing reports. During the project, interaction has been frequent among the teachers and also among the teachers, the local site coordinators, and the Berkeley team.

The teacher researchers are still working on their research, and the university team, in addition to continuing to provide support for them, is beginning to synthesize the teachers' varied pieces of writing and their talk together across the year. As we have begun to categorize the teachers' research questions, we are finding that their areas of focus are in themselves interesting. Many focus on issues of curriculum and classroom orientation:

- How can I make issues of racism and conflicts about multiculturalism explicit in my classroom?

- What happens when race, culture, and class become an ongoing topic of discussion in my classroom?

- How can I integrate attention to these issues with the subject areas I teach?

- In a multicultural African American history class, what happens when students are given the opportunity to express their conflicts about multiculturalism and their own cultural identities in their journals? What kind of role does the teacher play?

- How does a multicultural literature and social studies curriculum influence how students think about themselves, including the role writing plays in their conceptions of self?

- What kinds of conflicts do children from varied ethnic groups face in a multicultural high school setting? How can talk and writing in a multicultural Louisiana history curriculum contribute to their dealing with these conflicts?

- What do students reveal in their writings and discussions when they are exposed to multicultural poetry?

- How can I modify a curriculum built for white middle-class students to meet the needs of students in urban, multicultural settings?

- What modifications do I have to make to a reading/writing workshop approach for an inner-city, below-level English class? How will my approach affect the students' understandings of one another across cultures? How will it affect their writing across time?

- How can I address issues particular to nonnative speakers of English?

- How can I help my students (who are nonnative speakers of English) internalize correctness so that it becomes a part of their repertoire?

- What role does talk play as nonnative speakers of English in my freshman Introduction to High School English class learn to write?

Other teachers felt the need to understand aspects of the students' lives, sometimes reaching outside the context of the classroom itself and beyond the literacy curriculum per se:

- What can we observe about the relationship between black male students and the practices of white female teachers?

- Why do some students excel while others do not, and what motivates students to read and write, anyway?

Others are dealing with the effects of school structures on their students' lives and on their learning:

- Why do so many black males in the urban inner-city who are competent individuals in the community end up in special-needs classes? What is the effect on these students of being placed in these special classes?

The teachers' answers to their questions address basic characteristics of the learning-to-write and writing-to-learn activities in these settings: the tensions these teachers experience as they attempt to create productive literacy activities and use literacy activities to improve learning; what they see as the literacy learning needs of their students, within and across cultural groups, considering needs as different as engaging with literacy to learning grammar to using literacy to learn; and how they document their students' progress.

Regardless of the kind of question the teacher poses, a key theme that has emerged in both the teachers' talk and their writing includes the importance of creating a "safe" environment in the classroom. What safety means varies according to the setting, but often creating a safe environment involves encouraging the students to take the "risks" that are necessary to learn to think independently and to speak honestly. Often the safe environment in the classroom contrasts with a violent environment on the surrounding streets. Part of creating a safe inside environment includes allowing in parts of that outside environment and dealing openly with the tensions the students experience, including racial tensions that may surface in multicultural settings.

As we move into the 21st century, those of us in the area of literacy will likely continue to be faced with the challenge of how best to educate our diverse populations. The Center's sociocultural frame is proving particularly important in helping us understand the needs of ethnically and socioeconomically diverse populations of learners. It is pointing to ways we can specify how what Rose describes as the "painful but generative mix of language and story" can yield "new speech, new stories, and once we appreciate the richness of it, new invitations to literacy." I would like to end with a plea that the profession work together actively to meet Rose's challenge, using the multidisciplinary methods and the multiple research paradigms that have helped us advance our knowledge across the past several decades and listening carefully to the multiple voices of our students and our varied colleagues.

17 The Death of Paradigm Hope, the End of Paradigm Guilt, and the Future of (Research in) Composition

STEPHEN M. NORTH

The conference session and, subsequently, the section of this volume that gave rise to this essay—"What Direction Will Research in Composition Take and How Will Research Affect Teaching?"—can probably be best understood as opportunities to enact the central constitutive ritual of the enterprise we call research in composition. I think of it as the Invocation of the Myth of Paradigm Hope for Composition Research. So far as I know, you will not find that particular expression "paradigm hope" anywhere in our professional literature, but its general import should nevertheless be familiar enough. One of its earliest and most visible invocations—indeed, what I have argued is the enterprise's charter, its founding gesture (North 17)—is that oft-quoted passage from Richard Braddock, Richard Lloyd-Jones, and Lowell Schoer's 1963 *Research in Written Composition* in which the authors offer this withering assessment of the work they had reviewed:

> Today's research in composition, taken as a whole, may be compared to chemical research as it emerged from the period of alchemy: some terms are being usefully defined, a number of procedures are being refined, but the field as a whole is laced with dreams, prejudices, and makeshift operations. Not enough investigators are really informing themselves about the procedures and results of previous research before embarking on their own. Too few of them conduct pilot experiments and validate their measuring instruments before undertaking an investigation. Too many seem bent more on obtaining an advanced degree or another publication than on making a genuine contribution to knowledge, and a fair measure of the blame goes to the faculty adviser or journal editor who permits or publishes such irre-

sponsible work. And far too few of those who have conducted an initial piece of research follow it with further exploration or replicate the investigations of others. (5)

In rhetorical terms, the admonitory tone of this passage has always put me in mind of an angry Moses: the voice of the prophet scolding the chosen people for their failures while at the same time making that founding gesture, holding out for them the vision of who they are destined to become—should they, that is, ever prove themselves worthy. In this case, the chosen people are composition researchers, and the vision is what I am calling paradigm hope. It can be read most usefully as an extended if/then proposition: if researchers will always keep up with what is going on in their field and really inform themselves about previous work before they do their own; if they will always conduct pilot studies and validate their measuring instruments; if they will always focus on making genuine contributions to knowledge, not on degrees or publications, and if their editors and dissertation advisors will be responsible for guaranteeing such authenticity; if researchers will always follow things up, follow things through, and, most important for the collective good, replicate the work of others, subordinating their own ambitions to the needs and demands of the paradigm—if they will only do these things, then research in composition will come to be what chemistry is to alchemy: presumably, what we know as a "modern science," one that would discover the truth about the structure of things compositional as opposed to what it has been heretofore, a (discredited) search for panaceas, elixirs of longevity, and philosophers' stones.

In characterizing both the conference session and volume section as opportunities for the performance of composition research's central constitutive ritual, then, I mean that they are part of a series of occasions whose purpose is, in effect, to locate the assembled (listeners or readers) with relation to this legacy: to create—or re-create, or reinforce, as you wish—a composition research "we" by invoking, explicitly or implicitly, this founding Myth of Paradigm Hope. What are researchers doing right? What are they doing wrong? Where, given the trajectory we have been following, should we go from here?[1] I do not mean to suggest that any of this—the existence of either such a founding mythology or a constitutive ritual—is all that unusual. So far as I can see, any collective enterprise, and certainly any research enterprise, needs some version of both: a way to create and then sustain some sort of collective identity. What has been unusual, however, is the extent to which composition has struggled to come to terms with its particular founding Myth of Paradigm Hope. I am not the only one who thinks so. In a recent review of Gesa Kirsch and Patricia A. Sullivan's *Methods and Methodology in Composition Research*, Russel K. Durst makes the following observation:

Our young field has produced an unusual number of books and articles which contribute not to the literature *of* composition research, but to the literature *on* composition research: taxonomies, bibliographies, handbooks, sourcebooks, research reviews. We produce more of these works, not just proportionately but in actual numbers, than our surrounding disciplines of literary and critical theory, anthropology, linguistics, or psychology. Perhaps this tendency stems from the pedagogical urge at the heart of composition studies—a desire to make our subject, whatever it may be, learnable. Perhaps it stems from an insecure need to reassure ourselves that our field is more than the academic equivalent of Gertrude Stein's Oakland. Whatever the reasons, we spend an inordinate amount of time defining the field, cataloging it, classifying it, and critiquing it. All of these are of course perfectly valid activities, and I have done more than my share of such work, but I submit that, as a field, we simply don't get down and do enough primary research. (260, Durst's emphasis)

While I will not vouch for everything Durst claims here, I concur with his assessment of what might be called composition's "inordinate" self-consciousness regarding its research enterprise. As he suggests, this concern over who we are and what we are doing seems gradually to have become, in a very literal sense, a dominating *preoccupation*. That is, although paradigm hope, as a founding myth, ostensibly tells us who we are, or at least who we ought to be—so that, as Durst puts it, we should long since have been able to just "get down and do" our "primary research"—we have proven increasingly unable to do so. Instead, commentator after commentator seems compelled to play out another version of this constitutive ritual. The *College Composition and Communication* book review format does not allow Durst much room for documentation, but it is not hard to supply a list of the kind of citations he has in mind, nor to see why the growth of this "literature *on*" composition research, especially over the past decade, should have thus drawn his attention. That is, while a fair number of titles from the 1970s remain relatively familiar—Dwight L. Burton's 1973 "Research in the Teaching of English: The Troubled Dream," for instance, or E. D. Hirsch's *Philosophy of Composition* (1977, esp. 169–73), or Patricia Bizzell's "Thomas Kuhn, Scientism, and English Studies" (1979)—they seem to come ever thicker and faster through the 1980s and into the 1990s: Janet Emig's "Tacit Tradition" (1980); Maxine Hairston's "Winds of Change" (1982); Robert Connors's "Composition Studies and Science" (1983); the mid-1980s quartet of Ben W. McClelland and Timothy R. Donovan's *Perspectives on Research and Scholarship in Composition* (1985), George Hillocks's *Research on Written Composition* (1986), my own *Making of Knowledge in Composition* (1987), and Janice M. Lauer and J. William

Asher's *Composition Research: Empirical Designs* (1988); Anne Herrington's "First Twenty Years of *Research in the Teaching of English* and the Growth of a Research Community in Composition Studies" (1989); Carol Berkenkotter's "Paradigm Debates, Turf Wars, and the Conduct of Sociocognitive Inquiry in Composition" (1991); the 1992 Kirsch and Sullivan collection that Durst reviewed. And there are at least dozens, and perhaps hundreds, of others.

Where Durst and I disagree, however, is on what to make of this preoccupation. He seems to take his cue from *Research in Written Composition*, admonitory posture and all. Maybe, he suggests, it is because we are so pedagogically oriented (the nice reason), or maybe because we are "insecure" (the nastier reason), but either way it is still *our* fault that "we simply don't get down and do enough primary research." In other words, the promise of paradigm hope is as powerful in 1993 as it was in 1963; we have simply found yet another way to prove ourselves unworthy. To the list of collective paradigmatic failings that Braddock, Lloyd-Jones, and Shoer posted 30 years ago, Durst would now add something like this: too many researchers seem more bent on figuring out exactly what research enterprise they are joining, and why, than on just getting down to work.

As my title is intended to suggest, I would interpret this preoccupation in a rather different way. I think the reason so many people have struggled so hard and so long and, increasingly, so often with these questions concerning who we are in composition research and what we are about is not, as Durst would have it, that we have this "pedagogical urge" nor that we are chronically insecure but, rather more simply, that paradigm hope has become less and less tenable as a constitutive myth: its requirements so peculiar, its characterization of our efforts so perverse, its promise finally so empty that people have found it harder and harder to live with—have found it harder and harder, in other words, to recognize any extant research "us" in it.[2] In short—to make the obvious play on Shakespeare—the fault lies not in us but in our stars: our research "we" has been emplotted in the wrong narrative; our constitutive myth has failed us. Two of its features in particular have proven to be serious liabilities.

The first and perhaps the more obvious of these has to do with the way the myth has characterized the research enterprise, characterized the way knowledge is made. It is easy enough to recognize in Braddock, Lloyd-Jones, and Shoer's founding gesture something of a cross between the idealized image of inquiry in the 19th-century German university—the notion of a positivist "pure science"—which did so much to shape its emerging American counterpart (and for which composition might understandably have some nostalgia; see Connors, "Rhetoric in the Modern University"), and some of western European culture's most durable tales of transformation. The result is a mythos in which the selfless and pure of heart (the disinterested researchers who, unblemished by the desire for degrees or publications, subordinate their desires to the needs of the paradigm), steeped in the true teachings of the past ("really" informed about previous research), scrupulously stay on the path of virtue and discipline (pilot experiments, validated instruments, follow-up studies) until, guided by just and upright counselors (editors and faculty advisors as Merlin?), they are rewarded (collectively, in this case) by a magical transformation: Arthur becomes king, alchemy becomes chemistry, composition research becomes a science.

The problem, of course, is that this tale of transformation has little to do with—is, indeed, dangerously misleading about—what might be called the contemporary scene of research, especially in the way that it ignores or suppresses the material and political conditions that shape that scene. Two examples will suffice. Consider, first, Braddock, Lloyd-Jones, and Schoer's complaint that "not enough investigators are really informing themselves about the procedures and results of previous research before embarking on their own." "Really" here seems to be—has the right etymology to be—an empirical term, suggesting that there is a finite body of information with directly discernible relevance for any proposed inquiry. But consider, to invoke the obvious test case, *Research in Written Composition* itself. In 1961, the NCTE Executive Committee, "[c]oncerned over the nature of public pronouncements about how writing should be taught" (Braddock, Lloyd-Jones, and Schoer 1), appointed Braddock, Lloyd-Jones, and Schoer as an ad hoc Committee on the State of Knowledge about Composition. This appointment was by no means accidentally concurrent with efforts to get the National Defense Education Act (NDEA, 1958) extended to include work in English: James Squire, who was both NCTE's executive secretary and the chair of its Committee on Publications, was also the chair of the (multiorganizational) Committee on National Interest, which produced—also in 1961—*The National Interest and the Teaching of English*. And indeed, the ad hoc group was convened in Washington, D.C., in April of that year.

It was in this context, then, that the ad hoc committee received its charge: "to review what is known and not known about the teaching and learning of composition and the conditions under which it is taught, for the purpose of preparing a special scientifically based report on what is known in this area" (qtd. in Braddock, Lloyd-Jones, and Schoer 1). The group itself reports making a subsequent series of decisions about what kinds of research it would include: only work on written composition; only studies in which "some actual writing was involved"; and only research "employing 'scientific methods.' " Moreover, when this already restricted search turned up a list of over 1,000 bibliographic citations, we are told (somewhat cryptically) that "enough apparently tangential references were eliminated to reduce the number to 485 items." These items were subsequently screened further "to determine which should be read carefully" (2).

Here, then, is the question: was this ad hoc committee "really" informed about research in written composition? Had they "really" reviewed "what is known and not known about the teaching and learning of composition and the conditions under which it is taught"? Despite their claim elsewhere in the report that they would indeed review " 'all' the research on composition" (1), I think the answer has to be no, of course not: they knew it; we know it.[3] They were informed well enough to satisfy the NCTE Executive Committee, which might feel better equipped to handle those problematic "public pronouncements," or to satisfy the Office of Education, from whom they had received $13,345 to do this work. This is not to disqualify the work that committee did—*Research in Written Composition* remains an impressive accomplishment—but it is to qualify it: that is, to point out (what is in any case obvious) that being "really" informed is always a relative condition, a function of context, in the end a political designation; and to suggest that the slippage between the committee's Mosaic rhetoric and its own reports of its practice has some bearing on the significance of their founding gesture.[4]

As a second example, consider Braddock, Lloyd-Jones, and Schoer's claim that "too many [investigators] seem bent more on obtaining an advanced degree or another publication than on making a genuine contribution to knowledge." The intended meaning here, presumably, was that some people had done research that Braddock, Lloyd-Jones, and Schoer had judged unsuccessful because it had been adversely affected by professional ambition of one sort or another. The formulation, however, implies a good deal more, namely that researchers are always faced with a tension between two separate and apparently competing enterprises: obtaining advanced degrees and publications, on the one hand, and making "genuine contributions to knowledge," on the other. This becomes clearer if we follow out the logic of the complaint. Thus, if a bad investigator is one who is more interested in obtaining degrees and publications than in making genuine contributions to knowledge, it follows that a good investigator will be equally interested in both activities, that is, will work hard for that degree or publication but never at the expense of making a genuine contribution to knowledge. But there is more, right? For if a good investigator still devotes half of his or her energy to obtaining degrees and publications, surely a better one would lean in the other direction—would, that is, have a greater interest in making those genuine contributions than in obtaining degrees and publications. And the very best investigator, then, would be the one who, forsaking all advanced degrees and publications, was devoted exclusively to making those genuine contributions.

What is bogus here, of course, is the notion that there are, indeed, these two distinguishable enterprises: that while the activity of research might (however unfortunately) be tangled up with the institutional and professional apparatus of degrees, publications, and the like—what might be called academic politics—that apparatus should not be mistaken for the real ("genuine") search for knowledge. Both the appeal and the absurdity of such a separation are illustrated in this figure of the very best investigator. We do have a special reverence for the *idea* of this single-minded, unsung, apolitical inquirer after truth: so deeply into work (Curie in her lab? Mendel in his garden?), so far out on the cutting edge, that he or she has neither the time nor the patience for such things as coursework or program requirements or dissertations, nor for the rigmarole of writing up results, journal refereeing, and so on. Unfortunately, to adopt such a position with regard to the enterprise we know as research in composition would be, in effect, to declare oneself a nonparticipant. It is simple: until a claim is both written down and subsequently certified by the relevant authorities (a dissertation committee, journal referees, and the like), it simply is not "knowledge," is not "known."

In short, the notion of "genuine contributions to knowledge" untainted by the apparatus of institutional life, like the notion of being "really" informed, exemplifies the larger tendency of this whole transformative tale to disguise the politics of knowledge making. Such a tendency can certainly be defended on tactical grounds. That is, as a rhetorical strategy for gaining federal support for research on composition, this narrative of the disinterested, apolitical research enterprise was (however ironically) demonstrably successful. The NDEA was indeed extended to English, and with a far greater emphasis on composition than, say, literary studies. However, as the subsequent script for a research enterprise in American colleges and universities in the second half of the 20th century—as, in effect, a code of conduct and a set of promises to be lived up to—it has proven to be rather more problematic.

The myth's second major liability is a by-product of this first, and it has to do with the price we have paid for the way Braddock, Lloyd-Jones, and Schoer's gesture constituted "composition" as its object of inquiry in the first place. Making a set of institutional practices the focal point of a research enterprise conceived in this paradigmatic way has a powerful conservative effect. In one direction, that is, it acts to fix those practices internally, to preserve "composition" as "composition" so that it can be studied: it needs to hold still so that research can first examine and then, gradually, discover the truth about it.[5] The goal is *disciplined* improvement: change in those practices should only come as the result of, or, failing that, only with certification by, research findings.[6] At the same time, such a focus works to preserve those institutional practices externally—to keep them on the (college catalog) books—by providing an impetus to maintain them quite apart from their other and/or prior institutional functions. To put it somewhat crassly, grounding a research enterprise—and, in fairly short order, a generation or two of professional careers—in something called "composition research" generates a considerable momentum for keeping the object of study, composition, around.[7]

Unfortunately, we have come to entertain increasingly serious, albeit extraparadigmatic, doubts about the set of practices thus conserved. A number of commentators—most pertinently here, perhaps, Robert J. Connors and Susan Miller—have detailed composition's troubled genealogy as a peculiarly limited mode of literacy instruction: the institutional residue of a disenfranchised rhetoric (Connors, "Rhetoric in the Modern University"), the necessary "low" textual counterpart to the "high" literary mode (Miller, *Textual Carnivals*). And these same commentators, along with a host of others, have asked hard questions about the relationship between this mode of literacy instruction and the no less problematic labor practices by which it has been maintained. The result has been a growing tension between this determinedly apolitical research enterprise brought into being to solve the problems of composition and the dawning political realization that composition—literacy instruction institutionalized in this way—might well *be* a problem. More and more, in other words, it looks as if our research enterprise is directed at perfecting a set of institutional practices that we have reason to believe, on the basis of other kinds of inquiry, are objectionable; and, more to the point, that that same research enterprise—because of the way it has been constituted—has a vested interest in perpetuating those practices.

As I say, these liabilities have gradually rendered paradigm hope untenable as a constitutive myth. In the context of this volume, therefore—that is, in answer to the question "What is the future of research in composition and how will it affect teaching?"—I would argue that the Myth of Paradigm Hope is dead or dying and predict, only a bit hyperbolically, that in the terms bequeathed by this legacy, there *is* no future for research in "composition": we will constitute ourselves and our research enterprise in other ways. One fairly obvious change, indicated in the second term of my title, will be the end of paradigm guilt: no more Mosaic recriminations, no more self-flagellation, no more (confused) shame at coveting degrees and publications over "genuine" contributions to knowledge, and so on. If research in composition is not destined to be transformed into a science, then we do not need to cast(igate) ourselves as the chronically unworthy, those mythical "too many investigators" who too often ruin everything by being underinformed, sloppy, too anxious to get ahead, irresponsible as editors and advisors, chronically insecure, and/or pedagogically obsessive.[8]

Other consequences, such as what form our research enterprise *will* take, or what roles, under the aegis of what new mythology, we *will* play, are a good deal less obvious. Nevertheless, I will conclude here by predicting some general trends, all of which seem to me to have already been set in motion. The first has to do not with research as such but with classroom practices and institutional programs—with the effects of research on teaching. In the absence of paradigm hope's conservative energies—and in conjunction, to be sure, with other political and economic changes—the institutional efforts at literacy instruction heretofore identified under and indeed constrained by "composition" will be redeployed in a rapidly growing variety of ways. Some changes, certainly, will be what I characterized a few pages back as internal; that is, they will consist of alterations within course structures that occupy composition's curricular space. (The Syracuse Writing Program's series of "studio" courses, for example, could be said to prefigure this kind of change, as might the kinds of courses outlined in, say, Patricia Donahue and Ellen Quandahl's *Reclaiming Pedagogy*.)

More and more frequently, however, such changes will be external; that is, they will result in the disappearance of the word "composition" from college catalogs and of traditional composition programs and their constituent courses from college campuses. In their place will emerge a variety of other arrangements, the lineaments of some of which are already visible: programs more closely aligned with cultural studies, or which focus on literacy studies. In my own utopian thinking, the result will be a transformation (that word again) of English studies as a whole. Composition, creative writing, expository writing, and the like—all those "kinds" of writing that the English curriculum has tended to consign to an essentially pre-or extradisciplinary role—will come together in "writing." "Writing" will become, as it must, "writing and reading" or, to invoke two disciplinary traditions, rhetoric and poetics. And, last but not least, rhetoric and poetics will subsume what we now call English studies, with the curricular aim of training (obviously) rhetors and poets—as opposed, say, to the (junior) literary historians and aesthetically sensitized readers so many English curricula still seem designed to produce. I make no particular claims for this vision, save that it is the one I will pursue. Other people in other places will work—are working, have been working—toward other ends; and indeed, there will be, at least for a time, an exciting diversity. In the absence of that pressure for standardization that is another feature of paradigm hope's conservatism (for the purposes of paradigmatic research, it is more efficient if composition at your school is the same as composition at mine), people will experiment more freely. In short, the landscape of college literacy instruction will change, and change rapidly.

Research, meanwhile, will by no means disappear. Even if that were desirable—and I adamantly do not think it is—certain institutional demands will guarantee its continued existence. Clearly, however, it will not be business as usual. As a constitutive myth, after all, paradigm hope has been reciprocally constraining: if "composition" was supposed to hold still, be examined, and then follow research's lead, research had the concomitant responsibility to do the examining, and then to provide leadership—systematic change—based on its findings. In the absence of that rather narrowly conceived responsibility, our research energies will be redeployed in two general directions. A portion of them will go, as a small percentage long since has, to inquiries at a considerable distance from our instructional efforts—to what sometimes gets called more "basic" research. By far the larger part of those energies, however, will continue to be tied closely to our increasingly diversified instructional efforts—with research, however, playing a very different role. Instead of leading an orderly march toward a perfected practice, research will find itself hurrying to keep up, serving as a companion—perhaps a commentator—trying to engage those practices in what will very often be a breathless dialogue.[9] We have had a foretaste of this role, I think, in work on Writing Across the Curriculum, where we have had to resituate our inquiries over and over again in academically alien, discursively complex, hard-to-control situations and to conduct them at something like this breathless pace in an effort to keep up with large, rapidly growing programs and sometimes larger institutional promises. This new relationship will feature rather dramatic differences in at least four areas of our research enterprise.

First, we will considerably expand the range of our research interests. That is, as our research follows these redeployed instructional efforts, we will not only move out of the familiar confines of the "composition" classroom but also be forced to face new complexities. We will need to respond to ideas about the means and ends of literacy instruction from which our tradition of reciprocal constraints has insulated us. Consequently, we will need to deal seriously, for instance, with issues of development during the college years (see for example Haswell) in programs that feature writing as a long-term, disciplinary concern as opposed to a short-term, predisciplinary one. We will need to wrestle with all those concepts we have given over to "creative" writing, concepts such as aesthetics, say, or talent. And we will need to consider the nature of instruction—the *politics* of instruction—in programs where the notion of the students' right to their own language is not a source of nostalgia but a point of curricular departure.

Second, we will study and report on this wider range of issues in a wider variety of forms. We have, of course, witnessed considerable methodological variation in this field already (see for example Herrington). However, I have in mind—and am willing to predict—rather more radical developments. In this new companion/commentator role, the credibility of research will become less a function of its paradigmatic orthodoxy—its ties to some (imagined) cumulative disciplinary effort—than what I would call its fitness for a given situation, a quality that must be determined by those involved. One effect of the diversification of our instructional efforts, then, will be to promote a parallel diversification in what "counts" as research, the negotiation of new forms to fit new situations. So, to suggest one trajectory such developments might follow, we have already moved from Shirley Brice Heath's *Ways with Words* (an ethnography) to Mike Rose's *Lives on the Boundary* (an autobiography) to various so-called teachers' stories (for example Joan Cutuly's *Home of the Wildcats*). It is not hard to imagine a future in which not only these three variations on narrative but indeed straight fiction will serve—with equivalent if not identical value—this companion/commentator's role in one or another context and in doing so equally warrant the designation "research."

Third, research in this new relationship will develop a very different rhythm. A research enterprise shaped by paradigm hope proceeds, at least ideally, at a stately and deliberate pace, with study building carefully upon study and each investigator "really" informed about earlier work. The academic system of publication is in essence a technological expression—the ritualization—of this ideal: reports, often years in the making, and licensed by a properly comprehensive list of works cited, are submitted for careful review, returned for revisions, resubmitted for further review, and so on, until the best and the true are selected out to appear in print a year or two or three after initial submission.

However, as research moves away from paradigmatic accumulation as its primary source of credibility, this rhythm changes: more inquirers working at a wider range of sites in a greater variety of forms—all less constrained by the cumulative weight of past inquiries—will produce a greater quantity of research and produce it faster. We have already begun to see some such acceleration, especially over the last decade. That is, the number of people seeking to publish their work has clearly increased, but the result has been less to create long queues at existing journals—people waiting patiently for their paradigmatic turn—than a proliferation of alternative publishing venues with alternative criteria for publication (journals, ERIC, essay collections, and the like), a kind of knowledge overflow that would appear to have swamped any extant apparatus for exerting paradigmatic control. More to the point, the continued existence of these alternative venues—the new journals, especially—will provide the systemic basis for further acceleration: that is, an ever-quicker cycling of a greater quantity of work, the cumulative coherence of which will be harder and harder to trace. And by the end of the decade, a further technological change, on-line publication, will accelerate this cycle even more. Soon enough, that is, researchers of all kinds will simply post their studies directly through one or another network clearinghouse, eliminating those last vestiges of paradigm hope, editors and referees, in favor of a kind of free market of ideas: readers will read what interests them, judging and debating its value in that same electronic space. The *activities* of research—the conduct of various inquiries themselves—will continue, of course, to feature their own temporal constraints; but in the next century the publication part of our knowledge-making cycle will make its own leap into the Information Age.

Which brings us to the fourth and last feature of this new relationship between research and instructional efforts: it will significantly alter the way research is valued. If developments follow the outline I have been sketching here, we will have more research more accessible more quickly, but it will also be both far less transportable and—though the term may seem unpleasant—far more disposable. Thus, while we will be able to learn about a study conducted at Albany, New York, much more quickly than heretofore—I will be able to post it directly on the Internet, likely without refereeing, without the year or two lag typical of publication in current journals—the increased (and increasingly acknowledged) diversity of institutional contexts and practices will render those findings far less directly relevant for, say, Albany, Georgia. The object of inquiry, "composition," will have lost its (imagined) identity. Moreover, this study (or any other) will have a far shorter shelf life, or at least a very different one.

The Myth of Paradigm Hope fostered a monumental image of knowledge making, one that led us to look to research for what was "proven" or, perhaps, "true." In its absence, we will look (as I have argued we often already do; see North, 21–55) for qualities such as plausibility and utility. This is not to say that research will matter less, or that it can, therefore, be carried out with any less methodological integrity. It is to say, however, that it will matter differently: that its value will not be a (paradigmatic) constant, so that it can indeed be discarded; and that its integrity will be less a matter of a researcher's commitment to other researchers, or the demands of a cumulative system, than to the teachers who are its prospective users.

The brave new world of literacy instruction I have predicted here will surely not be universally popular; research, after all, is by no means the only part of our professional collective with a vested interest in preserving composition as we know it. Nevertheless, I not only believe that such changes *will* happen but also that they *should*—in large part, of course, because of our increasing sense that composition represents a questionable model of literacy instruction kept in place by even more problematic labor practices, but also because I think we owe it to Braddock, Lloyd-Jones, and Schoer. *Research in Written Composition* was written at a certain time for a certain purpose, and it has served us well, gotten us this far. But times and purposes change. I like to think its authors knew that, and that they would be the first to urge us that it was time to move on.

Notes

1. Obviously, I am not arguing that such occasions are simple-minded convocations: the assembled are not asked, for example, to raise their right hands and recite these injunctions as a pledge. For most purposes in contemporary American culture, at least, neither founding myths nor constitutive rituals function to thus supplant individual belief, and that is surely the case here: individual researchers will espouse varying beliefs and indeed change those beliefs over time. I am arguing, however, that such beliefs will inevitably arise in the context of, in effect be in answer to, an orthodoxy shaped by Braddock, Lloyd-Jones, and Schoer's founding gesture and its constitutive mythology.

2. To be sure, people have responded to the myth's failing explanatory powers in very different ways: some, such as Durst, looking for someone (themselves included) to blame; others, such as Herrington, working at something closer to triage, trying to (a)mend it, as it were, and thereby keep it alive; and still others, such as Thomas Newkirk, aiming to (sup)plant it. But these represent, I would argue, a predictable range of reactions to the same underlying phenomenon.

3. Perhaps the most obviously problematic exclusion has to do with histories. What does it mean to be "really informed" about the conditions under which composition is taught and learned if any history of such conditions is excluded as not "scientific"?

4. Two quotations seem particularly apt as guides here. The first is a refrain (with variations) from chapter 2 of Jasper Neel's *Plato, Derrida, and Writing*, "The Structure of Origin and the Origin of Structure," in which Neel traces Plato's attempts to do away with writing through the use of writing: "I wish I didn't think Plato knew all this." The second is from the scene in the film version of *The Wizard of Oz* in which Toto has pulled back the curtain to reveal the "wizard" at work: "Pay no attention to that man behind the curtain!"

5. Although I do not have the space to pursue the issue, I need to acknowledge here the relationship between this image and various accounts of the feminization of composition. See for example S. Miller, "The Feminization of Composition."

6. This effect in particular has been enhanced by what might be called the federalizing of the enterprise and the desire for standardization that tends to come with such a centralization of authority. Simply put, it would have seemed—as it still often does seem—an awful waste of NCTE or Department of Education resources if composition research produced findings that are of largely or exclusively "local" significance. There is always some pressure, therefore, to preserve composition's identity across a very wide range of institutions and thereby promote the portability of research findings.

7. Research is by no means the only conservative force at work. Another obvious choice, and one with particularly interesting ties to this matter of careers, is the textbook industry: profitable large-scale adoptions depend on a relatively standardized composition.

8. Even George Hillocks, perhaps the most forceful and visible apologist for a

paradigmatically conceived research enterprise, is at least conflicted on this point. That is, while his characterizations of experimental research, in particular, clearly echo Braddock, Lloyd-Jones, and Schoer ("Too often the treatments are poorly conceived, [occasionally silly], and the studies are badly designed" [93]), he does acknowledge not only that he does not "know what the next step in [Braddock, Lloyd-Jones, and Schoer's alchemy to chemistry] analogy" might be, but that "the analogy may be inappropriate today anyway" (xvi). Thus, even though he doggedly returns to precisely that analogy a paragraph later to offer a suitably upbeat and orthodox conclusion—"although many problems remain," he argues, "we have reason for optimism. We have the power to teach and to continue research well beyond the stage of alchemy" (xvii)—there appears to be some chance that the promise of transformation might at least be amended.

9. I am indebted here, as in all discussions of research/instruction relationships, to Patricia Harkin's "Postdisciplinary Politics of Lore."

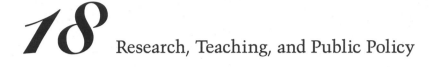

18 Research, Teaching, and Public Policy

RESPONSE BY SANDRA STOTSKY

Unlike the positions expressed by several other pairs of speakers at this conference, those of Sarah Warshauer Freedman and Stephen M. North seem to be at almost complete odds with each other. Freedman sees a continuing role for current paradigms for research in the 21st century, and she naturally believes that what the National Center for the Study of Writing and Literacy is doing or plans to do represents the kind of research that should be done. On the other hand, North believes that we have learned little of value from composition research precisely because of the ways in which researchers have defined objects of research, what knowledge in composition consists of, and how to go about creating it. North also sees no future (or hopes there is none) for the college composition course. Indeed, he claims that it is composition research that has kept this course alive.

Freedman's and North's papers elicited a number of questions from their audience. I will organize my own comments around four sets of concerns expressed by these questions. One group of questions focused on the future relationship between research and teaching. North's position was clear—future research would no longer dominate practice; it would follow or at best accompany it. But some participants wanted further elaboration of Freedman's remark in her talk describing the role of research as one of providing information to teachers without concern for whether this information had pedagogical implications. This remark does not appear in her written paper, and Freedman's essay indicates that she expects to move toward "specific implications for practice" in her current research with teachers, thus suggesting the more traditional relationship between empirical research and practice. Nevertheless, both stances reflect a relationship that North does not view as desirable or useful. The questions directed to this relationship seem to stem from a growing source of tension between researchers and composition teachers, at least at the college level. Like North, who has articulated his views at length in his published work, many college composition instructors are highly critical of the "privileging" of researchers over teachers in the making of knowledge about composition, denying the legitimacy of the hierarchical relationship they perceive and questioning the value of what most existing research has offered them.

I sympathize with North and other teachers who believe they have been patronized if not ignored by researchers. Their perceptions are not without some foundation. Many researchers have offered dogmatic recommendations to teachers on the basis of one or two studies rather than letting their results serve as a limited and tentative source of knowledge to inform pedagogical judgment. Moreover, much educational research has been addressed chiefly to other researchers, not to teachers. Like others with professional roots in pedagogy (I began my own career years ago as a third-grade teacher, later taught at the high school level, and have more recently taught undergraduate and graduate courses on writing pedagogy), I believe that educational research is justifiable only if it is relevant to practice and intelligible to teachers, enlarging their understanding of pedagogical issues.

But I do not agree with North that our current research paradigms have offered composition teachers little useful knowledge. As does Freedman, I believe that we have learned much from composition research and will continue to learn more, regardless of the paradigm or mode of collaboration between researcher and teacher. In fact, I believe that North is implicitly (but unintentionally) suggesting a change in our central research question, not "How can we improve or assess writing?" but the more fundamental "Is writing teachable?" And indeed, that should be our central research question, as suggested by both the featured article by Aviva Freedman and responses to it in the October 1993 issue of *Research in the Teaching of English*.

Nevertheless, empirical research, whether experimental or ethnographic or mixed in approach, cannot be the only means by which we try to explore what aspects of writing can be taught, under what conditions, and how. I agree with North that pedagogical, critical, and aesthetic judgments are crucial. These kinds of judgments are not the results of research in any scientific sense of the term (and it is debatable whether they should even be considered as the results of nonscientific modes of research, as some are now proposing), but because these judgments reflect other ways of learning, they can be at least as useful, if not more so, in the development of our understanding of a pedagogical issue and in the formulation of educational policy.

Educational research has suffered from both the excessive prestige that has been accorded to it in the university and the excessive faith that has been placed in it by educators. Empirical research on composition needs to be removed from the pedestal on which it was long ago placed. Researchers should be far more modest about what any empirical study could tell us about writing. No one study, nor any one group of studies, could ever tell us everything we would want to know about a phenomenon as complex as writing. Moreover, as someone who has had the privilege in recent years of drawing upon the critiques of hundreds of colleagues in order to evaluate the manuscripts submitted to *RTE*, I have learned time and time again how limited are the claims any one study can make. But in removing empirical research from its pedestal, it is not necessary to smash it. Rather than losing the benefit of what it can tell us, teachers need only read educational research more critically, understand the inherent limitations of even the best-designed and conducted studies, and accord these studies less definitive authority.

A second set of questions raised in response to Freedman's and North's papers focused on the forms that research might take in the 21st century. They were directed more to North than Freedman, since she embraced an inclusive approach. Although North sees no future for current modes of research, he is admittedly rather nebulous about the forms future research might take. He foresees many different forms, ranging from ethnography to autobiography to fiction, suggesting that all could profitably be considered research. However, we may want to view such an expansion of its definition as a tactical rather than a principled consideration; if what we understand today by research can be both discredited (as futile "paradigm hope") and diluted in meaning, its disintegratation and disappearance can be hastened. I say this because it is important to think about what we may lose from successful efforts to colonize research with what we know are nonresearch genres of writing. As one perceptive questioner noted pointedly, by abandoning generalizability in research, North seems to be abandoning theory as well. It is not accidental that North never uses the word "theory" even once in his *Making of Knowledge in Composition*, even though theoretical thinking is the sine qua non of all academic inquiry. Surely, the devaluing of the scientific method and the colonization of research with nonresearch genres are the wrong price to pay for trying to elevate teachers as equal or even dominant partners in educational decision making, if indeed it could be accomplished by that means. Moreover, although I am intrigued by the scenario North lays out and see some value in a possible explosion of publication in "electronic space," I doubt that the "methodological integrity" he believes future genres of research can display can be a meaningful concept outside of our empirical research traditions and the kinds of studies they create.

Regardless of the relationship between research and practice and the forms research might assume, we still need to think about our responsibility for addressing much of what is driving public debate at the local as well as national level—the inadequacy of student writing in K–12 and in college courses. A third set of questions at the conference session focused on concerns about the future of freshman composition and professional identity. While college composition serves both traditional and nontraditional students, what is ultimately at stake in teaching nontraditional students academic writing is their chance for economic advancement and full civic participation, as Mina Shaughnessy observed many years ago in her germinal work. More than anyone else, she helped us understand the enormous challenge that the extension of higher education to nontraditional students created—how to give all students access to "the language of power," not just those who come to college with better preparation for acquiring it. It seems premature to conclude that writing is unteachable, or that it can be taught best in the disciplines themselves, without full institutional evaluations and without careful scrutiny of the kinds of writing that students are now taught and of the ways in which they are taught. But I am dubious about the wisdom of the approaches I have heard some propose with reference to those formulating policies for institutional assessment.

So I would like to close by suggesting an alternative to the notions of "intervention" or "creative resistance" that have been put forth. In so doing, I also address a fourth set of questions, which focused on how teachers might best influence the political process from which the final decisions will be made on the form institutional assessment will take and the future of the freshman composition course. I happen to wear many hats, among them one as town meeting member in my home community. Every year we have to decide upon how much we will spend on such equally valued facilities or services as our parks, recreational programs, and streets. The experience of self-government is, as both John Stuart Mill and James Bryce have noted, morally and intellectually stimulating. It is also very sobering. One must constantly rethink basic priorities; needs seem to be infinite, but resources and revenues are always finite. In my political life, I have found that most legislators and other policymakers are reasonable human beings. Instead of complaining that "they" seem to distrust teachers, let us ask why we distrust "them" and try to overcome it. Why not engage in a mutually sympathetic dialogue and develop a collaborative approach for addressing our concerns about institutional assessment and freshman composition? Surely, the fruits of various kinds of research as well as pedagogical judgment about the value and optimal location of composition instruction should be able to assist us in these deliberations.

Part 7 What Political and Social Issues

Will Shape Composition in the Future?

19 English Studies, Work, and Politics in the New Economy

JAMES A. BERLIN

Unrelenting change has been the one constant of the 20th century, the key marker of social and cultural experience. This, of course, is as much a product of the market conditions of capitalism as it is of the avante-garde aesthetic of modernism. Despite this unchanging change, until just recently one realm of stability has been found in the payoff provided by a college degree. Unfortunatcly, as all of us too painfully know, this is no longer the case. College graduates cannot now be certain that they will find a comfortable position in the work force. Indeed, they are not sure they will find any position beyond the level that would have been available to them without a degree. A Labor Department study released in 1992 indicated that between 1984 and 1990, 20 percent of college graduates were underemployed or unemployed. This figure is expected to rise to 30 percent between 1993 and 2005 (Greenwald 36). Graduates who do find the good jobs today, furthermore, are discovering the conditions of work to be quite different from those of just a few years ago. In other words, the kinds of tasks and responsibilities they are expected to undertake are assuming new dimensions. Indeed, both graduates and their employers are more and more complaining about the preparation colleges are offering, questioning the match of the old curriculum to the new work force.

Teachers in English studies ignore these changes in the world of work at the peril of the future of students as well as the welfare of the nation. I want here to situate these transformations in hiring and work patterns within the larger economic, political, and cultural conditions of our moment and to recommend a response I would hope English departments would consider. These comprehensive alterations commonly fall under the rubric of the postmodern, a designation referring primarily to the cultural realm but also indicative of changes in work and political relations. In my analysis, I will rely especially on the discussion of the postmodern found in David Harvey's *Conditions of Postmodernity* and in a collection of essays titled *New Times: The Changing Face of Politics in the 1990s*, edited by Stuart Hall and Martin Jacques. Both consider postmodernism in terms of its place in the development of international capitalism as well as its manifestations in the cultural arenas of art, philosophy, and forms of popular entertainment.

Harvey and the contributors to the Hall-Jacques collection are especially useful in helping us to understand the changing economic conditions for which we are preparing our students. While most of them would argue that these changes are extensions of the forces of modernism—an inevitable development of the trajectory of 20th-century capitalism rather than a new stage of it—the disruptions presented nonetheless call for radically new responses at every level of our experience. Most important, we are today witnessing a shift from a Fordist mode of production to a post-Fordist one—to what Harvey calls a "regime of flexible accumulation."

Fordism

The term "Fordism" refers to the mass production system perfected (although not invented) by Henry Ford in his Michigan auto plants early in the 20th century. This system, Robin Murray explains in *New Times*, was based on four principles. First, products and the parts and tasks that go into them were all standardized. Second, this standardization allowed many of the tasks that are needed for production to be mechanized. Third, the remaining jobs were "Taylorized," a term derived from the methods for increasing efficiency introduced by F. W. Taylor. These activities were thus "redesigned by work-study specialists on time-and-motion principles, who then instructed manual workers on how the job should be done" (39). Finally, factory production was organized along a nodal assembly line so that the products being assembled flowed past the workers. This method led to an economy of scale. As Murray explains, "[A]lthough mass production might be more costly to set up because of the purpose-built machinery, once in place the cost of an extra unit was discontinuously cheap" (39). This mode of mass production depended on mass consumption, a pattern of buying in which consumers became accustomed to purchasing standardized products. It also demanded protected national markets so that companies could recover their production costs at home before any attempt to compete internationally.

Fordism created new kinds of workers. Unlike the craft mode of production, work was de-skilled and fragmented into a set of mechanized movements. This made for a rigid division between manual workers and mental workers. Most manual workers were interchangeable parts of the production machine and were paid according to the job they performed. As Murray explains, the "result was high labor turnover, shopfloor resistance, and strikes" (40). Managers constantly sought new laborers from rural areas, from immigration, and from the marginalized in the cities. The Fordist mode also gave rise to a distinct group of managers, employees who were more and more likely to be the holders of college degrees. Taylorism, however, was applied even at this level: "Fordist bureaucracies are fiercely hierarchical with links between the division and departments being made through the center rather than at the base. Planning is done by specialists; rulebooks and guidelines are issued for lower management to carry out" (40). The bureaucratic structuring of mental work meant that managers too were often extensions of the machine, performing tasks that required little skill and training and that allowed for almost no initiative. In this scheme, very few managers were required to display creativity or imagination in implementing their areas of expertise. Finally, the most important consequence of the Fordism regime was that an accommodation was reached between management and labor in which higher wages were exchanged for managerial control of production. After World War II, this system of collective bargaining on a national scale led to a period of growth and prosperity for large numbers of workers.

Post-Fordism

The Fordist mode of production still survives, of course, but it is rapidly being challenged by the regime of flexible accumulation, or post-Fordism. The differences fall into three general categories. First, production becomes an international process made possible by the compression of time and space as a result of rapid travel and communication. Today, a company might have its assembly plant in one country, its parts production in two or three other countries, and its markets in all of these and still others. Communication and the movement of technical experts, parts, and products among these various divisions are made possible by advances in electronics technology and modes of rapid transportation. Second, there is a turn to small batch production of a variety of goods rather than the mass production of homogeneous products. While corporations are larger, productions operations are smaller and responsive to demand, not, as in the Fordist mode, to resources, the means of production, and the work force. Subcontractors are more common, and they now share the risks of overproduction and underdemand, saving the larger corporations manufacturing capital. Third, internationalizing corporations through decentering operations is in turn accompanied by the decentralizing of urban areas. Regional industrial zones and inner cities are abandoned in favor of "green sites" that come with tax concessions and promises of a better quality of life. And, once again, all of this is made possible through the rapid means of communication and transportation encouraged by the technological compression of time and space. Clearly, the managers in this dispersed system must then display extraordinary ability in communicating in written form, usually through the mastery of various electronic media.

The effects of these developments on the work force are dramatic. Employers now exert control over labor not seen since a much earlier period of capitalism. Harvey explains: "Flexible accumulation appears to imply relatively high levels of 'structural' (as opposed to 'frictional') unemployment, rapid destruction and reconstruction of skills, modest (if any) gains in the real wage, . . . and the rollback of trade union power—one of the political pillars of the Fordist regime" (50). In the era of flexible accumulation, workers are expected to perform multiple tasks, train on the job, and work well with others—all requiring at once more adaptability and responsibility than under the Fordist mode.

At the same time, the work force has been radically restructured. At the center is the core group of full-time managers. They enjoy greater job security, good promotions and re-skilling prospects, and relatively generous pensions, insurance, and other fringe benefits. In return, they are expected to be adaptable, flexible, and geographically mobile. This is the group made up primarily of college graduates. Its numbers are kept small, however, and many companies even subcontract management tasks that under Fordism they performed themselves—for example, advertising. The competition for these safe jobs is becoming more and more intense so that today a college degree provides only a permit to compete for one of them, not, as previously, a voucher for a guaranteed position. Thus, in contrast to the modernist era, a college education does not automatically promise upward mobility.

The consequences of not making it into this increasingly smaller upper tier of employment are becoming more drastic than under the Fordist regime. The dismal alternatives are seen in examining the periphery of the new employment pattern. This sector consists of two levels. The first is made up of clerical, secretarial, and routine and lesser-skilled manual workers. Because these jobs offer few career opportunities, there is great turnover in them. Their numbers are thus easily controlled in response to business conditions. The second group is made up of even less secure part-timers, casuals, temporaries, and public trainees. These jobs are the most unstable and offer the least compensation. While obviously some employees might enjoy the flexibility provided, the effect for most of the workers in these two peripheral layers is discouraging in terms of wages, insurance coverage, pension benefits, and job security. The net result of these new forms of industrial organization has been a significant reduction in the ability of workers to organize for better wages, benefits, and conditions, particularly because they are isolated by the terms of their employment.

The effort of women to achieve parity in the workplace has been especially damaged by these developments. Women are central to this entire process. Because they are still the primary caregivers for the home and family throughout the industrial world, they are more likely to seek part-time work. As a labor force they are thus easier to exploit, a sector serving as substitutes for their better-paid and more secure male counterparts. In many advanced capitalist nations, women make up 40 percent of the labor force, increasing their numbers at a time when well-paying, secure jobs decline and low-paying, unstable positions constantly increase.

One of the most obvious features of the employment picture today is the decreasing number of jobs in manufacturing and the increasing number in the service sector. The vast majority of the latter fall into the two unstable employment tiers and offer few attractions for most workers. There are, however, conspicuous exceptions. One obvious feature of flexible accumulation is that accelerating turnover time in production requires accelerating turnover time in consumption. The result is the growth of well-compensated workers—almost exclusively educated workers—who are in the business of producing the artifices of need inducement: advertising, public relations, and the like. The media through advertising and other means has thus encouraged "a postmodernist aesthetic that celebrates difference, ephemerality, spectacle, fashion, and the commodification of cultural forms" (Harvey 156). Additional well-compensated service jobs have been created by the new information industries that meet the increasing need for data to coordinate decentered operations as well as to provide up-to-date analyses of market trends and possibilities. In flexible accumulation, markets are as much created as they are identified, and so "control over information flow and over the vehicles for propagation of public taste and culture have likewise become vital weapons in competitive struggle" (Harvey 160).

So far we have seen that the managerial job market our students wish to enter values employees who are expert communicators, are capable of performing multiple tasks, can train quickly on the job, and can work collaboratively with others. In sum, workers must combine greater flexibility and cooperation with greater intelligence and communicative ability.

Any consideration of the postmodern must also examine its social and cultural manifestations. These, I would argue, are largely the response to the changing economic forces I have just discussed and are, like them, both continuations of the modern and a sharp break with it. These social and cultural developments especially demonstrate the results of space/time compression.

Thus, we are told we live in a decentered world, a realm of fragmentation, incoherence, and the absence of a nucleus or foundation for experience. Cities are without centers, except for shopping centers and industrial centers, neither of which is any longer at the center of anything but itself. Our national culture seems decentered as we see more differences than similarities among our members. This perception, furthermore, is not without foundation; the 1980s witnessed the largest wave of immigration in 200 years, totalling nearly nine million. The result is that close to half of the foreign-born in the U.S. arrived after 1980. Anxiety about this influx may be partly responsible for the lament for the lost Anglo-Saxon ideal—for instance, in the form of the insistence on the literary canon to ensure national unity through a common discourse (see for example Hirsch, *Cultural Literacy*). Indeed, not since the huge immigrant influx at the turn of the century has there been such alarm about the endangered Anglo-Protestant cultural heritage as we daily encounter the internationalization of our cities and experience a variety of international cultures on TV and in other media. We even have an "English only" movement in some states, as if legislation could somehow undo the work of economic and social forces, changing a group's culture in the swipe of a pen. Space has thus been compressed so that the geographical borders of the U.S. no longer provide the security and simple-minded insularity they once did. Multiculturalism is a reality of daily experience, not a mere politically correct shibboleth of the left.

We also experience time compression in a world of fast foods, fast cars, and fast fads. Ours is declared the age of the image and spectacle, and we are daily bombarded by a variety of sensory assaults, from the shopping center to the TV. Manners, modes, and styles are constantly in flux. This compression extends to history as styles of earlier times in clothing, architecture, and art are appropriated indiscriminately, merging the past and the present in the "pastiche" (see Jameson). This is even seen in shopping as the products of different societies and different times are randomly presented to us. The culture of the "simulacrum," the cultivated image and spectacle of other eras and places, is celebrated as the opportunity to live from one intense experience to another (see Baudrillard). For those with the means and time, life becomes a rich succession of manufactured events, a simulation of the past or future, the end being detachment from the concrete material and social conditions of one's own historical moment. One defeats time and space and escapes the depressing features of daily life, the dark side of the new economy, through the manufactured public performance.

This process of decentering and fragmentation has indeed shaken the foundations of our experience as workers, consumers, and citizens. It has encouraged dramatic disruptions not only in the worlds of work and culture but also in traditional conceptions and practices across the academy. Here I want to interrogate the adequacy of the modernist curriculum to the economic and cultural conditions just described.

The modified elective curriculum that has been the center of a college education from around the turn of the century was able to resist all criticism because it delivered what graduates, government leaders, and employers most wanted: a secure class of skilled managers whose well-compensated expertise would increase profits. Any accusation that universities failed to provide an educated citizenry or cultivated patrons of the arts or well-rounded individuals could be ignored as long as both employers and workers were pleased with the economic benefits of higher education. As we have seen, the configurations of the work force today have threatened this happy arrangement. A college degree no longer ensures a secure job and a comfortable way of life. The discontent on the part of graduates facing an uncertain job market after the effort and expense of four or five years in school is meanwhile echoed by the dissatisfaction of employers with the educated workers they are hiring. College graduates, employers commonly tell us, are technically competent but lack the ability to communicate and are reluctant to seek out and solve problems creatively (Blitz and Hurlbert).

The attempt to address this dissatisfaction is not simple. College graduates argue that the university should have offered better preparation for the work force. This, of course, suggests consultations with prospective employers about bringing the curriculum more in line with job demands. Unfortunately, these efforts offer little help. In "Cults of Culture," Michael Blitz and C. Mark Hurlbert analyze the script of the nine days of hearings held by the Subcommittee on Education and Health of the Joint Economic Committee of the United States Congress in 1987. It is immediately obvious from these hearings that many of the complaints leveled against schools and colleges are often simply an attempt to shift to new workers the blame for the failures of top managers or for the vagaries of the market. More significant, when corporation leaders try to dictate what ought to take place in universities, they commonly offer a host of contradictions. As Blitz and Hurlbert found time and again, the standards voiced by corporate leaders call for workers who are at once creative and aggressive in identifying and solving problems and submissive and unquestioningly cooperative in carrying out the orders of superiors. The two sets of demands simply do not square with each other. Furthermore, the frequently asserted insistence that college professors teach traditional knowledge rather than searching out and disseminating new discoveries flies directly in the face of the needs of a work force for up-to-date information and training.

The changing complexity of the work force with its three-tiered hierarchy further complicates any simple effort to adjust the curriculum to the employment market. As Samuel Bowles and Herbert Gintis have demonstrated, higher education is already organized along hierarchical lines. Job placement and earnings correlate with the kind of school a person attends: community college, low-prestige private or state college, or high-prestige private or state college. These divisions are partly the result of the conscious vocational choices students make. No one ought to expect, however, that colleges should build such vocational choices and hierarchical divisions into the English curriculum—say, one set of texts and reading practices for one tier of students and another set and reading practices for another tier. In other words, while professional training may vary from school to school, there is every reason to expect that the kind of knowledge and competencies that English studies will provide will be fairly consistent in objectives and methods, even as they vary in concrete practices and the materials studied.

In short, trying to adjust the college curriculum exactly to the minute configurations of the job market is simply out of the question. At the same time, I do not think that we in the academy can just ignore the advice of employers. We must, indeed, provide a college education that enables workers to be excellent communicators, quick and flexible learners, and cooperative collaborators. In fact, many of the recent changes in the English curriculum reflect this effort. The increase in the number of undergraduate writing courses as well as graduate programs in rhetoric and composition has been encouraged by college administrators who are responding to the appeals of graduates, employers, and professional schools. The emphasis on learning diverse writing practices in literature courses is also on the rise, as indicated, for example, by almost any issue of *College Literature*. Furthermore, as Lester Faigley has demonstrated, courses that prepare students for the dispersed electronic communication characteristic of a post-Fordist economy are also increasing (*Fragments of Rationality*). One of Faigley's midlevel writing courses at the University of Texas at Austin, for example, relies on a network computer system. Students spend half of the term conducting large-group discussions through the system, learning the difficulties of communicating exclusively through electronically produced texts. In addition, Mas'ud Zavarzadeh and Donald Morton have argued that the abstract mode of thinking encouraged in postmodern literary studies prepares students for the decentered conditions of the new economy. I would concur in their judgment (as well as in their reservations about some of the unfortunate effects of this development). Writing courses have also encouraged collaboration both through peer editing and through group-composed assignments, the latter a common feature of courses in professional communication, and even some literature courses are experimenting with group efforts. An openness to the differences of other cultures, both at home and abroad, is also being fostered in literature courses that extend the reading list beyond the literary canon and in writing courses that take cultural difference as their subject. All of these changes in teaching English promote the quick and flexible learning required in the postmodern workplace as students respond to the diverse reading and writing activities encouraged in such classrooms.

In short, English courses are indeed moving in the direction of preparing students for work in a postmodern economy. I would argue once again, however, that this can never be a simple accommodation to the marketplace. We must instead measure all such efforts against a larger institutional objective. Colleges ought to offer a curriculum that places preparation for work within a comprehensive range of democratic educational concerns. Regardless of whether students are headed for the highest or lowest levels of the job market, we ought to provide them at the least with an understanding of the larger operations of the work force. This will require preparation in dealing with the abstract and systemic thinking needed for the dispersed conditions of postmodern economic and cultural developments, in distinct contrast to the frequently atomistic, linear, and narrowly empirical mode of the modern. Students need a conception of the abstract organizational patterns that affect their work lives, indeed, comprehensive conceptions of the patterns that influence all of their experiences. In addition, students deserve an education that prepares them to be critical citizens of the nation that now stands as one of the oldest democracies in history. In the United States, it has seldom been considered sufficient to educate students exclusively for work. The insistence that they must also be prepared to become active and critical agents in shaping the economic, social, political, and cultural conditions of their historical moment has been a commonplace in educational discussions. And while I will admit that this position has not always been overwhelmingly dominant, it has never been altogether absent in curriculum formation in U.S. schools and colleges.

From this democratic political perspective, knowledge is regarded as a good that ought to serve the interests of the larger community as well as individuals (a prime motive, incidentally, for the formation of land-grant colleges in the last century). It must be situated, however, in relation to larger economic, social, political, and cultural considerations. Students must learn to locate the beneficiaries and the victims of knowledge, exerting their rights as citizens in a democracy to criticize freely those in power. I realize that we have just been through a period in which the end of education has been conspicuously declared to be primarily the making of money. The counterproposal offered here, however, is in keeping with one of the oldest notions of education we in the United States possess, eloquently proclaimed in the American pragmatist philosophy of John Dewey. Here, the interests of the larger community and the value of the individual must be paramount, and this is true whether we are discussing the activities of government or of large corporations. This educational scheme is designed to make human beings and their experience in a community the measure of all things (in this, as Susan C. Jarratt indicates, echoing the Sophist Protagoras). In short, education exists to provide intelligent, articulate, and responsible citizens who understand their obligation and their right to insist that economic, social, and political power be exerted in the best interests of the community as a whole. To use the term proffered by Henry Giroux, the work of education in a democratic society is to provide critical literacy.

I would also invoke in support of my position the many liberal critics who propose economic democracy as the most appropriate response to present global conditions. One of the best versions is offered by Robert N. Bellah, Richard Madsen, William M. Sullivan, Ann Swidler, and Steven M. Tipton in *The Good Society*. They suggest an alternative to the radically individualistic and hierarchical modes of production and work relations found under both entrepreneurial and Fordist regimes. Indeed, they argue that post-Fordism requires new forms of cooperation in production, distribution, exchange, and consumption that encourage democratic arrangements throughout the workplace. While the argument of the Bellah group is too complex to rehearse in detail here, I would like to summarize some of the major features of its proposal.

This recommendation would require comprehensive planning to take into account the quality of life of all of the members of society. Such planning demands that the interaction of the political and the economic be recognized so that the economic not be treated as beyond the intercession of the public in serving its own good. Corporations, we are reminded, are legal entities that must be held accountable for the consequences of their acts on the environment, workers, and citizens. Furthermore, given the radically collaborative nature of the post-Fordist production process, corporations must themselves become participatory in decision making in order to ensure maximum productivity. At the same time, the division of the work force into a small group of the comfortably secure, on the one hand, and a large group of the poorly compensated and expendable, on the other, must be challenged in the name of social justice. Finally, the new economic democracy would require consumers whose buying habits are the intelligent responses to the needs of the community, not simply to personal interest. This last matter leads to a consideration of the cultural conditions of a postmodern economy and its relation to English studies.

I would argue that our colleges, despite the inadequacies of the modernist curriculum, are much better equipped to prepare workers for the new job market than they are to prepare citizens for the cultural conditions of our new economy. In other words, our students are more likely to acquire the abilities and dispositions that will enable them to become successful workers than they are to acquire the abilities and dispositions to make critical sense of the age of the image and the spectacle, of their daily experience in a postmodern culture. When it comes to understanding the creation and fulfillment of desire through the use of the media, for example, our students receive virtually no guidance from their schools. Students in the U.S. ought to be formally prepared to critique the images that today occupy the center of politics, as students are, for example, in parts of Canada and the United Kingdom (see Brown). While there is no denying that many of our young people arrive at sophisticated strategies for negotiating the messages of the media on their own (see for example McRobbie), this is too important a part of daily life to be left to chance. In the age of the spectacle, democracy will thrive or fall on our ability to offer a critical response to these daily experiences.

My argument is that English studies has a special role in the democratic educational mission. It is, after all, required of all students in the schools, even including in most states four years in high school. The college English department, furthermore, prepares the teachers who staff these English classrooms so that its influence always extends far beyond its own hallways. And for the vast majority of college students, freshman composition has become a necessary ritual of passage into higher education. English studies has also historically served as the center of liberal education, assuming the role the rhetoric course played in the 19th-century college. English courses have been looked upon as the support and stay of certain ethical and political positions since at least the turn of the century. They have even served in times of crises—for example, major wars, the Great Depression—as a rallying point for encouraging certain values. As Arthur N. Applebee, Gerald Graff (*Professing Literature*), and I (*Rhetoric and Reality; Writing Instruction*) have indicated in our disciplinary histories, Matthew Arnold's call for literature as the surrogate for religion in a secular society was embraced with great seriousness of purpose in the United States. English studies became a powerful ethical force in influencing the private experience of individuals. It must now become equally committed to preparing students to critique the conditions of their economic, political, and cultural involvements.

20 Work, Class, and Categories: Dilemmas of Identity

SHIRLEY BRICE HEATH

In 1881, William Lloyd Garrison, editor of *The Liberator*, reminded Maria Stewart, an African American writer, of something she had written 50 years earlier:

> You made yourself known to me by coming into my office and putting into my hands, for criticism and friendly advice, a manuscript embodying your devotional thoughts and aspirations, and also various essays pertaining to the condition of that class with which you were complexionally identified. You will recollect, if not the surprise, at least the satisfaction I expressed on examining what you had written. (qtd. in Sterling 153)

In 1916, Mary Church Terrell, an African American woman who helped found the National Colored Women's Club of America in the late 1890s, wrote to T. A. Metcalf, president of the Home Correspondence Writing School: "If I had all the talent of all the short story writers put together, it would avail me nothing in this country, provided I should try to write anything which would represent the Colored-American's side of the question" (Terrell, 25 May 1916). Mary Church Terrell wrote hundreds of essays, was active on the national lecture circuit, and published her autobiography. She took an active part in a writing and reading club called the Book Lovers' Club in Washington, D.C., and eventually had some of her short stories published. Maria Stewart was a member of a literary society visited by Garrison, and she and others of her club contributed over the years to the abolitionist publication *The Liberator*.

These two snippets of the history of African American literary societies since the 1830s suggest two key points. The first is the huge accumulation of evidence of writing unnoticed by the academy but powerful in its personal, political, and social roles. The second is the extent of the subordinated, silenced diverse populations of writers whose points of view have not been represented in the published literature and hence have been unavailable for classroom use. From 1828 through 1940, literary societies, such as those to which Maria Stewart and Mary Church Terrell belonged, flourished, often in connection with literary journals. Most, though not all, were created and sustained by women who, denied access to formal education, turned to literature, political essays, devotional or spiritual writing, and aesthetic expression in their own creative writing and around their reading of literary works. However, in spite of frequent close associations with publishers and prominent black leaders, most of those women who tried to have their writing taken seriously as literature or imaginative fiction failed to succeed and thus remained unpublished and unrepresented among selections for classroom use.[1]

These historical figures—writers and artists whose voices are silenced or ignored by the mainstream—have their modern counterparts and variants. The illustrations that follow come from inner-city youth organizations, collaborative ventures between industry and community colleges, and the benefits programs of universities.[2]

In this first illustration, imagine a large room on the third floor of an abandoned school, now used as a city parks and recreation center, in a section of an inner city just off the border of two of the most violent gang territories of a midwestern city. Gathered with their arts director, an African American writer and actress, are 25 young people who have come to Liberty Theatre from all over the city for a summer jobs program in drama. They are eligible because their families qualify for assistance under federal guidelines; few have known each other before this first week of their program. About half of these youth say they intend to quit school in the fall; the other half's responses to school range from accepting to hostile. At Liberty Theatre, their wide-ranging talk, as well as their journal writings, center around their three-week task of producing the script for a 45-minute drama they will present before younger participants in all the city's parks and recreation programs during the second three weeks of their full six-week term. In their first three weeks together, they must agree on a theme, develop the script and characters of the play, and rehearse to an acceptable level for their first performance. During the second three weeks, they will present two to three shows daily, returning to Liberty Theatre daily as well for evaluations of their work and further rehearsals. Dancing, drumming, and singing will supplement their spoken words—words that emerge into final script out of transcripts their director makes each day of their discussions. They revoice these transcripts the next day, discarding, reworking, and expanding, so that by the end of the first week, they have almost completed the full first draft of the written script for their play.

A portion of their play written and produced during the summer of 1993 follows. The segment of the script provided here occurs midway into the play, just after an African American male and a mixed-race African American/Puerto

Rican Spanish-speaker have been in an altercation about whether or not speaking Spanish is "American." In the play, just as in the real clash between the two that took place during their second day of class, these two males exchange insults, push each other a bit, and then move into an Afro-Cuban-inspired dance routine when others of the group begin drumming and clapping as tension between the two mounts. (Slash marks [/] indicate an overlap of the speech of two speakers. An equals sign [=] at the end of one speaker's utterance and the beginning of the next indicates a latching of talk in which the second speaker continues the utterance of the first without pause.)

SHEILA: [*pointing to the two*] Hey, you're doing the same step. [*She joins in.*]

ARTURO: Yeah.

MANUEL: How did that happen?

ONYX: There are a lot of things our cultures have in common; there is no way we could avoid/

JIM: /all you have to do is think about explorers and travelers=

SHEILA: =from Spain, to Africa, to South America=

ONYX: =and back again=

VICTOR: =exchanging food, clothing, dances/

MARIA: /The Moors in Spain=

NADINE: =the Africans in Brazil=

DENNIS: =the Mexicans, Puerto Ricans=

ARTURO: =Cubans=

JAIME: =and Africans in North America.
[*They end their dance and move away to side stage, leaving alone one young African American man who turns toward the audience, clapping slowly as the music softens.*]

DAVIS: Sometimes it feels good to be alone, and sometimes it's just lonely. [*singing*]

> When I am alone, lonely, the sun is colored gray,
> When I am alone, lonely,
> I feel a million miles away,
> from a smiling face,
> from a joyous place,
> a reason to keep running the race.
> When I'm alone, lonely,
> when I am alone

[*Other ensemble members begin humming softly and move center stage, as he backs away.*]

NADINE: When I am alone, lonely=

SHEILA: =I am locked in a cage with no way out.

NADINE: When I am alone, lonely=

JIM: I feel like a ghost town.

ONYX: I feel trapped in a big white, cold, empty room=

TYRONE: =or like the porch is missing from my house.

NADINE: When I am alone, lonely=

VICTOR: =lonely, because there is no one there to make me happy=

EDUARDO: =all alone in an empty house=

ARTURO: =deep inside my mind=

MANUEL: =with no one.

Later in the play, they all take part in a dance from northern Brazil, and the play ends with each young person stepping forward to announce a triumphant call of and for themselves, such as, "I was born in the ghetto, but the ghetto wasn't born in me."

Imagine now another scene in a community theatre in a distant urban center where youngsters and adults working together produce a play, *Waiting in Vain*, written by Rebecca Rice. This African American playwright based her work on a news article that recounted the suicide of a young woman, Linda, who had kept a journal from her early elementary days. After her death, her journal and a packet of her poetry were discovered and told the story of all that she had wanted, hoped for, despaired of, and finally given up on because she was convinced that she was "waiting in vain."

Given here is a brief summary of this complex play that uses as its theme portions of the popular song by Bob Marley, "Waiting in Vain." The following lines can be heard softly as background from the band that is on stage with Linda during much of the play:

Don't treat me like a puppet on a string
Don't talk to me as if you think I'm dumb
I want to know where you're coming from
I don't want to wait in vain. . . .

The play opens with the reading of the poem "Night Vision" by Lucille Clifton. Linda stands near the band, and the bandleader encourages her to tell her story because if she does not, no one else will. Throughout the play, much of the tension centers around whether or not writing can help Linda, or whether her writing could help others if her story were told. Linda briefly recounts her suicide shortly after the play opens; the remainder of the play celebrates her life through portions of her journal and poetry.

Among the entries in Linda's journal is the following: "I am fifteen years old and I am becoming a poet. I'm gonna be somebody. I gonna be a book person. That's me. Somebody . . . I'm gonna write smart things here, like I have sense. Like dreams and aspirations." Her quest here is to achieve, through her own efforts as an individual, with little reliance on school. College does not figure in Linda's future; her goals are much closer—just being able to stay in high school. Near the end of the play, her mother takes her out of school to work so that she can contribute to the support of her nephew. Linda's money goes to buy him school clothes and tennis shoes.

The next illustration is drawn from a quite different scene: a large state university in which the wage-earning custodial staff, when told their benefits package cannot be increased or their hourly wages raised this year, stage a rally. At this time in which everyone at the university must take a 5 percent pay cut, they agree not to ask for additional wages, but they demand an additional—and unusual—benefit. They ask the university to provide them a writing/reading/talking/listening, or "literacy," course. There, with the guidance of an English composition instructor, the workers (principally African American women over 35 years of age) write and read and talk about the Bible, church materials, and their children's homework. They fret over forms they must fill out and information that comes to them and to which they must respond in tasks involving "civic literacy." Their course is about communication, primarily to meet their aesthetic, emotional, and spiritual needs. When the Freirian literacy instructor suggests taking some of their newfound power to their jobs to call for changes and improvements there, the group resoundingly rejects this idea, pointing out that they—unlike many of their younger female African American friends—*have* jobs, and they wish at this time to do nothing to jeopardize these. For now, they are content for literacy to meet their aesthetic, spiritual, and daily pragmatic goals.

The last illustration comes from a situation in which a national chemical corporation downsizes its work force after installing electronic control and monitoring equipment and initiating a massive communication overhaul in the company. Upper management attempts to level old hierarchies and establish work teams for sections of the plant and across sections linked by common concerns. Managers soon find that plant staff are hesitant about writing and reading their required reports and about talking and planning together in the weekly meetings now involving all workers on a rotating basis. The company turns to its local community college for assistance. Several liaison personnel work to design courses to help improve report writing, planning strategies, efficient uses of conference times, and collaborative talk sessions. The program expands rapidly, and the provost creates a professional outreach communications department, made up of the most innovative members of the English and business management departments.

What these examples across times, places, and needs illustrate are the following trends or issues affecting the future directions of writing in society and formal education, including composition classes:

- People segment their periods of reading and writing across their lives according to perceived personal needs. Hence, reading and writing around and about literature, for religious solace, or societal critique take place in response to felt needs. For many, the kind of aesthetic and personal expression outlets available through the drama, personal journals, and poetry noted here become at some point an essential part of their existence.[3] These writers do not see or need writing that is gate-opening within institutions as the only—or even the most important—writing for them. Instead, they see their writing as soul-opening at particular periods in their lives.

- Institutions of higher education—especially community colleges—are adapting to meet the communication (as distinct from composition) needs of individuals in workplaces, employment and counseling centers, and joint health and education institutions. As employers place increasing emphasis on information exchange, oral communication, and group problem solving, workers previously uninvolved in such communication networks find themselves in need of new skills.

The above illustrations show that a variety of types of institutions are responding to personal, spiritual, and civic needs, as well as business changes, to develop opportunities and add courses or build programs to meet these needs. They do so not by announcing an end to existing structures but by adding on to the existing infrastructure of community youth programs, businesses, or postsecondary institutions. In the new settings, these groups enable writers to merge formal and informal writing across genres, audiences, and institutional and personal contexts. They allow learners to use writing and speaking as symbolic expressions of critical social self-understandings. They permit learners to make their own choices about taking these understandings forward for different kinds of advancement and achievement in a variety of types of institutions. These efforts are not "purely" or even primarily academic, but they are vocational, community-building, health-improving, and spirit-renewing. Learners in these programs use tools of communication to mediate their social identities across ethnicities, ages, and contexts. Especially the young people of the first two illustrations given here see as their work the work of living, of surviving, and of having what Linda Flower in this volume reminds us is an "identity kit" of discourses across modes and channels. These communities of literate practices, from theatre groups to the university literacy-as-benefit class to the chemical corporation and community college collaboration, *compose* themselves for reflection and response as writers, readers, speakers, and actors.

From within the usual college composition program of a college or university, we may well ask what has created these largely unheralded scenes of shifting and shifted uses of writing, reading, speaking, and listening. First, changing demands in community and work settings have led the writers and actors described here to develop felt needs for new forms of symbolic mediation, whether these be computer graphics, printed forms, dramatic role playing, or new numeracy requirements. To these more pragmatically driven needs may be added the mental health needs met by outlets of creative expression offered in the programs mentioned above. The youth of Liberty Theatre, for example, found that in the safe place of their dramatic scripts, they could explore their shared sense of loneliness in a time when many had no backing from traditional support systems of family, school, and church. The women of the literacy-as-benefit course brought to their discussions a shared lament over the crises their daughters and younger sisters faced from drugs, violence, and unsafe neighborhoods in which to raise their children. Writing, reading, talking, and listening around common needs, including the pragmatic goals of employees of the chemical corporation, produced a sense of shared awareness about current conditions.

But aside from such self-reported evidence of the affective, community-building, and pragmatic dimensions of these programs, what else might participants gain? Is there *hard* evidence of any cognitive or linguistic development? Linguistic data from the programs of youth groups such as the one at Liberty Theatre suggest ways to document the path of changes in particular kinds of critical thinking, such as hypothetical reasoning and agent-driven propositions. From transcribed audiotapes of young people involved in planning and practicing within their youth organizations, it is possible to document the increase over time of particular kinds of language uses associated with complex problem solving and an improved sense of self-as-agent. For example, as young people move forward in their planning and practice toward the time of performance, their use of hypothetical statements, full assertions in declarative sentences, and collaborative knowledge building (based on both personal experience and verifiable external sources, such as print and video media) increases. Perhaps most important for young people who come together for the first time in these learning and working environments of community organizations, linguistic data permit the careful documentation of the growing degree of their shared understandings. For example, in the Liberty Theatre script given above, the high preponderance of latched statements in which one speaker completes the thoughts of another indicates what may be considered the extent to which they are "in each other's heads." Additional evidence of such cooperative discourse comes through their repetitions of each other's words and phrases, frequency of parallel syntactic and lexical structures across speakers, and syntactically compatible interruptions.[4]

A further question of the settings for reading and writing described here might relate to their implications for college attendance by participants. The institutional settings the young people, custodial workers, and chemical corporation chose allowed individuals to obtain the knowledge and skills they saw as meeting their current specific needs—personal, vocational, and aesthetic. Beyond their role in the organizations in which they participated, they could avail themselves of the self-teaching, individual practice, and small-group exploration their courses encouraged. Their futures held no trajectory of either two-year or four-year college attendance progressing through a sequence of predetermined courses. For those who saw some sort of postsecondary education ahead for them, they expected to dip into and out of college, pulling from it what they saw as current needs. For example, following the Liberty Theatre summer, Davis, who had recently completed high school, decided to enroll for a course in radio broadcasting at a local college, taking classes while he worked. The summer convinced him he needed to keep up his journal writing and even try his hand at more dramatic scripts, but he had no current plan to try to enter college, take college composition, and act as though he expected to remain enrolled in college on a year-to-year basis. Hence, college composition, as currently constituted as gatekeeper to college entry and progress through a pattern of courses in the first year, bore no relevance to his goals or needs. He, like others of the Liberty Theatre group, had been in and out of jobs and had concluded that what he needed for security and advancement was communication skills and knowledge about how to "get along with people." At Liberty, the acting director demanded of the group oral accountability, reading and writing of specific types within a collaborative framework that could work only if they learned to work effectively with people unlike themselves. At the end-of-season oral exit interviews, young people consistently answered the question "What did you get out of this summer?" with comments attesting to how much they had learned about "working with people who are not like me." At Liberty, they had learned that there is no one language, dialect, register, or genre of power. There are several, and in some cases many, and to survive work, class, and category dominations from the larger society, they had to know and use as many as possible. Liberty Theatre and its strong interweaving of oral and written language made this learning possible.

To those entrenched within composition and concerned about protecting their own jobs in a shrinking economy, it is tough to look "out there" to such cases as the ones cited here. Those in leadership positions in the institutional situations illustrated above are not in English departments of the college or university. Will their innovative efforts replace those of teachers of freshman composition? Probably not substantially so before the end of the second decade of the 21st century. By that time, the cohort of current college graduates will have children of college-entry age, and economic projections suggest several reasons why college may not be the choice for these young people. For the first time in U.S. history, this future generation may well choose to be less

well-educated than their parents, whose college diplomas were not able to ensure for them the upward mobility of the prior generation. Postsecondary
choices will consequently have to look very different from their current configuration, for they will need to be much more tightly tied to vocational, personal, and community-building goals than the current four-year college norm.
Parents in the second decade of the 21st century will, no doubt, advise their
young to cast their net of abilities wider than simply a liberal arts college degree. These parents may well ask that the paths of learning for their children
intersect with work, mental and physical health, and civic and ethical needs
and concerns.

This future scenario seems imminent; current college graduates, as well as
those who know they cannot now plan on college, worry and think a great deal
about work—who works, when, where, how, why, and for what. Though unable to put their finger on the sources of their worry, they feel the abstract
forces of deindustrialization, a new international division of labor, a reliance
on contingent workers, loss of trade unions, declining real wage, and rising
importance of the service sectors. In the first nine months of 1993, approximately 50,000 jobs were lost each month. Such facts are reported widely, and
young people comprehend at some level that work has become more insecure,
more intense, and for those with jobs, just simply more—an extra month of
work a year in 1993 than was the case in 1969. The increase in the amount of
work has been created by the loss of high-paying jobs and jobs associated with
union contracts. Compensation for jobs has polarized into a minority of very
highly paid workers and a majority of poorly compensated ones. For example,
while the approximately 950 new African American Ph.D.s each year of the
1980s experienced a rise in family income, the five million African Americans
living below the poverty line suffered a deterioration of family income.

These views parallel those of the middle Americans interviewed by Katherine S. Newman in a study undertaken to look at the effect on those in their 30s
of realizing that owning a home and having a secure job would be unlikely
achievements in the near future—if ever—for them. In her study, *Declining
Fortunes: The Withering of the American Dream*, she explores how American society has "reneged on its promise to the baby-boom generation." The
inability to match the comfort of their own parents' lives looms heavily for
these young people who increasingly resent affluent Asian newcomers, for example, and resist the redistribution of the economy for those perceived as un-
willing to work. Newman also points out the extent to which the baby-boomer
generation is divided against itself and finds that the scattering of their dreams
has left them separated and highly focused on individual needs. Economist
Robert Heilbroner, in *21st Century Capitalism*, underscores why full employment is simply not likely to be possible again. He further suggests that acquisi-
tiveness—that desire to get further and further ahead and especially ahead of

one's parents—may have a limit beyond which it no longer serves and may well hold back the adaptability of the society.

It is this holding back that colleges and college composition now seem to do. College and the usual four-year curriculum for which freshman composition is the entryway implicitly promise more from academic achievement for future employment than they can deliver. They consequently downplay other paths that may offer highly desired stable financial subsistence as well as a base for reasonable next steps for young people seeking job security.

Perhaps the best examples of such alternatives come from the small business sector of the economy. In the 1980s, small and midsized companies created 80 percent of U.S. jobs. Between 1988 and 1990, when big business had a net loss of 500,000 jobs, small businesses (those employing 500 or fewer) accounted for 3.2 million new jobs. By 1993, nearly 60 percent of small business owners said they would limit the growth of their company in order to maintain the advantages they see accruing to the flexibility that comes with small size.

Of the four million small businesses in 1992, more than half were of the type that depended on direct communication with clients in service and negotiating encounters through retail sales, health and home services, and finances. For small businesses in the first decade of the next century, temporary help and business services, food services, and health care continue this trend of projected growth. All of these labor-intensive employment settings require quick, on-the-spot critical thinking skills, effective communication, and careful record keeping.

For many young people and those wishing to remain employed, their only current feasible employment opportunities depend on gaining the skills that will make them desirable to these companies—oral communicative and interpersonal skills. Those who begin working for others in service jobs, such as restaurant workers, tour guides, janitors, hairdressers, housecleaners, gardeners, and repair personnel, gain experience and, with sufficient improvement, can look forward to having control of their own business. Over 98 percent of all small businesses are owned by a sole proprietor. The route to acquiring the tools to set up a small business, especially for minorities establishing themselves in their own communities with the aid of loans from the Small Business Administration, does not necessarily include college. Manuals and guidebooks, as well as seminars organized for segments of minority communities, instead recommend networking, developing tools of self-assessment, keen observational skills, and the ability to think clearly and plan ahead on the basis of fairly assessed information.[5]

Increasingly, distinctions in job levels will divide between those in direct service to others, such as retail clerks, health care workers, banktellers, and waiters, and those for whom tools mediate their work with others. As the 20th century ends, those at the lower end of the pay scale, with few exceptions, are in direct service, where oral communication is vital to the interaction. These jobs will be filled more and more by the growing percentage of the population from non-Anglo cultures. Their learning must depend on contexts outside formal education, and they will continue to be subjected to tests of their competence—on-the-spot judgments about their effectiveness. The problems they must identify and solve are immediate and human and require artistry, humanity, and commitment to their clients and community. In contrast, employees more removed from their clients, customers, or patients and far less frequently in direct contact rely much more on the mediation of tools and their own interpretation and production skills.

The issues identified here may best be summarized as follows. The first is a move on the part of those we would be likely to think of as possible college attendees in inner cities to steer away from formal education as currently conceived. Instead, they are placing their reliance on gaining sufficient communication and self-management skills through their arts performances and participation in community organizations. Through what they learn there, they are managing to get jobs, and within those settings, they hope to learn the skills they further need to get into places that can teach them more skills through new experiences and opportunities to observe those more advanced in the organizational scale. Many of the young, such as those of Liberty Theatre, reject failure, having had much too much heaped on their heads. Their dramatic work, like the literacy classes of the university custodial staff, offers expressive outlets that enable them to work through many of the political factors and social structures that have kept them outside the gates of either financial stability or advancement.

The second issue has to do with changes in the larger economy—the direct effects of which young people especially see and feel. Though they often cannot talk in terms of 21st-century capitalism, they see that in their late 20s and early 30s, they are highly likely to face joblessness, despair, and family problems, even if they should be able to gain college educations.

These central issues will surely shape education in the coming decades. If reasonable reorganizations and new directions follow from what appears to be greatest need, then colleges and college classes will do things quite differently. They will first build networks, as many technical and community colleges have already done, to job opportunities, community-based organizations, and health-delivery systems. Within these networks, they will link communication skills, oral and written, to a host of needs—social, aesthetic, and personal, as well as vocational. For those linked to community organizations, such as the arts and drama groups named here, or those mentioned in Anne Ruggles Gere's presidential address to the Conference on College Composition and

Communication in 1993 as extracurricular, such experiences will become the curricular. Would-be writers and readers in some classes selected for aesthetic and personal expression will receive the benefit of instructors' guidance in choosing materials and composing their own poetry, stories, and dramas. Reference skills, editing skills for would-be publishers, and aids to journal keeping and poetry techniques will be the norm within such groups who see their involvement with literature for its aesthetic and personal functions, with no illusion about direct transfer to job skills.

Other courses will be linked to job settings or specific communicative situations, for example, in the health arena (such as providing a medical history). Networking classes among learners will increase so that learners can work with each other and with distant experts collaboratively across a variety of genres. Increasingly, these classes may be cross-age, as are many family literacy programs, in which older, more experienced writers and speakers work with younger or differently experienced individuals. Just as is the case with the projections for adult literacy programs linked with technology, described in the 1993 Office of Technology Assessment report (United States, *Adult*), individuals will work with certain types of technology in their homes, networking through their writing via technology. In such work, they will improve skills necessary for their jobs and tap into networks that provide information they need to achieve their personal goals—ordering gardening seeds or fishing tackle, for example. Composition as gatekeeper and hence gateway will give way more and more to what are now experimental programs often viewed as marginal and run jointly between community-based organizations and workplaces, on the one hand, or postsecondary education institutions, on the other. These programs, currently relegated to university or college offices with titles such as "continuing education" or "outreach education," will by the second decade of the 21st century increasingly move to more central awareness among college administrators.

Aside from the social and political forces noted here, certain dimensions of college composition have, no doubt, contributed to the past marginalized and somewhat fixed role of courses such as those developed by the local community college to help workers enter collaborative worker-managed networks. Foremost among the reasons for the peripheral state of such courses and new ventures of the sort mentioned here has been the relative absence of effort and hence of success that such courses have had in teaching students to write beyond the classroom. These courses have been centrally concerned with preparing students to advance within the *academic* setting through forms historically established as tests of the reasoning and reporting skills of schooled youth. Thus, such courses have felt no effect from the dominant pattern of academic entry within the U.S., which remains (primarily for those in the lower middle class and below) some work before and during college, along with stop-out periods for work (and sometimes family) before multiple returns to college.

Several years ago, I was asked to visit a branch of a midwestern state university whose deans and department heads were despairing at their four-year retention or graduation rate, which was less than 25 percent. They knew how to evaluate themselves only in terms of the percentage of their students who had completed four years at their school or reported transfer to complete their degree at another four-year institution. Looking through the outsider's eyes—those of the anthropologist—I asked surprising questions of these administrators: What is it that your students want out of this university when they come? What percentage of your students have worked and/or are currently working while attending school here? How many courses do most of your students take at a time, and how many of these students choose courses that we regard as typical of the beginning college freshman? Their answers, on the spot, had to be impressionistic, but they called in professors from their largest programs—those of nursing, industrial arts, pre-engineering, and health services. These professors did not share the concerns of the administrators (most of whom were from the liberal arts). They saw their students as getting what they came for, coming back for more when they felt the need, and reporting high satisfaction with what this particular university offered them (based on informal surveys they had conducted in their classes). They reported that as students became older and more secure in their jobs (in what was in that area of the Midwest primarily manufacturing and retail and food service), they came back for liberal arts classes. Pointing out a fact that college English teachers have long wished to push under the rug, these students reported that only when they had leisure and security could they take the time to read for pleasure, write in journals, and think more deeply about films and popular arts. Moreover, in leisure they could follow up on some curiosities they had held since high school, matters such as the Civil War, medieval romances, and Renaissance drama.

To be sure, a small state university in the Midwest does not offer the only model for generalizing to the broad dimensions of the question of what the political and social issues shaping composition in the future might be. However, it does represent a pattern that is increasingly the case as more and more young people take their future in their own hands and recognize that college does not ensure job placement or competencies that match the realities of job market demands.

This same pattern is echoed in the many adult basic education programs across the country that find their students want something special and new in their current education. These adults, who are now writing poetry, producing their own life histories, and studying children's books in order to read to their children, report previous school failures. They indicate that while in school, they often saw no reason to explore the questions then put before them by their teachers. They were then too intent, worried, and preoccupied with adolescence, status seeking, or finding a job to give themselves over to their education. Thus, increasingly, learners outside of the expected trajectory of high school and college are learning what we would not expect (or perhaps want) them to learn without formal education. They are doing so in sizable proportions to express their wonder and despair at the absence of a place for them in today's social, educational, and political systems. For many, their disconnections from family, communities, and school are fed by the fact that formal educational advancement no longer guarantees a job, much less achievement of the American dream, security of family, and the possibility of living in a safe neighborhood.

Eudora Welty once described the juxtapositions between reality and literature as "rival validities." We are faced today with what are rival validities between what social science tells us and our preference for remaining comfortable within our current institutional frames and tasks. We prefer to ask "What are we doing?" (and hence talk about pedagogical tactics) than "What is college composition doing here—in this place in this institution and in its role in the society?" Current social science and organizational research along with economic projections force us to hear things that do not nurture complacency about the latter question. An odd, uneasy quality emerges for those within colleges when disciplinary studies in community life and workplaces contest fundamental propositions of the institution in which we serve. It is hard, from within the ivory tower, to go on remembering every day that there are suppressed or unheard sides to every argument. The challenge is to balance our own desires for job stability in a culture and economy more complex than we could ever have imagined with a sense of the imperative for a sane path of change. We have to move past the limitations of vogue and politics and past our own fears of loss of predictability in our daily lives. We have to try to use our little freedoms, moderating them whenever possible.

We must learn to represent humankind not so as to flatter or fool it—as we have perhaps unwittingly done in our promises through college—but to dignify it by insisting on people's capacity for seeing possibilities where we may not and for finding ways to create innovative ways to survive. Survival today must precede planning for tomorrow. The changes I have outlined here will not be revolutionary, and most will have little direct effect on those currently teaching. The changes will be incremental in a continuous networking process, not a collection of independent, autonomous tasks. The first and most likely changes will be interlinking institutions. Just as we have seen ourselves cross disciplines, now we will watch more and more of us move across institutions and departments.[6] In these efforts, we will see ourselves moving from a single-channel focus on writing to multiple-channeled foci on symbolic systems—encouraging and thinking of speaking and acting across genres and contexts as well as writing across these with a variety of traditional tools plus new possibilities from electronic media. Ours will become a field of communicative and visual arts.

In these new directions, we will come to grips with a much more complex perception of so-called minorities within the United States population. I purposively began this paper with brief passages from history that I could sadly predict would surprise readers. I could be sure readers would not expect to hear of a rich African American literate history dating as far back as the 1830s. In this current era of all things "multicultural," we rush to classify "others" by wrapping about each group a key image. That of "an oral people" has become the wrapper for African Americans past and present, so that even African American critics celebrate themselves as "oral in nature," neglecting the abilities and achievements of African Americans in writing and other visual forms of representation. Much work remains to be done to restore accuracy of representation to not only the rich African American literate heritage of reading and writing but also to the ways in which the oral channel and even "oral features" are omitted from consideration in composition—as though we did not compose our oral thoughts.

A common error in looking forward is to think that current practice and research and, above all, current hierarchies of valuation are the most important elements in future success. If anyone had told us 50 to 100 years ago that at the close of the 20th century, only about 5 percent of U.S. families would be of two-parent, opposite-sex members with one parent working outside the home, we would have said, "Impossible—the family will be our most abiding institution." By implication, that response would have meant "the family as *we* define it now."

Similarly, on a far less significant scale, had someone told us as recently as 1988 that by 1993, the very existence of International Business Machines (IBM) would be in jeopardy, we would have thought, "That will never happen." Colleges and universities, along with the family and IBM, will change, and they will change more drastically than we can now imagine. As John Trimbur suggests in this volume, the college or university of 2015 or 2020 will not be the autonomous, self-regulated, tenure-giving, self-interested, overprofessionalized institution dealing in the currency of credentials we know it to be today. Some such institutions may remain, but in active and prominent competition and respect will be community-building learning centers linked to health delivery and work systems, enabling communication across media, channels, and modes and embracing diverse sets of talents such as those from the theatre, corporation, and community college programs mentioned above.

More than a decade ago, the literary critic Carolyn Heilbrun made a statement to English teachers regarding literature that applies as well to composition studies. Thus, I have taken the liberty of a minor adjustment of her words.

> Today's youth, whatever the reason, no longer go to literature [composition], and what we used to call "culture" as to the fountain of wisdom and experience. Youth . . . responds rather to an alternative culture, outside the English classroom, vital, challenging, relevant. . . . If students are to see English literature [and composition] as capable of informing them about any of the aspects of life, they must become convinced that it is as capable of revolutionary exploration as their own lives are. (qtd. in Ford)

To accept this challenge is to move forward on the strength of perhaps the most valuable gift of humanity and the humanities we celebrate—imagination.

Notes

1. Much of their writing related to current events and issues, such as the dramatic increase in lynchings following the Civil War, and their essays or opinion pieces on these matters were more often published than their fiction. Yet in their literary societies, they discussed their own imaginative writings as well as those of published authors. Numerous archival deposits tell the stories of the writing, advice giving, joint readings, and collaborative planning of these literary societies, most of which were independent, some of which were tied to churches. For further discussion of their work, see Porter; McHenry and Heath.

2. Data for two of the illustrations given here were collected in connection with a fieldwork project (1987–1993), "Language, Socialization, and Neighborhood-based Organizations," funded by The Spencer Foundation, with Milbrey W. McLaughlin and myself as principal investigators. Pseudonyms are used for all organizations and individuals. For further background on these and other organizations, see Heath and McLaughlin; McLaughlin, Irby, and Langman. Data for the third illustration were provided by Sheryl Gowan of Georgia State University.

3. Strong evidence of the developing trend for individuals to seek out opportunities for creative writing as an outlet of personal expression comes from the persistence of oversubscriptions for state and national creative writing workshops. Since the 1970s, major literary figures have spoken publicly and written about what they regard as the phenomenal growth of these programs. Additional evidence of the appeal of such writing comes from the extent of informal "publishing" projects of programs in English as a Second Language. See for example volumes of *Voices*, begun in 1989 by the Lower Mainland Society for Literacy and Employment of Surrey, British Columbia, Canada.

4. For further discussion of such linguistic analysis showing both degree of

growing compatibility as well as junctures of marked dissonance in group cohesion, see Heath and Langman.

5. Materials for information included here have been drawn from the 1992 *Statistical Abstract of the United States* (United States Department of Commerce), *The Small Business Information Handbook* (Berle), *The State of Small Business: A Report of the President* (United States), *SBA Hotline Answer Book* (Berle), and issues of *Black Enterprise* from mid-1993.

6. An example of such a "crossover" occurs through the accomplishments of Barbara Cambridge at Indiana University-Purdue University at Indianapolis, where the English department works closely with professional schools, such as nursing, to enhance students' learning of a broad range of communication skills. An example of university-community organization linkage appears in the work of Linda Flower and her students reported in this volume and in references cited there.

$\mathcal{21}$ Imagining the Future: Composition in a New Economic and Social Context

RESPONSE BY CAROL PETERSEN HARTZOG

In their conference papers, James A. Berlin and Shirley Brice Heath look toward an America that is both like and unlike anything we now know. They foresee the early 21st century reflecting many of the economic, cultural, and political forces of our present society yet certainly having a character of its own. They anticipate that, under pressure, American society and the educational system supporting it will change in ways none of us can now accurately predict.

Together, Berlin and Heath suggest that the test of American higher education will come in its call to meet responsively the changes in our society and in the school population while holding to the academic principles that are essential to education in a democracy. Both remind us that a college degree no longer promises students the secure employment and improved living conditions that earlier generations could expect. These circumstances lead Berlin and Heath—and their audience—to a questioning of higher education and of the needs, aspirations, and cultural milieu that influence young people's decisions about college.

In "English Studies, Work, and Politics in the New Economy," Berlin asks that colleges and universities respond to the needs, but not all the demands, of the changing job market. This response, he says, "can never be a simple accommodation to the marketplace." Berlin describes in detail the new economy and recommends a college education that "enables workers to be excellent communicators, quick and flexible learners, and cooperative collaborators." He advocates not only preparing students for work in this economy but also helping them to understand the dynamics of the work force and to develop into critical citizens of our democracy. Believing that "English studies has a special role in the democratic educational mission," he argues that we are now doing better at preparing students for working than for coping with the other realities of a postmodern society.

Heath's approach in "Work, Class, and Categories: Dilemmas of Identity" is very different. She turns to lived experience in American society, giving us words by and about writers long unnoticed and experiences of inner-city youth, university wage earners, and chemical plant staff. Like Berlin, Heath sees growth in service jobs, requiring oral communicative and interpersonal skills, and an increasing distinction between direct and mediated services. She anticipates that young people will move away from formal education as we now know it toward community organizations and that "colleges and college classes will do things quite differently" if they respond to the needs revealed through our changing economy and society. She stresses networking and new forms of outreach programs.

Heath points out that people read and write in discontinuous periods of their lives as needed and that some campuses, especially community colleges, are already adapting to meet these perceived personal needs. Such efforts, she writes, are "vocational, community-building, health-improving, and spirit-renewing." Heath encourages us "to move past the limitations of vogue and politics" to meet the challenges before us. Though she expects change to be incremental, she calls on us to engage our energies and our imagination in responding to human needs.

While neither Berlin nor Heath addresses directly the national or academic politics that may influence composition in the decades ahead, both describe circumstances that will give context to political attitudes, debates, and actions in those years. They give us strikingly different yet compatible analyses of the economic and social forces now shaping American society and promising to influence composition into the new century. Berlin's deductive and Heath's inductive strategies converge in their discussions of work and its implications for writing. Heath goes much further in speculating on those implications, showing the challenges that writing teachers and colleges will confront and suggesting possible responses.

These two papers effectively address the agenda of this book, stimulating questions, comparisons, and speculations leading outward to individual campuses and pointing forward in time. The small-group discussions that followed the conference presentations seemed to have three primary foci: the power and threat of new technologies, connections between the academy and the community, and what was termed (after Carlos Fuentes) the new geography of composition.

The force of technology is seen in a report that Shannon L. Wilson made. Her group discussed technological resources they now use—asking first-year students to keep electronic journals, for example—and acknowledged that these uses are yet limited. This group speculated that technology may "produce an insecurity which makes us fall back on old paradigms and standards" but that, even so, it is changing the way we envision the space and time of communication, the classroom, and the community. The group recognized technology as "inequitably distributed and expensive" but described its new capabilities as smashing forms that teachers and some students know and comfortably accept. Writing teachers must "reimagine and reinvent" their work and their classroom roles.

Conference participants welcomed Heath's invitation to strengthen links with the community. Already many academic boundaries are dissolving, and direct connections with learners in their own neighborhoods and work environments could well increase, especially where technological links are viable. Participants resisted narrow ideas of vocational education, though, fearing these could limit rather than liberate students from their present environments and from their traditional academic programs. Like Berlin, the groups emphasized the broad democratic purposes of education. As Phyllis Hastings reported for her group, higher education not only meets certain immediate needs but also gives students new contexts for understanding themselves and their futures. A readiness, even an enthusiasm, for reaching into the community remained balanced by a commitment to liberal education. However, there was a healthy uncertainty about how to achieve these educational goals in the 21st century. George Kalamaras reported, for example, that his group asked how we can "best learn from our students what their . . . 'multiple identities' are and what they need to know."

Discussions about the profession focused on what it might become, given the many and disparate possibilities before this field in the 21st century. Will the undergraduate writing curriculum be eliminated, more than one group asked, or will it explode? If freshman composition as we know it disappears, how will students learn to cross discourse boundaries, and what academic community will fill the special role in democratic education that Berlin describes? If, on the other hand, it explodes into new forms and new areas, how will this happen? Writing may be increasingly taught in studios or mini-courses, with technology integrated into its pedagogy. The roles and practices of writing centers may be much expanded. More on-site programs may develop, as Heath recommends. We may need to find new definitions of "literate" and "basic writers" to connote writing with particular purposes and with particular abilities. Perhaps a new kind of community will develop to support writing instruction.

Participants agreed on the need for reimagining how writing is taught. They saw reasons for flexibility, alternative approaches serving multiple purposes, and open agendas. They were concerned that corporate needs not be met at the expense of human needs. They saw tensions between providing what employers want and helping students develop the writing and analytical skills needed in a democratic society of the 21st century. They understood that writing teachers' roles will change in the new century and that new attention must be given to preparing faculty and graduate students who may well teach in unfamiliar settings. They believed that new attention must also be given to the role of adjunct and part-time faculty. Susan Bachman's group, describing these faculty members as a rich resource, suggested they might be empowered as a corps of experts to teach in the community or across disciplines as projects emerge. One reporter ended by welcoming change, welcoming the new diversity of students, teachers, methods, and means of communication, and noting that these changes will surely have profound meaning for us as individuals and as a profession.

In the new century, the economic, social, cultural, and political forces of change will require a presence and responsiveness unlike those of earlier times. This volume is meant to anticipate those hurricane winds of change. It is itself a measure of the profession's awareness and responsiveness. It also represents a call for humility, courage, and dedication. The profession has matured over the past two decades, becoming practiced and self-confident; it can now look toward the unprecedented demands of the approaching century. In a sense, nothing we have done prepares us for what is ahead; at the same time, all of our experience on campus and in the profession has helped prepare us for those challenges.

Part 8 What Will Be the Meaning of

Literate Action and Intellectual Property?

22 Literate Action

LINDA FLOWER

Composition courses reflect our public visions of literacy, and once again that vision is under reconstruction. Traditionally, the academy has wrapped itself in the cloak of what Deborah Brandt calls textual literacy, idealizing the autonomous text and valorizing the essayistic mind. Textual literacy uses the current-traditional paradigm in composition to initiate its students, demanding, at the door, the union card of correct form and appropriate convention (Young, "Paradigms"). Expressive literacy, on the other hand, according to John Willinsky, embraces self-discovery and an aesthetic of craft and creativity. More recently a third vision, which we might call rhetorical literacy, is emerging as the social, the cognitive, and the rhetorical strands of English studies weave themselves together and begin another reconstruction of composition. Rhetorical literacy revolves around literate action. In place of a decontextualized, logically, and linguistically autonomous text and in place of a crafted personal statement, rhetorical literacy places a writer—a rhetor, if you will—as an agent within a social and rhetorical context. What would a 21st-century pedagogy of literate action require of us?

This pedagogy poses an interesting problem because literate action, as I am using the term, has three key features:

- First, it is a socially embedded, socially shaped practice.

- Second, and at the same time, literate action is an individual constructive act that embeds practices and conventions within its own personally meaningful, goal-directed use of literacy.

- And third—and herein lies the interesting problem—because literate action is a social/cognitive, personal/public process, it is rarely guided by single goals or simple forces. Instead, it is often a site of conflict among multiple goals, alternative goods, and opposing shoulds; it calls for negotiation among unavoidable constraints, options, and alternatives. To teach composition as literate action, then, is to invite students into this vortex. My question is, how shall we teach them to deal with it?

I would like to explore this problem through the experience of some under-graduate writers who in their different ways were attempting to move beyond their school-based practices into literate action. Listening to the story in their own words suggests that their literate action and learning grew out of a prob-lematic negotiation among conflicting theories and values.

The Context for Writing: Mentoring Another Writer

Let me start by describing this context for writing and its invitations to liter-ate action. The class started like any seminar in rhetoric and composition might, inviting students to enter the controversy over literacy by reading his-tory, educational research, and theory, with a special emphasis on the topic of the course, which was community literacy. The students in my Carnegie Mel-lon University class were writing weekly discovery memos on an electronic bulletin board shared by the class. At the end of the term, they would write a final paper on an issue of their choice. However, in the midst of this academic inquiry, members of the class shifted out of the role of student to become mentors at Pittsburgh's Community Literacy Center (CLC) where they worked on an extended eight-week writing project with inner-city teenagers in a CLC project called INFORM. In the INFORM project, teenagers may use writing to talk to other teens about drugs or to adults by publishing a newsletter that articulates the teenager's perspective on public issues such as school restruc-turing, on problems of risk and respect in school, and on gangs and violence. Each CLC project culminates in both a published 10- to 12-page newsletter and a public Community Conversation that the young writers plan and run.

The urban teenagers who come to the CLC are usually not school-comfort-able, but here they find themselves addressed as "writers" where they can pres-ent their ideas in text and later in a public event that typically attracts school board members, parents, city council members, university people, community activists, and the media.

At the CLC, roles are reversed in yet another way that affects this story. When college mentors join the CLC, they do not enter as tutors or editors. Instead, both teenagers and mentors learn to work as collaborative planning partners where the teenager holds the role of writer and planner and the college student is a partner and supporter. As both partners learn to use strategies for rhetorical planning, rival hypothesis thinking, and problem solving, the end in view is helping the writer develop his or her own plan and text (Flower et al.). This relationship makes the notion of writing expertise problematic and can raise the question of what counts as literacy—my practices or yours?

Invitations to Literate Action

For the college mentor, this experience offers some compelling invitations to literate action, invitations that can take the form of a pressing question. Consider the cross-cultural question: How do you, a relatively privileged, white, middle-class, academically successful college student, go about entering into a meaningful conversation with an inner-city African American teenager who has not been nurtured by academic institutions, who is skeptical about the power of writing, and is probably uncertain about you? How do you open up the cross-cultural inquiry you both want into the reality of each other's lives? James Paul Gee talks about discourse as a kind of identity kit that supplies you with "the appropriate costume and instructions on how to act, talk, and often write, so as to take on a particular role that others will recognize. . . . A Discourse is [a way of] saying (writing)—doing—being—valuing—believing" (6–7). What is the right discourse for this literate act? A second unsettling question brings us closer to writing. Mentoring invites you to work as a collaborative planning partner, but the catch is, how do you support someone else's ideas and development when you are the one with all the technical knowledge and writing experience? A final question: In your weekly bulletin board messages and final paper, how will you as a writer make sense of this experience for yourself and others?

The three situations just raised all offer invitations to literate action located in the practices of cross-cultural conversation, collaborative planning, and writing an academic paper. Each presented significant conflicts that mentors talked and wrote about. Going to the CLC is often a plunge into an eagerly embraced but unsettling, intercultural discourse, an attempt to cross boundaries of race, background, and education on the bridge of collaboration and writing. That is a conflict everyone anticipates and welcomes. It is a reason students take this course. However, what students may not expect is the way the controversy over literacy moves out of the safe world of assigned reading and into reality when they begin to encounter the conflicts between community literacy and their own practices, standards, and assumptions about writing, based on academic images of textual or expressive literacy.

I have been looking at what happens to students' images of literacy through examining their bulletin board journaling and final papers, transcripts of their mentoring sessions, and interviews in which students helped interpret their own writing. In the cases examined here, students appear to be reconstructing their understanding of writing by entering into three kinds of negotiation and reflection:

- testing and refining academic theory in the crucible of practice
- reflecting on the assumptions and strategies that shape their own writing
- developing situated "working theories" of literacy in context

These are acts of dilemma-driven negotiation, the kind of literate action that supports learning. These students can help us understand such events as sites of negotiation that we as teachers may want to encourage; these students can help us define what our 21st-century pedagogy for literate action might want to include.

Testing and Contextualizing Theory

The first site of negotiation for most mentors was the contested meaning of literacy itself and the conflicting assumptions of what is essential to teach. Gerald Graff has argued that English studies needs to acknowledge its own internal controversies as the heart and the history of the discipline, to make these theory wars a part of undergraduate education (3–15). In this class, one of the first conflicts centered on textual literacy with its focus on textuality rather than on intellectual action or social involvement; its prescriptive concern with correctness, conventions, or style; and its history of atomistic, linguistically reductive preoccupation with error (Brandt; Mike Rose, "Language" 343). Mentors, eager to support the writing of students who do not control mainstream conventions, found it easy to be critical of academic discourse and the heavy hand of textual literacy. But in the next instant, they heard black educators such as Lisa D. Delpit and John U. Ogbu argue that minority groups need to learn the language of power; that black teachers "see the teaching of skills to be essential to their students' survival" (Delpit 383; see Ogbu). Meanwhile, still other theorists identified textual literacy and its ideal of autonomous text with the intellectual power of an abstract, logical, and internally consistent statement. Nevertheless, the bottom line in these views of literacy was not insight or persuasiveness but text: "the criterion for the success of a statement in explicit prose text is its formal structure" (Olson 188).

Then rhetorical literacy entered the fray, shifting the focus from texts to social practices and personal acts. Mentors read ethnographic and cross-cultural research that redefined the monolith of "literacy" as literate *practices*— as "recurrent, goal-directed . . . activities" and "socially developed ways of using knowledge and technology (such as a script) and to accomplish tasks" (Scribner and Cole 236; see also Heath, "Protean Shapes"). (Perhaps, then, mentors should focus on helping teens master a literate *practice* such as writing a community newsletter?) But, as their reading in cognitive rhetoric went on to argue, writing is also an individual constructive act that lets writers embed generic practices and conventions within a personally meaningful, goal-directed use of literacy (Flower, *The Construction*).

Bear in mind that for students wondering, "Where will I as a mentor place my priorities in working with my writer?" each of these theories suggested an implicit plan of action. Community literacy, with its roots in the collaborative consensus building and problem solving of the inner-city community, complicated the issue still further. Community literacy values "written discourse from the margins of society" that lets members of an inner-city neighborhood literally "compose" themselves for action (Peck vi). Texts are not autonomous but are parts of social actions and events, like the Community Conversation on the high rate of school suspension for African American males that combined rap, drama, policy arguments, and text at a meeting attended by the school board president and picked up that night on the evening news. The practice of advocacy in community literacy, Peck argues, "grows out of the dilemmas in the lives of neighborhood people [and] depends on a conversational, collaborative process seeking action" (1). Devoted to social change, community literacy depends on transactional, persuasive writing; it calls for strategic thinking and problem solving.

However, unlike textual or cultural literacy, community literacy does not see a monocultural discourse (much less the academic essay) as the way to achieve its ends. Community literacy often leads to hybrid texts that may speak in the street talk of teens, mixed with arguments of policy developed by personal narrative, and alternately supported by conventions of academic persuasion and the black church. Its educational focus is not on the grammar and convention of standard white English but on strategies for planning and collaboration that let writers make strategic decisions in the face of multiple conventions and discourses. The goal of this literacy, as it is practiced at the CLC, is not only to speak to multiple communities but also to build an intercultural conversation among writers, among groups separated by race, culture, and social and economic power. As a community/university collaborative, the CLC attempts to confront cultural difference by bringing people into a collaborative working relationship and asking them to make productive use of difference in the creation of texts that make a difference (Peck, Flower, and Higgins).

The first few weeks of the course should have made Gerald Graff happy. This theoretical controversy over literacy led college students to see their own assumptions and academic strategies as no longer simply "normal" "good writing" but as expectations created by a particular, mainstream academic discourse. Although mastering these expectations can buy one a great deal in university forums, they may be ineffectual in the debates of the local city council (Peck). Entering the theory wars can have strong effects on students. Ideally, it lets one build a more qualified understanding. On the other hand, as we all know, reading about conflicts of theory can sometimes have the opposite effect, leading students to take simpler, more dogmatic oppositional positions.

For these mentors, however, conflicts between theories were not just an abstraction to debate or a side to take, because their definition of what counted as literacy dictated what they would set as priorities when they sat down to plan, write, or read the text of their teenage writers. And the choices they made often raised questions. Judy, for instance, was a facile creative writer, a fast typist, and an experienced editor with a strong commitment to a shapely, artistically crafted sentence. Because she could "type so much faster than Darcia," her writer-partner, Judy found herself taking over at the keyboard. But as other people began to notice, in doing so she soon became an on-line editor, and Darcia fell silent, waiting for Judy to supply the phrasing that turned her idea fragments into sentences.

On the other hand, what if the mentors resisted their own schemas for "good" school writing and refused to take control over the teenagers' texts? What if they turned their attention away from errors of grammar or style and tried to act as collaborative planning partners, not editors, trying to support their writers' own—slowly, so slowly, developing—intentions and text? But suddenly they realized publication was only two weeks away. And how should they respond to the position of a fellow mentor—an African American who felt she struggled to make it to a competitive university—who dismissed the power of "being heard" as an illusion and argued that empowerment for these inner-city teens would come through control of the mainstream discourse? As she put it, focusing on ideas and arguments might let you talk to the board of a corporation or civic group; working on correctness would let you get on it.

Even if you are trying not to impose your own standards, it is hard to respond to difference. Terry had finally achieved a remarkable success in getting Sheila (a shy girl whom some teachers had dismissed as learning disabled) to begin to talk in text at all. Although Sheila surprised everyone with an observant portrait of a neighborhood beauty shop owner, the text did not look at all like what Terry—a fluent college writer—expected of a draft: "She doesn't seem to understand organization, connections, themes at all. I am just trying to get her to see that. What is the best way? . . . Even if it is not grammatically correct, shouldn't it at least have a point? I thought that was the point—to help her write effectively."

Over the eight weeks, Terry's image of what her supposedly "poor writer" could do, of what she needed to learn, and of what a draft should look like were challenged and redefined.

Trying to serve as a mentor in the midst of conflicting theories, values, and priorities—but having to take action—was uncomfortable. Chris put the problem succinctly in one of her early posts on the bulletin board:

I'm concerned about the power relations going on here at the CLC. Our purpose is to give writers their own voice in the texts they are producing, but I wonder how much of that is a realistic goal. As mentors, we impose—even though we try not to—our own standards of good writing. . . . We are producing a written text, when some of the writers are not comfortable in that medium at all. Can any one help me?

What the bulletin board posts and the mentors' meetings made clear was that, for most mentors, none of the theoretical accounts of literacy was fully acceptable. The clean conflicts of theory and the option of choosing an argument to stand on did not translate well to taking literate action in a complex, intercultural discourse or to building a working relationship with another writer. Surrounded by multiple, often conflicting voices within their own minds, mentors had to create what I am calling a *negotiated* meaning of literacy (Flower, *The Construction*). Negotiation means that in the face of a contested meaning, writers rise to active awareness of conflict. They recognize, if only momentarily, the multiple forces that would shape their understanding or dictate meaning. And in response, they construct a reflective, provisional resolution; they set priorities and construct an understanding in the presence of trade-offs.

This process of negotiation operates in two common senses of the term. On the one hand, mentors often had to negotiate (or arbitrate) the power relations between these conflicting voices dictating what literacy should be or what they should do. They had to balance opposing claims, often resisting the normally unquestioned expectations of mainstream discourse and arguing with its voice of authority and status. On the other hand, this process of meaning making was not always oppositional but was often a process of negotiating (or navigating) a best path, of acknowledging alternative values and finding a route that honored as many as possible.

In situations like these, both mentor and writer move toward negotiated images of what good writing means—a conditional, qualified, experimental understanding. Theory is no longer a commodity exchanged by theorists whose conflict students only observe. Learning to take literate action is learning to live in a complicated world where theory is tested and ideas such as literacy take on a negotiated meaning. Instead of merely taking sides in the theory wars, these students are evaluating theory in the crucible of their practice and constructing a new, conditionalized meaning for themselves.

Reflecting on One's Own Writing

In the set of negotiations we just looked at, students dealt, as Graff suggested, with conflicting voices within the establishment. However, the received wisdom of theorists is not the only knowledge that needs to be examined. Literate action also means interpreting the assumptions and strategies that guide your own writing.

Faye Miller was committed to her work at the CLC. But somehow, when it

came to writing her final paper, she was "left still feeling that there was nothing that—nothing that grabbed me. . . . Like, there's nothing that I feel passionate about." The turning point for Faye came when her collaborative planning partner pushed her to get specific, as she said, "to get down to what
actually I experienced and have the paper come from my experience, rather
than my thoughts about things, which is what I hadn't been doing before, I
hadn't been dealing with the experience that I had." The troubling irony of this
little episode is that Faye—a writer who cares a lot about being passionate—
had not realized why she was coming up empty until she sat down to reflect
on the tapes from her collaborative planning sessions and started to articulate
the strategy that was leading her to dead-end writing:

> I was basing my focus of my paper on what I had learned from readings,
> rather than what I had experienced and [this little "and" is the source of
> Faye's conflict] I want it to be based on my experience. . . . I wasn't using—I
> didn't know how to use information that I've gotten from being a mentor
> and working at the CLC for my paper. I was just thinking about the paper
> in broad general terms.

In this act of self-reflection, Faye began a new negotiation with some of the
buried conflicts in her own values, assumptions, and habits, in which the
voices of received wisdom tend to drown out the insights of her experience.

The paper Faye wrote not only spoke with intellectual passion but also carried this inquiry into her own meaning making a step further. Faye was drawn
to Jim, a perplexing teenager who wrote "Why I Sleep in Class." Jim, a master
of unobtrusive failure, never missed a CLC session but doggedly resisted the
role of writer, speaker, actor, or authority. As Faye argues, "Each of us has our
own set of valid, useful strategies for dealing with the world and interacting
with others, and we bring these with us to the CLC. Jim's is just one way of
dealing. . . . We're all just trying to get by as best we know how." And yet
understanding, says Faye, is not that easy.

But there are real barriers in truly knowing a student such as Jim—what
drives him, what his capabilities are, how he experiences things—especially
in the limited duration of the CLC sessions. Jim resisted being known. Faye
brought us into the dilemma of interpretation. It is a site of negotiation between our desire to understand, our need to act out of understanding, and the
limitations of our own ability to do so.

In the face of this tension, Faye did not seek the "truth" about Jim but
attempted to construct a contested meaning, reflecting on her own strategies
of meaning making and on the voices that actively enter into her own negotiations: "Our perceptions are certainly more under our own control than is his
behavior. I'd like to explore how the ways we perceive each other may affect
our literate success. What do we assume in the face of gaps in our knowledge?

How do we make decisions when we are uncertain? . . . What does it mean to be a 'good mentor' to a student like Jim?" Faye took literate action by constructing a new understanding of her process of making meaning. Her insight into this negotiated, constructive process did not erase conflicts but gave her a new measure of control within them.

Building Working Theories

By most standards, a pedagogy for literate action would have done well if it succeeded in helping Chris challenge and contextualize received theory and if it helped Faye gain a new reflective control over her own writing. But a third case shows how students can take literate action by beginning to build working theories of their own, dilemma-driven efforts for understanding, rooted in students' own experience and observations even as they grapple with larger theoretical issues, much as Faye did with the difference between understanding Jim and responding to Jim (Flower, *The Construction*). These reflective, written accounts of hypotheses and provisional readings as a working theory aim not for generalities but for the interpretation of personal experience.

For Robert Dixon, literate action is a playing field for the exercise of power. His final paper addresses literacy as a site of ongoing negotiation among alternative accounts of who has power and alternative theoretical perspectives on how it is exercised in literate acts. One account locates authority in crafted, autonomous, mainstream texts. Another voice echoes Robert's reading of cultural theory and its critique of colonizing practices that impose one culture's language on another. And yet another voice argues the collaborative philosophy of the CLC with its vision of hybrid texts and intercultural conversations in which all parties are learners. Robert's working theory is built around his interpretation of three such revealing moments of conflict, when power shifted.

Robert describes his first day at CLC, already aware of an identity conflict. On the one hand, he was a card-carrying scion of textual literacy—a mentor and professional writing major and an experienced editor from Carnegie Mellon University, who had "power over language and the institutional credentials, the authority to exercise that power." On the other hand, he wanted to assume the role of collaborative planning partner and supporter. How would he "construct" himself as a writer? As he puts it, "I was afraid of pandering or patronizing or of getting stuck or being unsure about what to do."

But from the very first session, Robert began to notice how the literate acts of writers had a way of shifting power relations in unexpected ways. In these sites of negotiation, literacy created a subtle but intriguing friction between the different communities at the table, a surprising spark that often realigned the power relations.

For instance, we were all discussing how the writers could have made the superintendent of schools, during a recent interview they had with her, listen *to* them instead of talk *at* them. Robert passed a note to Ebony, his writer, that said, "If they do not take you seriously, who do they take seriously?" He wanted to help her bring that issue into the discussion, "to shift the power of asking a question I thought important from myself to Ebony," but this literate move backfired. He says, "I got looks from some of the mentors and . . . suddenly felt like I had been caught in grade school passing cartoons of the teacher to my neighbor, only worse, because I was a senior in college, responsible, a good student, supposedly a mentor-type role model."

But when Ebony did not respond, Robert tried to raise the question about power himself, which did indeed lead to a power shift, but in an unexpected direction, because the worst of all possible things happened—nobody responded. "As a mentor, having a question which I formulated left hanging in silence shifted my own position of power in the round table. Mentors are constructed as authorities on writing and planning, [and] a lack of response from the writers devalues that authority, at least to the mentor," rearranging authority relations of mentor and mentee.

However, a far more important example of how literacy both asserts and realigns power came for Robert at the Community Conversation when the teenage writers were fielding questions about the document they had titled "If I Had a Choice." In response to the writers' strong pleas for schools that were not boring and where teachers listened, some well-meaning members of the audience revealed their own assumptions about authority when they asked, "Shouldn't teenagers' literate acts of advocacy run in the proper channels, offered by the institution of school?" One woman raised the question of free press: "Couldn't students just talk about these issues of school reform and suspension in their student paper?" Sitting in the back row, Robert (an experienced student newspaper editor) fumed to himself, "A high school paper may not be subject to seizure (the school owns and finances it), but it is certainly subject to control by those in positions of power and authority. I wanted to tell the woman who asked these questions to put the flowers back in her hair and dig out her bell-bottoms. I wanted to call her 'whitey.' " But, of course, Robert, sitting in the audience, could not say anything.

The issue of how literate acts should operate came to a head in public, however, when a man stood up to ask why the students were not using institutional channels if there was a problem: "What about the student council?" Up on the stage, Michelle, who had the microphone, looked perplexed (perhaps at this lame question?) and answered that the student council does little more than plan activities such as the prom. Then Mark, who had written a rap about the causes of suspension (from extensive personal experience), stepped to the mike: "I also have an answer for that. Student council is mostly made up of straight-A students, anyway [laughter from the audience]. I mean, come on [more laughter]. Come on now. I mean."

Mark's statement, which brought the house down, was not an autonomous text. It was supported only by an argument from ethos. However, the literate action of those two students shifted the power relations at that moment, giving status to the problems of teenagers who are not the straight-A students, who find the proper channels either closed to them or ineffectual.

Consequently, Robert's final paper represented literacy not in terms of texts or the conventions of discourse but as a force that creates moments of "friction between the various sub-communities of the CLC, and in doing so brings about subtle shifts of power which can alter the status of Mentor and Mentee, and the status of students the school may see as marginal or problematic."

Robert's paper constructed a complex, personal representation not found in the literature or in other students' representations. For instance, the meaning Robert built did not merely reproduce the ideology of mainstream education or of his professional writing major, or even of the more marginal ideologies of cultural critique or community literacy that entered in his thinking. Robert's paper was a literate act that emerged out of a personal negotiation in which conflicting ideologies and conflicting theories of literacy became inner voices, along with the voice of Robert's own values and experience, including the extended negotiation that went on over the course of a semester.

Most of these mentors are not simply expanding their knowledge of literacy but also are building reflective, working theories that, like Robert's, link ideas to action and test theory in practice. In putting theoretical claims on the table and acknowledging generative conflicts, the course brought their meaning under more active negotiation and put students in the role of observation-based theory builders (Flower, "Cognition").

A pedagogy of literate action, this pedagogy for the 21st century could do more than recreate the academic theory wars Graff describes. As a pedagogy of writing, not just reading, it could invite students to test and temper the generalities of theory with observation of real situations and to apply observation-based reflection to their own writing. Thus, they could build more actively negotiated working theories of their own.

I will end, however, by raising one of the generative conflicts that I commend in our students. The working theories that a writer such as Robert builds are likely to be at best a provisional resolution. Like any negotiated meaning, they are constructed in response to multiple demands, options, and constraints. Robert's understanding of literacy and the ways it aligns power relations has to accommodate a tension, which will not go away, between his genuine authority (based on textual literacy) and his own goals of being a collaborative planning partner and supporter. It has to somehow recognize the danger of literate colonizing while listening to the voices of African American educators and students urging him to share the language of power. However, negotiation is a constructive act; in the midst of these conflicting voices, a writer has to forge an understanding, decide on priorities, create a relationship among voices and ideas, and, on the basis of that provisional resolution, act.

As educators, we are like Robert. We cannot afford to ignore any of these voices as we construct our own negotiated understanding of literacy. Look back at the tension in that final Community Conversation where adult voices, urging change through conventional channels, met the voices of Michelle and Mark cutting through to the reality of school. Students who were used to standing on the margin saw their literate acts shift the balance of power. In that moment, they carried the day—but, political reality whispers, it was only the day. The working theory we construct will not hold simple answers; our pedagogy for literate action will be a site of negotiation.

23 Intellectual Property in an Age of Information: What Is at Stake for Composition Studies?

ANDREA A. LUNSFORD

This book aims to ask tough questions about the future of composition studies. In the same spirit, I hope to contribute some questions of my own about issues that only a few years ago seemed peripheral but that now seem absolutely central to our work in composition studies. The issues I hope to explore are ones I have been vaguely fretting about for the last 10 years, ever since Lisa Ede and I embarked on a study of the writing practices of members in seven different professional organizations, including those for chemists, psychologists, engineers, city and regional planners, technical communicators, modern language scholars, and CEOs (*Singular Texts*). That study eventually led me to consider at length what I offer as the theme of my essay: intellectual property and its relation to human subjectivity and information. I will put forth the ways in which these issues impinge on composition studies in important and even dramatic ways to suggest that most of us—for particularly intriguing reasons—continue to turn a blind eye to these issues and to urge that we move quickly in confronting these issues in our professional organizations, in our publications, and in our home universities and classrooms.

Let me start with a seemingly simple question: What is intellectual property? To those of us steeped in the ways of the academy, where intellectual property is the very bread and butter of our existence, it may seem strange even to ask. What is intellectual property—and who owns it? Copyright, patent law, related rights agreements, proscriptions against plagiarism or intellectual piracy seem our stock in trade. It is interesting to note, therefore, that the concept of intellectual property is a fairly new one and that its vast system of regulation as we now take it for granted in the Western world has had a relatively short life.

Intellectual property, of course, is a metaphor that has evolved over the

course of the last 300 years. In a 1991 MLA presentation, I attempted to un-
cover the power of the property metaphor, noting that what we now think of
as intellectual property is, in fact, related to another earlier metaphor of paternity: those ideas we give birth to are our children. You may recall a very early
version of this notion expressed in Plato's *Symposium*. In that dialogue, Plato
has Diotima "teach" Socrates that the highest form of procreation is that of
ideas, the conceptions of wisdom and beauty that poets and philosophers produce. In a supreme irony, what arguably amounts to the masculine appropriation of giving birth comes as a lesson from a woman (who surely must have
been turning in her grave ever since). At any rate, this metaphor linking the
production of great ideas with parthogenetic and paternal birth has a long life
in the Western world; we can trace it through Augustine, Chaucer, and Milton
to Shakespeare and William Harvey—and to the U.S. Patent Office. Eventually, however, the paternity metaphor began to merge with a new one, one
concerned with ownership of property—of tangible objects such as land. Mark
Rose has recently traced such metaphors through the course of the 18th century, noting particularly the ways in which they come together in some of
Daniel Defoe's arguments in favor of copyright. Here is, for example, Defoe
conflating these metaphors in a fairly hair-raising description:

> A Book is the Author's Property, 'tis the Child of his Inventions, the Brat of
> his Brain; if he sells his Property, it then becomes the Right of the Pur-
> chaser; if not, 'tis as much his own, as his Wife and Children are his own—
> But behold in this Christian Nation, these Children of our Heads are seiz'd,
> captivated, spirited away, and carry'd into Captivity, and there is none to
> redeem them. (*The Review* 2 Feb. 1710; qtd. in Mark Rose 39)

From Latin *proprius* (own) and *proprietas* (ownership), our words "proper,"
"propriety," and "property" are closely related. (Until at least the late Renaissance, in fact, "property" and "propriety" were synonymous.) In each case, as
the Defoe passage makes clear, the words connote exclusionary possession
and rights that, not so incidentally, belong to men (women and children, in
fact, were themselves another kind of property men could own). As Mark Rose
points out, important to this concept is John Locke's theory of property, which
held that a man could, through his mental work, convert the common ground
of nature into private property. In *Two Treatises of Government* (1690), Locke
says:

> Though the Earth, and all inferior Creatures be common to all Men, yet
> every Man has a *Property* in his own *Person*. This *no Body* has any Right to
> but himself. The *Labour* of his Body, and the *Work* of his Hands, we may
> say, are properly his. Whatsoever then he removes out of the State that Na-

hath provided, and left it in, he hath mixed his *Labour* with, and joyned to it something that is his own, and thereby makes it his *Property*. (305–6)

Out of this property metaphor grew the first copyright law, the 1710 Act of Anne, which gave "proprietors" of copyright the right to act against those who trespassed on their intellectual "property" by protecting the sale of works for 14 years, with one additional 14-year extension possible. In the ensuing years, however, copyright—enshrined in our own Constitution to "Promote the Progress of Science and the Useful Arts"—has grown, from the 1833 Dramatic Copyright Act, to the 1886 Berne Convention, to the 1911 Copyright Act, to the 1967 Convention Establishing the World Intellectual Property Organization (WIPO), to that maddeningly confusing but lawyer-profiting Copyright Act of 1976. And the work goes on: in spring 1993, WIPO convened an important worldwide symposium on copyright and neighboring rights at Harvard. As Peter Jaszi and Martha Woodmansee note in "The Law of Texts," over the almost 300 years of its existence in Europe and America, "the trend in copyright law . . . toward longer and longer terms of protection, against more and more kinds of unauthorized uses, and to more and more different kinds of so-called 'works' " provides a dramatic example of the tenacious growth of copyright. WIPO now defines intellectual property as including all of the following:

1) Literary, artistic, and scientific works
2) performances of performing artists, phonograms, and broadcasts
3) inventions in all fields of human endeavor
4) scientific discoveries
5) industrial designs
6) trademarks, service marks, commercial names, and designations—and all other rights resulting from intellectual activity in the industrial, scientific, or artistic fields. (World, *Background* 3–4)

Who Owns Intellectual Property?

As WIPO's definition suggests, intellectual property has grown in our society to include a vast array of things, and those things—and, importantly, not some other things—are protected to a fare-thee-well, as I will point out shortly. For now, however, I want to ask, If intellectual property is that which is protected and owned, who is it that does this owning? It might seem absolutely obvious that the creator (recall the paternity metaphor) is the owner, but the debate over how this question would be answered was actually a long and exceedingly bitter one, and part of the story is brilliantly related by Martha Woodmansee in "The Genius and the Copyright."

In that essay, Woodmansee demonstrates that before copyright—the ownership of intellectual property—could come to seem not only just but inevitable, society had to accept the notion that there is a crucial distinction between the production of intellectual property, particularly as it is embodied in works, and, say, the raising and selling of a certain strain of apples, and that the author's role in producing such intellectual property is somehow privileged—special and different from, for instance, that of the printer or bookbinder. Such a connection of exclusionary ownership between the author and the work is one we have constructed, largely out of romantic ideology that linked the concepts of originality and genius to that of the ideas of an author (read owner of intellectual property). This maneuver was not a simple one, for the notion of the freedom of ideas is a very old and revered one in our culture. Ideas—knowledge—are given freely to us by God and should be freely shared for the common good. Martin Luther and a host of others who opposed the growth and spread of copyright and related rights laws insisted on this point. As Christian Sigmund Krause put it in 1783:

> No, no it is too obvious that the concept of intellectual property is useless. My property must be exclusively mine. I must be able to dispose of it and retrieve it unconditionally. Let someone explain to me how that is possible. . . . Just let someone try taking back the ideas he has originated once they have been communicated so that they are, as before, nowhere to be found. All the money in the world could not make that possible. (qtd. in Woodman—see 443–4)

What *did* make this concept possible was a set of moves that seemed to reconcile the tensions inherent in the traditional role of freedom of information (or ideas) in Western society with the desire to create incentives for producing information through the protection of property "rights." The happy constellation of the figure of the romantic author/genius, the theme of originality, and a concomitant distinction between ideas and expression—as articulated by Edward Young ("Conjectures on Original Composition," 1759) and Johann Fichte ("Proof of the Illegality of Reprinting," 1793) roughly 300 years ago—allowed this reconciliation to take place. Most simply put, these theorists identified the source of ideas/knowledge not in God, not the "book of nature," not in previous texts, not in "common" knowledge, but in the geniuses themselves. Through their own unique thought processes, such "authors" transformed ideas so that they reflected their own individual originality. To allow this originality or genius its due rights, the idea—as it was construed under the emerging copyright system—could go into the world of public exchange. But its "expression" remained the sole property of the author.

This is, as legal theorist James Boyle has compellingly demonstrated, a very appealing conjunction. But what has come to be known as the "author effect" was still unstable, particularly in terms of the law's decisions on how to resolve competing claims between control and access, until a new term, the "work," entered the equation. With the work's obvious connection to the expression of an author's ideas, the scene was finally set for the very rapid expansion and rigidification of copyright "protection." That this expansion took place during the 18th-century commercialization and commodification of goods in an increasingly capitalistic economy almost—but not quite, particularly for those of us in composition studies—goes without saying. Despite these developments, however, as Peter Jaszi notes in "Toward a Theory of Copyright," "the terminology of authorship" survived alongside that of the work. In some respects, in fact, the author concept is as prominent in contemporary discussions as it was in the mid-18th century: "not only did 'authorship' take on a new ideological importance with the objectification of creative property," says Jaszi, but it "continued (and continues) to be strategically deployed to extend copyright protection to new kinds of subject matter" (480), including concepts from science and technology as well as those from the arts.

In fact, this concept has spread like kudzu throughout our legal system and is embedded in all of those rights protected by the 1976 Copyright Act (in which copyright subsists in "original works of authorship fixed in any tangible medium of expression"), the WIPO Convention, and contemporary GATT (General Agreement on Tariff and Trade) and TRIPS (Trade Related Aspects of Intellectual Property) Agreements—and, most recently, in NAFTA. So widespread is the legacy of the author effect that it characterizes not only much of our legal system but also every other institution in our society, including the institution of higher education.

In spite of their ambiguity, however, the notions of authorship and of work, as they have developed in our legal and academic institutions, are not only highly constructed and contingent—as I have tried to suggest—but also currently at the point of disintegration, or at the very least at a point of transformation. In short, the concepts of author (as the representation of any creator) and work (as a tangible medium of expression of an author's idea) have never been more problematic than they are today. Several examples in the humanities and the sciences will illustrate this claim.

Mounting a critique on the author has been an ongoing part of postmodern and poststructuralist projects for some time now. It was heralded in 1968 by Roland Barthe's dramatic (and, as it turns out, greatly exaggerated) announcement of the "death of the author." And Michel Foucault performed a lengthy autopsy, arguing that it is more appropriate to speak of author *functions* than of authors and to see these functions as contested sites in a complex world of political, scientific, cultural, economic, ideological, and other forces ("What Is an Author?").

Barthes, Foucault, and other poststructuralist theorists note the compelling and persuasive tendency to continue to link "authority" to autonomous individualism, to a unique self who creates. This concept of author has been explored—and exploded—in many areas, including the work Karen LeFevre (*Invention*), Lisa Ede and I (*Singular Texts*), and others have done on collaboration. That work demonstrates that the dominant romantic concept of authorship as singular and originary has effectively erased the largely collaborative and dispersed nature of most creative endeavors, from art, drama, literature, and film to scientific experimentation and "discovery." Lisa Ede and I attempted to explore the deeply collaborative nature of most such work in *Singular Texts/Plural Authors*, where we particularly noted some of the problems attendant on continuing to try to fit the square peg of multiple creativity into the round hole of singular romantic authorship. Particularly striking to us during the time we were working on this book were problems surrounding library attribution (our entire Library of Congress system demands an author, for instance) and honorary authorship and corporate name authorship in the sciences. In our book, we report some of these findings:

> The nature of research in High Energy physics is such that it involves the collaboration of many scientists, resulting in papers with large numbers of "authors." In 1962 a group of collaborators published a communication in *Physical Review Letters* under the names of the three laboratories where they worked instead of their own names (much to the indignation of the Editor of that journal). *Physics Abstracts* made no mention of the three institutions in the bibliographic description and they were not indexed; in other words, the paper was treated as anonymous.
>
> In 1970, papers on the analysis of lunar rocks retrieved in the July 1969 moon landing began to appear. One of these published in *Science* was attributed to "The Lunar Sample Preliminary Examination Team." The individual members of the team, 62 in number, were listed alphabetically by name in a footnote as "the people who contributed directly to obtaining the data and to preparation of this report." The reaction of *Chemical Abstracts* to the report was to ignore the team designation and to list as authors the first name appearing in the footnote, along with "et al." to represent the other 61 team members, in both the bibliographic description and the authors' index. (24)

In spite of mounting evidence that the author construct is just that, a construct, and that it does not serve to describe contemporary discursive practices in the sciences and humanities very well, the construct has proven highly tenacious in the law as well as in our national consciousness. As a result, the rights protected by copyright have expanded to such a degree in the Western world that whatever balance may have existed between public benefit (free information) and private reward (the author's right to a work) has been virtually destroyed as various contestants scramble for more and more exclusionary rights. As an example, Robert Merges speaks of a "land rush" mentality among those working on the human genome project: "I guarantee there are people out there right now chugging out the [genetic] sequences, writing up applications and filing them just because they are afraid of what will happen if they don't. They are afraid of being the one company or one researcher who didn't file and didn't claim their stretch of the sequence, and now they're up the creek without a patent" (23). The result Merges foresees is a "nightmare scenario" of "conflicting claims to various parts of the genome" (23) and an incredible tangle as the courts try to find an "author." Such nightmare scenarios are increasingly frequent. James Boyle notes, for instance, the decision in *Moore v. The Regents of the University of California*, in which Moore, "whose cells were used to manufacture a drug worth billions," did not "own his body." In this instance, Moore was merely a "source," the court held. The "authors" with propriety rights were the doctors who used that source ("Alienated Information" 14). An example from the entertainment field further illustrates how long the arm of copyright has grown. In a case concerning parody, the rap group 2 Live Crew was sued for using Roy Orbison's song "Pretty Woman" without permission to create a parody of what the group called "white-centered popular music" (*Acuff-Rose Music Inc. v. Campbell*). The U.S. Court of Appeals ruled against 2 Live Crew, stating that the parody amounted "to purloin[ing] a substantial portion of the essence of the original" and thus demonstrating that copyright has expanded to include not only translations "but a seemingly infinite series of imaginable varieties thereon—including varieties as apposite as parody" (Jaszi and Woodmansee 8). In November 1993, the Supreme Court began hearing arguments in this case, and the 1994 decision overturning the Court of Appeals has been greeted with sighs of relief not only in the music industry but also by all those like us who teach and assign parodies to our students (Biema). The problems of infringement of copyright are particularly acute for scholars attempting to tiptoe through the minefield of fair use legislation to work with unpublished materials, which are all covered now by copyright. (For a particularly chilling account of the ways in which this extension of the author effect works to censor texts and to silence many voices, see LeFevre, "The Tell-Tale 'Heart.' ")

As I hope these brief examples have suggested, the romantic conception of authorship is both deeply entrenched in our legal system and increasingly problematic. They also point, however, to the fact that this romantic conception tends to value certain producers (authors) and their works while erasing or devaluing others. No copyright, for example, exists in a work produced by a true collective enterprise, nor "can copyright subsist in a work which is not 'fixed' " (Jaszi and Woodmansee 21). The result is that while certain producers' rights are very highly protected, others are not protected at all. These "others" include traditional folkloric productions that are appropriated more and more by the culture and entertainment industries of the West. James Boyle illustrates this appropriation in an example from medical research:

> Centuries of cultivation by Third World farmers produce wheat and rice strains with valuable quality—in the resistance of disease, say. . . . The biologists/agronomists and genetic engineers of a Western chemical company take samples of these strains, engineer them a little to add a greater resistance to fungus or a thinner husk. The chemical company's scientists fit the paradigm of authorship. The farmers are everything authors should not be—their contribution comes from a community rather than an individual, tradition rather than innovation, evolution rather than transformation. Guess who gets the intellectual property rights? Next year, the farmers may need a license to re-sow the grain from their own crops. ("Alienated Information" 14)

Similar stories from the Amazon and the South American rainforest abound (see for example Judson; Goleman; Pearce; Posey). One of the most striking examples of such stories I have heard involves the indigenous use of Madagascar's rosy periwinkle—and in particular its vinca alkaloids—to treat diabetes. After complex investigation and exploration, the Lilly Company used the alkaloids as the basis of a compound now used in chemotherapy, a treatment the British periodical *Independent* claims "yielded a trade in the drug worth $100m a year." As the writer of this article says, "Madagascar is the unique home of perhaps 5% of the world's species. Yet without an income from its huge biological wealth, it has chopped down most of its forests to feed its people" (Pearce). In other words, the people of Madagascar do not "fit" in the legal system created around romantic authorship and copyright and so end up resorting to deforestation. Thus, as James Boyle points out, the (non)decision to impose our "author vision without acknowledging, or even understanding, its implications, is also the decision not even to try to solve these problems" ("Alienated Information" 16).

If the author construct is problematic, so also is the construct of a work, as the foregoing examples suggest. Where in the growing, evolving periwinkle, for instance, is the fixed and tangible expression of an idea—the work protected by the 1976 Copyright Act? Nowhere is this problem more acute, of course, than in the area of electronic technology, and it is this area that may be forcing us to new considerations of how to balance the tension between public access to information and protection of the rights of its producers. I have already alluded to the controversy surrounding fair use laws, a controversy most of us may be familiar with from following the proceedings of *Basic Books v. Kinko's*, the decision concerning which arguably has led to denial of access to information across our college campuses today. When we start to see cartoon strips almost daily about such issues, we can be fairly sure that they have penetrated the national consciousness. You may be able to think of a number of examples; I have seen them recently in the *Chronicle of Higher Education* (10 June 1992, B7), in "Blondie" (18 Oct. 1993), and in the *New Yorker* (11 Oct. 1993, 119). This last cartoon shows a child reading to classmates " 'How I Spent My Summer Vacation,' by Lilia Anya, all rights reserved, which includes the right to reproduce this essay or portions thereof in any form whatsover, including, but not limited to, novel, screenplay, musical, television miniseries, home video and interactive CD-ROM." The problems presented by the *Kinko's* decision, however, pale in comparison to those posed by the advent of electronic information and particularly, as Jay Bolter suggests, of hypertext. As Bolter puts it in "Intellectual Property and the Electronic Writing Space," "Copyright Law recognizes fixed verbal expressions. Yet hypertext is not a single fixed text; nor is a hypertext fully characterized by the words it contains. In a hypertext, linking is writing. What legal status does a link have?" (8).

Indeed, what laws will govern the "works" emerging on Internet, now accessible in 100 countries, and on what some are labeling the "electronic superhighway" that is being called for by the Clinton administration and being jockied for by AT&T and other communications giants (see Markoff; Lehman; Samuelson)? At stake here, among other things, are the futures of libraries and the publishing industry as we have known them. As Paul Nijhoff Asser, secretary of the International Group of Scientific, Technical, and Medical Publishers, states, "If we lose the electronic publishing battle we will have worldwide uncontrolled piracy" (qtd. in Wilson A21). Or, conversely, some might say, we will have total freedom of information.

You see the problem, I think, and, indeed, while it is the old problem of the conflicting claims of access versus protection, the problem is made more visible—and much more extreme—by electronic communication. As a result, the next few years will surely see increasing efforts to establish new controls and to recognize—and protect—new forms of intellectual property as well as increasing efforts to *resist* such regulation, resistance exemplified by what Richard Stallman calls "copy left," the explicit renunciation of property rights by some users of Internet.

What Is at Stake for Composition Studies?

Whatever else I might say about the future of intellectual property in an age of information, it will certainly be exciting, as gripping as any high drama we might imagine. And as I hope I have suggested, the way this particular story plays out will have very significant implications for each one of us. Will the author and his [sic] work triumph, renew marital vows, and live happily—and profitably—ever after? Or will that dark and handsome stranger, electronic communication, finally help to shatter these constructs of romantic ideology or perhaps transform them utterly?

Whatever the outcome, we in composition studies have a vital stake in it. For notions of intellectual property play a primary role in the way we in the academy define knowledge, in the way we share knowledge, and in the way we assign value to certain producers and products. In terms of the research many of us conduct, funding will be a major part of what is at stake. As Mary Clutter, National Science Foundation assistant director, recently remarked: "The Federal Government has a fine and longstanding commitment to promote the progress of science through encouraging the free flow of information. At the same time, the Federal Government has an obligation to facilitate the transaction of the results of publicly supported research into useful products" (Genome 1). But if research funding is at stake in the battle over intellectual property, our own scholarly access to information is also at stake, as the controversy over fair use makes clear. I am arguing, then, that the way we redefine intellectual property in an age of information will affect the kind of research we are able to do and the way we value and are rewarded for that research. In particular, new conceptions of intellectual property may allow for truly collective enterprises and may value heretofore ignored cultural productions and cultural workers. This is an end toward which, in fact, many African American, feminist, and Third World scholars have been working.

If our research and scholarship stand to be affected by the debate over intellectual property, however, our academic daily lives may be affected even more. For I would suggest that in the academy, the concepts of romantic authorship and the fixed expression of an author's ideas in the work of the individual mind have been reified to such an extent that they inform almost all of our academic practices. To give only the most obvious examples, we gain promotion and tenure by trading on these constructs. Guidelines often dwell on the merits of individual and original contributions to scholarship. Our "original" contributions become the chips of intellectual property we trade in for recognition and advancement. Our compulsive attention to what I might call hypercitation and endless listing of sources offers further evidence of our devotion to author constructs and to the efficacy and necessity of owning ideas as property. In an interesting if, I think, seriously flawed recent study, Terry Caesar takes a close look at the scholarly genre of acknowledgments, demonstrating the degree to which we figure information and knowledge as commodities to be owned and noting that contemporary acknowledgments everywhere are deeply suggestive of a crisis in relationships among selfhood, knowledge, and textuality. This

crisis is largely repressed, however, and Caesar eventually finds that "acknowledgments continue to present the indebtedness of a single individual at the
center of his or her thought" (37).

Beyond issues of tenure and advancement, publication and the conventions
of citation, attribution, and so on, lie the issues related to intellectual property
and ownership of ideas that affect our students and our classrooms. Most notably, our students are led to realize their own subjectivity by establishing
their own individual authorial rights in the form of intellectual property that
is strictly commodified into grades and performance on tests, or even into
other measures such as portfolios, measures that ultimately depend for their
efficacy on the author construct and its relation to originality and to the fixed
expression of ideas.

At the heart of such issues lies our field's concept of voice as that which
gives rise to intellectual property that can then be owned and exchanged for
advancement in our academic and economic systems. I am not intending to
speak against voice here but rather to argue that this concept, which is another
construct, is deeply connected to the author construct and to traditional notions of intellectual property and, furthermore, that we can learn by looking
at voice from this perspective. Our field's obsession with plagiarism and our
insistence that students cite sources for everything except what we coyly refer
to as "common knowledge" is another notable case in point. (In a supreme
irony, most of the plagiarism statements I have looked at seem to be plagiarized
from one another.) In fact, the way we teach as well as evaluate writing and
reading seems to me almost universally to assume the author construct and
concomitant notions of private ownership of ideas, texts, and intellectual
property. I would suggest also that these traditional notions are too often unexamined and at least partially responsible not only for overt resistance to
collaborative practices on the part of many traditional teachers (collaboration
encourages plagiarism) but also for the more subtle but no less devastating
trivialization of collaboration that we see taking place in the pages of our journals and in sessions at our national conferences, not to mention in our work
force. As I have said more than once, when everyone from General Motors and
Turner Network Television to the U.S. Air Force starts to call for collaboration
and teamwork, I become deeply suspicious of just what they mean by those
terms. Thus, what is at stake for us includes literally everything, from the way
we get accepted into and rewarded in the academy, to the research we conduct,
to the way we conduct our classes, and all even more so in an age of information because information is at the heart of everything we do in the academy in
general and in composition studies in particular.

I am assuming, then, that as a society we are moving toward a global economy vitally concerned with the production and use of information. I am

further assuming that the romantic-author-and-the-expression-of-his-unique-ideas-in-fixed-works paradigm that has evolved over the last 300 years is not adequate to the needs of such a global information economy. Such a paradigm is particularly inadequate as one responsive to forms of information produced by collectives, by indigenous peoples, and, in this country at least, by many African Americans and many women. I am still further assuming that too often where these issues have been concerned, voices like ours have not joined the conversation, or at least they have not been heard. To alter this situation calls on us to work together to understand what James Boyle has so aptly called the "rhetoric of entitlement" in a society in which information—genetic, electronic, proprietary—is one of the main sources and forms of wealth. Even more important, we need to join forces in shaping this rhetoric of entitlement during what will surely amount to a bitter battle to control the future of all knowledge production. If we do not confront the issues I have tried to raise here, then the future of composition studies will, I fear, support and replicate a system that is thoroughly embued with radical individualism, with definitions of ideas as certain kinds of commodities to be owned, bought, and sold, and with representation of human agency as limited and narrow, a representation that excludes alternative forms of subjectivity and ownership.

That, in short, is what is at stake for us. I cannot imagine, really, any higher stakes, nor can I imagine a more pressing and compelling reason to get involved in the debate over copyright and intellectual property and to begin today to question our all-too-easy assumption about the relationship of a "self" or "voice" to what is known—and to question how ownership of what is known works to enrich and empower some while utterly beggaring others. In our recognition of a collective response to these issues may lie the key to using, rather than being used by, intellectual property in an age of information.

Conclusion: Mapping Composition's New Geography

LYNN Z. BLOOM

That the geography of composition indeed presents a configuration of the field unanticipated by many of the most prescient even a quarter century ago is clear from the position papers, assessments of the state-of-the-discipline, and calls for action addressed in *Composition in the 21st Century: Crisis and Change.* Composition teachers, students, researchers, school administrators, and national policymakers approach the new century far from complacent about the past, uncomfortable with the present, uneasy about the future. This book has addressed the need for a new map to provide direction through territory that superficially looks like familiar terrain. But to the extent that the authors have presented a map, its contours are at some intervals sharply etched, at others blurred—terra incognita to which we might refer, as did cartographers of old, "That way be monsters!"

Many of the issues addressed in this book, as in the conference that engendered it, are perennial in the teaching of composition in America: What is composition, anyway? And why do we teach it? Who should teach composition, and what should they know (accompanied by James F. Slevin's perceptive corollary questions, "Whom should composition teach, and what should *they* know?")? Other questions have emerged more insistently in the past quarter century as composition has grown into a vital discipline with a history (a recoverable past implies an interpretable future); an active research component; political and social dimensions—always present but now explicitly acknowledged in every essay and response here; and a cadre of professional administrators concerned with all of the above issues, and more. It is not by accident that the national Council of Writing Program Administrators created this forum for discussing these issues. Nor is it by chance that the authors included here for their national perspectives on the subject have reached not closure but ever widening arcs of expansion.

The contributors to *Composition in the 21st Century* conceive of the field of composition as multidisciplinary, eclectic, widely inclusive rather than exclusive. Anne Ruggles Gere defines the field not as "a bounded territory, one that can be distinguished and set apart" but instead as " 'a complex of forces,' . . . a kind of charged space in which multiple 'sites' of interaction appear" (*Into the Field* 4). Significant among these interactive sites is work in composition that involves, among other disciplines, literature, literary theory, linguistics, philosophy, education, psychology, ethnography, history, computer science, and mathematics and a host of "area studies"—African American studies, Asian studies, womens' studies, Native American studies—all of them disciplinary blends. Composition, which might be called "composition studies," not only contains multitudes, but it also is subject to the interaction of still other forces—politics, public policy, the law. These concerns emerge, as David Bartholomae observes, in "curricular agendas (stated and unstated)" and in "the marketing of careers and materials, . . . institutional arrangements and negotiations, sponsored research, the importing and exporting of theory and method," resulting in an "array of often competing desires for order and control" (this volume). Local, state, and national governments and school and university systems have an impact on the field in what Mary Louise Pratt calls the "contact zone"—"social spaces where cultures meet, clash, and grapple with each other, often in contexts of highly assymetrical relations of power" ("Arts" 34; see also Bartholomae, "Tidy House"). If so many factors, diverse, contradictory, reinforcing, and conflicting, make the field of composition difficult to map, they also make it exciting, if unsettling, to explore.

To the extent that any endeavor, any academic field, is alive, it is ever changing; any map of that field must be continually redrawn. An unexamined subject, composition included, is not worth teaching. Even the familiar questions cannot be asked in the old ways, nor can we expect familiar answers. That the fundamental question "What is composition?" can itself encompass a universe of writing (and speaking and reading and nonverbal) practices is apparent from the variety of fields now embraced by the discipline. The concept of the solitary writer, quill—or computer—at the ready, may not have been banished to the garret, but it lurks only in the peripheral vision of the researchers included here, who focus on context and community. They treat as a given that all of us live and learn to read and write in a complex and fluid universe of discourse(s): preschoolers, schoolchildren, and many adults emerging into literacy at home, in the classroom, everywhere in this wide world; community, four-year college, and university students in settings traditional and nontraditional; fluent writers at work, collaborating on documents in offices and laboratories, creating hypertext on Internet in outer space—documents that, with or without virtual reality, are themselves no longer fixed but ever evolving.

The question of who should teach this broad spectrum of writers—and where—reflects the perpetual conflict between theoretical idealism and budgetary realpolitik. Well-trained, well-paid professionals? A floating underclass of underpaid part-timers (whose numbers continue to increase, professional resolutions notwithstanding)? Anyone who reads, thinks, and writes, in contexts formal and informal? Whether in kitchens or classrooms, playgrounds or prisons, or in a variety of workplace settings, the prevailing model of collaborative learning and writing implies that writers-in-process teach and learn from each other. When a teacher is present, he or she may function more as a coach, an interpreter, a translator, or a fellow collaborator than as an arbiter of grammatical laws and rhetorical order. The classroom itself is no longer seen as a place where teachers necessarily replicate and reify their own culture, especially if that is white and middle class; it, too, may become a "contact zone." John Trimbur, Shirley Brice Heath, and others in this book envision colleges and universities transformed from today's "autonomous, self-regulated . . . self-interested" credentialing institutions to 21st-century "community-building learning centers linked to health delivery and work systems . . . embracing diverse sets of talents . . . from the theatre, corporation, . . . community college programs" and elsewhere, responsive to a host of alternative cultures outside the traditional English classroom (Heath, this volume).

The concept of writing emphasized here is broadly instrumental, utilitarian; writing is a way for writers to gain freedom, authority, power, and political access. Nevertheless, although the contributors to *Composition in the 21st Century* concentrate on writers at work, not at play, there are places even in this action-oriented universe of discourse for poetic, spiritual, and other forms of expressive writing (see in this volume Gere; Heath; Holladay). Yet what these writers should learn is, characteristic of the profession, the subject of perennial disagreement.

Linda Flower suggests that 21st-century composition pedagogy should treat writers as "agents of literate action within a [complicated] social and rhetorical context" (this volume). If her view, shared by many others in this book, prevails among researchers, will they be able to change the hearts and minds of those teachers and school systems pledged to perpetuate the traditional concerns of textual correctness, convention, and style? Will the citizenry, as reflected in local school boards and state departments of education, continue to insist that their children learn the same composition their parents were taught? If Sharon Crowley is right, what pupils will learn will not be the writing process but current-traditional rhetoric, which she claims still dominates the contemporary pedagogical landscape, as it has done for decades. There are, however, other models. For instance, people of all ages could learn in what Gere calls an extracurriculum, learning communities "extending beyond the academy to encompass the multiple contexts in which persons seek to improve their own writing" as it fulfills a host of needs—social, aesthetic, and personal, as well as vocational—" 'all the life that happens outside of us, beyond us' " ("Kitchen Tables" 80, 91). Indeed, Heath envisions this extracurriculum as becoming the conventional 21st-century *curriculum* (this volume).

Whatever students are supposed to learn, how will their teachers be accountable? Whether schools and school systems will—and should—resist or accept the imposition of national standards and various measures (ranging from SATs to portfolio assessment) is a matter of prolonged debate. Will tests be used as gateways or barriers, demonstrations of achievement, or a means to exert social control by perpetuating hierarchies of class and race? Edward M. White assumes that assessment will always be with us and that if composition professionals do not monitor their own terrain, the composition police, the external assessment community, will do it for them, determining allocation of educational resources, "which programs live and die, and what national goals for writing should be" (this volume).

If there is a conspicuous gap in *Composition in the 21st Century*, other than its rather slight concern with the liberatory and textual power of creative writing, it is the indifference to the economics of these various visions of disciplinary and consequent social reform. Academicians in the humanities, who by the nature of their profession live by the conceptual, die by the budget, over which they have minimal influence or control.

If the profession cannot ensure the funding for its broad-based, unsettled, unsettling, and undoubtedly expensive agenda, what chance is there not only for reformation of the status quo but also for the utter transformation that Flower, Gere, Trimbur, Heath, and Lunsford, among others, envision? Do these visions of a new millenium represent, as Samuel Johnson says of a second marriage, a triumph of hope over experience? To ask the questions asked throughout this book, and to keep asking them in changing times, changing contexts, may be as important as to answer them, since in any dynamic field answers will always be provisional.

In proposing four utopian models for 21st-century assessment, Peter Elbow offers in his chapter a defense of utopian visions in general: "Surely there is something misguided when the term 'utopian' is used to criticize and is taken to mean 'unrealistic' and 'unsophisticated.' We need the utopian or visionary impulse to keep from being blinded by what seems normal—to help us see that what is natural is constructed, not inevitable." Thus, even though any utopian vision is guaranteed to create new problems, it is necessary to ask "How *should* things be?" in order to solve or work around those problems that already exist. Indeed, the most powerful assumption of *Composition in the 21st Century* is that we, as a profession, a multidisciplinary field, a nation, need, as Elbow says, to "honor the utopian impulse. What looks at first like unrealistic utopianism can turn out to be realistically feasible; what looks like a 'nowhere' (what 'utopia' literally means) can turn out to be a somewhere"—not over the rainbow but right here on the streets, however mean or mundane, where we live.

The map of the universe of composition at the emergence of the 21st century might have been rendered by Escher's engraving of one hand drawing another hand. At first glance, the hands look like mirror images of one another; they are not. Nor is either image finished, though initially it appears to be. The process of conceiving, constructing, changing any field is ongoing, dynamic; it represents a world of hope, a world without end.

Works Cited   Contributors   Index

Works Cited

Adams, Peter Dow. "Basic Writing Reconsidered." *Journal of Basic Writing* 12.1 (Spring 1993). Special Issue: 4th National Basic Writing Conference Plenaries. 22–36.

Adelman, Clifford, ed. *Performance and Judgment: Essays on Principles and Practice in the Assessment of College Student Learning.* Washington: U.S. Dept. of Education, Office of Educational Research and Improvement, 1988.

Anderson, Benedict. *Imagined Communities: Reflections on the Origin and Spread of Nationalism.* Rev. ed. London: Verso, 1991.

Anderson, Melville B. "The Leland Stanford, Junior, University." *English in American Universities.* Ed. William Morton Payne. Boston: Heath, 1895. 49–59.

Applebee, Arthur N. *Tradition and Reform in the Teaching of English: A History.* Urbana, IL: NCTE, 1974.

Asante, Molefi. *The Afrocentric Idea.* Philadelphia: Temple UP, 1987.

Avedon, John F. *In Exile from the Land of Snows.* New York: Vintage, 1986.

Bakhtin, Mikhail. "Discourse in the Novel." *The Dialogic Imagination: Four Essays by M. M. Bakhtin.* Ed. M. Holquist. Trans. C. Emerson and M. Holquist. Austin: U of Texas P, 1981.

——. "The Problem of Speech Genres." *Speech Genres and Other Late Essays.* Ed. Michael Holquist and Caryl Emerson. Trans. Vern W. McGee. Austin: U of Texas P, 1986.

Barthes, Roland. "The Death of the Author." *Image—Music—Text.* New York: Hill, 1977. 142–8.

Bartholomae, David. "The Tidy House: Basic Writing in the American Curriculum." *Journal of Basic Writing* 12.1 (Spring 1993). Special Issue: 4th National Basic Writing Conference Plenaries. 4–21.

Baudrillard, Jean. *Selected Writings.* Ed. Mark Poster. Stanford: Stanford UP, 1988.

Bellah, Robert N., Richard Madsen, William M. Sullivan, Ann Swidler, and Steven M. Tipton. *The Good Society.* New York: Knopf, 1991.

Berkenkotter, Carol. "Paradigm Debates, Turf Wars, and the Conduct of Sociocognitive Inquiry in Composition." *College Composition and Communication* 42 (1991): 151–69.

Berkenkotter, Carol, Thomas N. Huckin, and John Ackerman. "Social Context: The Initiation of a Graduate into a Writing Research Community." *Textual Dynamics of the Professions: Historical and Contemporary Studies of Writ-*

ing in Professional Communities. Ed. Charles Bazerman and James Paradis. Madison: U of Wisconsin P, 1991. 191–215.

Berlak, Harold. "Toward the Development of a New Science of Educational Testing and Assessment." *Toward a New Science of Educational Testing and Assessment*. Ed. Howard Berlak, et al. Albany: State U of New York P, 1992. 181–206.

Berle, Gustav. *SBA Hotline Answer Book*. New York: Wiley, 1992.

———. *The Small Business Information Handbook*. New York: Wiley, 1990.

Berlin, James A. *Rhetoric and Reality: Writing Instruction in American Colleges, 1900–1985*. Carbondale: Southern Illinois UP, 1987.

———. "The Teacher as Researcher: Democracy, Dialogue, and Power." *The Writing Teacher as Researcher: Essays in the Theory and Practice of Class-Based Research*. Ed. Donald A. Daiker and Max Morenberg. Portsmouth, NH: Boynton, 1990. 3–14.

———. *Writing Instruction in Nineteenth-Century American Colleges*. Carbondale: Southern Illinois UP, 1984.

Biema, David Van. "Parodies Regained." *Time* 21 Mar. 1994: 46.

Bizzell, Patricia. "Thomas Kuhn, Scientism, and English Studies." *College English* 40 (1979): 764–71.

Bizzell, Patricia, and Bruce Herzberg. *The Rhetorical Tradition: Readings from Classical Times to the Present*. Boston: Bedford, 1990.

Black, Laurel, Donald A. Daiker, Jeffrey Sommers, and Gail Stygall. *New Directions in Portfolio Assessment: Reflective Practice, Critical Theory, and Large-Scale Scoring*. Portsmouth, NH: Heinemann, 1994.

Bledstein, Burton J. *The Culture of Professionalism: The Middle Class and the Development of Higher Education in America*. New York: Norton, 1976.

Blitz, Michael, and C. Mark Hurlbert. "Cults of Culture." *Cultural Studies in the English Classroom*. Ed. James A. Berlin and Michael J. Vivion. Portsmouth, NH: Boynton, 1992.

Blumenthal, Sidney. "The Syndicated Presidency." *New Yorker* 6 Apr. 1992: 42–7.

Bolter, Jay. "Intellectual Property and the Electronic Writing Space." Conference on Cultural Agency/Cultural Authority: Politics and Poetics of Intellectual Property in the Post-Colonial Era. Bellagio, Italy, 8–12 Mar. 1993.

Bordo, Susan. *The Flight to Objectivity: Essays on Cartesianism and Culture*. Albany: State U of New York P, 1987.

Bourdieu, Pierre. *Outline of a Theory of Practice*. Trans. Richard Nice. Cambridge: Cambridge UP, 1977.

Bové, Paul A. *Intellectuals in Power: A Genealogy of Critical Humanism*. New York: Columbia UP, 1986.

———. "The Rationality of Disciplines: The Abstract Understanding of Stephen Toulmin." *After Foucault: Humanistic Knowledge, Postmodern Challenges*. Ed. Jonathan Arac. New Brunswick, NJ: Rutgers UP, 1988. 42–70.

Bowles, Samuel, and Herbert Gintis. *Schooling in Capitalist America: Educational Reform and the Contradictions of Economic Life*. New York: Basic, 1976.

Boyle, James. "Alienated Information: The International Political Economy of Authorship." Conference on Cultural Agency/Cultural Authority: Politics and Poetics of Intellectual Property in the Post-Colonial Era. Bellagio, Italy, 8–12 Mar. 1993.

———. "A Theory of Law and Information: Copyright, Spleens, Blackmail, and Insider Trading." *California Law Review* 80.6 (Dec. 1992): 1415–540.

Braddock, Richard, Richard Lloyd-Jones, and Lowell Schoer. *Research in Written Composition*. Champaign, IL: NCTE, 1963.

Brandt, Deborah. *Literacy as Involvement: The Acts of Writers, Readers, and Texts*. Carbondale: Southern Illinois UP, 1990.

Brannon, Lil. "(Dis)missing Freshman Composition." Presentation given at CCCC. San Diego, 2 Apr. 1993.

Brown, James A. *Television "Critical Viewing Skill" Education: Major Media Literacy Projects in the United States and Selected Countries*. New York: Erlbaum, 1991.

Bruffee, Kenneth A. "On Not Listening in Order to Hear: Collaborative Learning and the Rewards of Classroom Research." *Journal of Basic Writing* 7 (1988): 3–12.

———. "Social Construction, Language, and the Authority of Knowledge: A Biographical Essay." *College English* 48 (1986): 784–90.

Bruner, Jerome S. *Acts of Meaning*. Cambridge: Harvard UP, 1990.

———. *On Knowing: Essays for the Left Hand*. Cambridge: Harvard UP, 1962.

Buber, Martin. *Between Man and Man*. Trans. Ronald Gregor Smith. Boston: Beacon, 1947. 83–103.

Burger, Julian. *Report from the Frontier: The State of the World's Indigenous Peoples*. London: Zed; Cambridge, MA: Cultural Survival, 1987.

Burke, Kenneth. *Rhetoric of Motives*. Berkeley: U of California P, 1950.

Burton, Dwight L. "Research in the Teaching of English: The Troubled Dream." *Research in the Teaching of English* 7 (1973): 160–89.

Caesar, Terry. *Conspiring with Forms: Life in Academic Texts*. Athens: U of Georgia P, 1992.

Camp, Roberta. "Changing the Model for the Direct Assessment of Writing." *Validating Holistic Scoring for Writing Assessment: Theoretical and Empirical Foundations*. Ed. Michael Williamson and Brian Huot. Cresskill, NJ: Hampton, 1993.

Campbell, Oscar James. "The Failure of Freshman English." *English Journal* 28 [College Ed.] (1939): 177–85.

Carruthers, Mary. *The Book of Memory: A Study of Memory and Medieval Culture*. Cambridge: Cambridge UP, 1990.

CCCC Committee on Assessment. *Post-Secondary Writing Assessment: An Update on Practices and Procedures*. Spring 1988. Report to the Executive Committee of the Conference on College Composition and Communication.

CCCC Executive Committee. "Statement of Principles and Standards for the Postsecondary Teaching of Writing." *College Composition and Communication* 40 (1989): 329–36.

"CCCC: Voices in the Parlor, and Responses." *Rhetoric Review* 7.1 (1988): 195–213.

Clinchy, Evans. "Needed: A Clinton Crusade for Quality and Equality." *Phi Delta Kappan* Apr. 1993: 605–12.

Coles, William E., Jr. *The Plural I: The Teaching of Writing*. New York: Holt, 1978.

Committee on National Interest. *The National Interest and the Teaching of English: A Report on the Status of the Profession*. Champaign, IL: NCTE, 1961.

Connors, Robert J. "Composition Studies and Science." *College English* 45 (1983): 1–20.

——. "Rhetoric in the Modern University: The Creation of an Underclass." *The Politics of Writing Instruction: Postsecondary*. Ed. Richard Bullock and John Trimbur. Portsmouth, NH: Boynton, 1991. 55–84.

——. "Textbooks and the Evaluation of the Discipline." *College Composition and Communication* 37 (1986): 178–94.

"The Conversation Continues: *Voices in the Parlor*." *Rhetoric Review* 7 (1989): 406–8.

Covino, William. *Forms of Wondering*. Portsmouth, NH: Boynton, 1990.

Cronbach, Lee J. "Five Perspectives on the Validity Argument." *Test Validity*. Ed. Harold Wainer and Henry J. Braun. Hillside, NJ: Erlbaum, 1989. 3–17.

Crowley, Sharon. *The Methodical Memory: Invention in Current-Traditional Rhetoric*. Carbondale: Southern Illinois UP, 1990.

——. "A Personal Essay on Freshman English." *Pre/Text* 12 (1991): 156–76.

Cutuly, Joan. *Home of the Wildcats*. Urbana, IL: NCTE, 1993.

Daggett, Willard R. *Preparing Students for the 1990s and Beyond*. Schenectady, NY: International Center for Leadership in Education, 1992.

Darling-Hammond, Linda. "Reframing the School Reform Agenda." *Phi Delta Kappan* June 1993: 752–61.

Deemer, Charles. "English Composition as a Happening." *College English* 29 (1967): 121–6.

Defoe, Daniel. *The Review*. 2 Feb. 1710. Rpt. in *Defoe's Review*. Reproduced from the Original Editions. Ed. Arthur Wellesley. Secord, NY: Columbia UP for the Fascile Text Society, 1938.

Delpit, Lisa D. "Skills and Other Dilemmas of a Progressive Black Educator." *Harvard Educational Review* 56 (1986): 379–85.

Dewey, John. *John Dewey on Education: Selected Writings*. Ed. Reginald Archambault. Chicago: U of Chicago P, 1964.

Dixon, John. *Growth Through English*. London: Oxford UP, 1967.

Dixon, Robert. "Intersections, Vectors, and Friction." Student paper, 1992.

Donahue, Patricia, and Ellen Quandahl. *Reclaiming Pedagogy: The Rhetoric of the Classroom*. Carbondale: Southern Illinois UP, 1989.

Durst, Russel K. Rev. of *Methods and Methodology in Composition Research*, ed. Gesa Kirsch and Patricia A. Sullivan. *College Composition and Communication* 44 (1993): 260–2.

Dyson, Anne Haas, and Sarah Warshauer Freedman. *Critical Challenges for Research in Writing: 1990–1995*. CSW Technical Report 1B. Berkeley: National Center for the Study of Writing and Literacy, 1991.

Elbow, Peter. "Trying to Teach While Thinking about the End: Teaching in a Competence-Based Curriculum." *On Competence: A Critical Analysis of Competence-Based Reforms in Higher Education*. Ed. Gerald Grant, et al. San Francisco: Jossey-Bass, 1979.

——. *What is English?* New York: MLA, 1990.

Elbow, Peter, and Pat Belanoff. "State University of New York at Stony Brook: Portfolio-Based Evaluation Program." *New Methods in College Writing Programs: Theory Into Practice*. Ed. Paul Connolly and Theresa Vilardi. New

York: MLA, 1986. 95–105. Rpt. in *Portfolios: Process and Product*. Ed. Pat Belanoff and Marcia Dickson. Portsmouth, NH: Heinemann, 1991. 1–16.

Eldred, Janet, and Peter Mortensen. "Reading Literacy Narratives." *College English* 54 (1992): 512–39.

Emig, Janet. *The Composing Processes of Twelfth Graders*. Urbana, IL: NCTE, 1971.

——. "The Tacit Tradition: The Inevitability of a Multi-Disciplinary Approach to Writing Research." *Reinventing the Rhetorical Tradition*. Ed. Aviva Freedman and Ian Pringle. Conway, AK: L & S, 1980. 9–18.

——. "The Uses of the Unconscious in Composing." *College Composition and Communication* 15 (1964): 6–11.

Enos, Theresa. "Gender and Journals, Conservators or Innovators." *Pre/Text* 9 (1990): 209–14.

Erasmus. "De Pueris Instituendis." Trans. Beert C. Verstraete. *Collected Works of Erasmus*. Ed. J. K. Sowards. Vol. 26. Toronto: Toronto UP, 1985. 291–346.

Erickson, Frederick. "School Literacy, Reasoning, and Civility: An Anthropologist's Perspective." *Perspectives on Literacy*. Ed. Eugene R. Kintgen, Barry M. Kroll, and Mike Rose. Carbondale: Southern Illinois UP, 1988. 205–26.

Eurich, Alvin C. "Should Freshman Composition Be Abolished?" *English Journal* 21 [College Ed.] (1932): 211–9.

Faigley, Lester. "Competing Theories of Process: A Critique and a Proposal." *College English* 48 (1986): 527–42.

——. *Fragments of Rationality: Postmodernity and the Subject of Composition*. Pittsburgh: U of Pittsburgh P, 1992.

Faigley, Lester, Roger Cherry, David A. Jolliffe, and Anna M. Skinner. *Assessing Writers' Knowledge and Processes of Composing*. Norwood, NJ: Ablex, 1985.

Flower, Linda. "Cognition, Context, and Theory Building." *College Composition and Communication* 40 (1989): 282–311.

——. *The Construction of Negotiated Meaning: A Social Cognitive Theory of Writing*. Carbondale: Southern Illinois UP, 1994.

Flower, Linda, David L. Wallace, Linda Norris, and Rebecca E. Burnett, eds. *Making Thinking Visible: Writing, Collaborative Planning, and Classroom Inquiry*. Urbana, IL: NCTE, 1994.

Ford, Richard. "What We Write, Why We Write It, and Who Cares." *Cultural Vistas* newsletter. Summer 1993.

Foucault, Michel. *Discipline and Punish: The Birth of the Prison*. Trans. Alan Sheridan. New York: Vintage, 1979.

——. *The Order of Things: An Archaeology of the Human Sciences*. New York: Pantheon, 1970.

——. *Power/Knowledge: Selected Interviews and Other Writings, 1972–1977*. Ed. Colin Gordon. New York: Pantheon, 1980.

——. "What Is an Author?" *Textual Strategies: Perspectives in Post-Structuralist Criticism*. Ed. Josue V. Harari. Ithaca: Cornell UP, 1979. 141–60.

Freedman, Aviva. "Show and Tell? The Role of Explicit Teaching in the Learning of New Genres." *Research in the Teaching of English* 27 (1993): 222–51.

——. "Situating Genre: A Rejoinder." *Research in the Teaching of English* 27 (1993): 272–81.

Freedman, Sarah Warshauer. *Exchanging Writing, Exchanging Cultures: Lessons in School Reform from the United States and Great Britain.* Cambridge: Harvard UP, 1994.

Freedman, Sarah Warshauer, Anne Haas Dyson, Linda Flower, and Wallace Chafe. *Research in Writing: Past, Present, and Future.* CSW Technical Report 1. Berkeley: University of California National Center for the Study of Writing, 1987.

Freeman, Lisa. "Point of View." *Chronicle of Higher Education* 28 Apr. 1993: A44.

Gee, James Paul. "Literacy, Discourse, and Linguistics: Introduction." *Journal of Education* 171 (1989): 5–17.

Geertz, Clifford. "Deep Play: Notes on the Balinese Cock Fight." *Daedalus* 101 (1972): 1–37.

Genome Patent Working Group, Committee on Life Sciences and Health, and Federal Coordinating Council for Science, Engineering and Technology. "Federally Funded Genome Research: Science and Technology Transfer Issues." Proceedings of a public meeting. Washington, DC, 21 May 1992.

Gere, Anne Ruggles. "Kitchen Tables and Rented Rooms: The Extracurriculum of Composition." *College Composition and Communication* 45 (1994): 75–92.

———. "Written Composition: Toward a Theory of Evaluation." *College English* 42 (1980): 44–58.

———, ed. *Into the Field: Sites of Composition Studies.* New York: MLA, 1993.

Giddens, Anthony. *The Nation State and Violence.* Berkeley and Los Angeles: U of California P, 1985. Vol. 2 of *A Contemporary Critique of Historical Materialism.* 3 vols. 1981–   .

Godzich, Wlad. *The Culture of Literacy.* Cambridge: Harvard UP, 1994.

Goodlad, John I. "On Taking School Reform Seriously." *Phi Delta Kappan* Nov. 1992: 232–40.

Gorrell, Robert. "The Traditional Course: When Is Old Hat New?" *College Composition and Communication* 23 (1972): 264–70.

Graff, Gerald. *Beyond the Culture Wars: How Teaching the Conflicts Can Revitalize American Education.* New York: Norton, 1992.

———. *Professing Literature: An Institutional History.* Chicago: U of Chicago P, 1987.

Grant, Gerald, et al. *On Competence: A Critical Analysis of Competence-Based Reforms in Higher Education.* San Francisco: Jossey-Bass, 1979.

Green, Andrew J. "The Reform of Freshman English." *College English* 2 (1941): 593–602.

Greenbaum, Leonard. "The Tradition of Complaint." *College English* 31 (1969): 174–87.

Greenberg, Karen. "The Politics of Basic Writing." *Journal of Basic Writing* 12.1 (Spring 1993). Special Issue: 4th National Basic Writing Conference Plenaries. 64–71.

———. "Validity and Reliability: Issues in the Direct Assessment of Writing." *WPA: Writing Program Administration* 16.1–2 (Fall/Winter 1992): 7–22.

Greenberg, Karen, Harvey Wiener, and Richard Donovan, eds. *Writing Assessment: Issues and Strategies.* New York: Longman, 1986.

Greenwald, John. "Bellboys with B.A.s." *Time* 22 Nov. 1993: 36–7.

Grego, Rhonda, and Nancy Thompson. "The Writing Studio Program: Reconfiguring Basic Writing/Freshman Composition." *WPA: Writing Program Administration*, forthcoming.

———. "Repositioning Remediation: Renegotiating Composition's Work in the Academy." *College Composition and Communication*, forthcoming.

Guba, Evon G., and Yvonna S. Lincoln. *Fourth Generation Evaluation*. Newbury Park, CA: Sage, 1989.

Hairston, Maxine. "Diversity, Ideology, and Teaching Writing." *College Composition and Communication* 43 (1992): 179–93.

———. "The Winds of Change: Thomas Kuhn and the Revolution in the Teaching of Writing." *College Composition and Communication* 33 (1982): 76–88.

Hall, Stuart, and Martin Jacques, eds. *New Times: The Changing Face of Politics in the 1990s*. London: Verso, 1989.

Halloran, S. Michael. "Rhetoric in the American College Curriculum: The Decline of Public Discourse." *Pre/Text* 3 (1983): 245–69.

Harkin, Patricia. "Bringing Lore to Light." *Pre/Text* 10 (1989): 55–67.

———. "The Postdisciplinary Politics of Lore." *Contending with Words: Composition and Rhetoric in a Postmodern Age*. Ed. Patricia Harkin and John Schilb. New York: MLA, 1991. 124–38.

Harvard Committee on the Objectives of a General Education in a Free Society. *General Education in a Free Society*. Cambridge: Harvard UP, 1945.

Harvey, David. *The Conditions of Postmodernity*. Oxford: Blackwell, 1989.

Haswell, Richard. *Gaining Ground in College Writing*. Dallas: Southern Methodist UP, 1991.

Haswell, Richard, and Susan Wyche-Smith. "Adventuring into Writing Assessment." *College Composition and Communication* 45 (1994): 220–36.

Heath, Shirley Brice. "Protean Shapes in Literacy Events: Ever-Shifting Oral and Literate Traditions." *Perspectives on Literacy*. Ed. Eugene R. Kintgen, Barry M. Kroll, and Mike Rose. Carbondale: Southern Illinois UP, 1988. 348–70.

———. *Ways with Words: Language, Life, and Work in Communities and Classrooms*. New York: Cambridge UP, 1983.

Heath, Shirley Brice, and Juliet Langman. "Shared Thinking and the Register of Coaching." *Perspectives on Register: Situating Register Variation Within Sociolinguistics*. Ed. S. Biber and E. Finegan. Oxford: Oxford UP, 1994.

Heath, Shirley Brice, and Milbrey W. McLaughlin. *Identity and Inner-City Youth: Beyond Ethnicity and Gender*. New York: Teachers College P, Columbia U, 1992.

Heilbroner, Robert. *21st Century Capitalism*. New York: Norton, 1993.

Herrington, Anne. "The First Twenty Years of *Research in the Teaching of English* and the Growth of a Research Community in Composition Studies." *Research in the Teaching of English* 23 (1989): 117–38.

Hill, Adams S. "An Answer to the Cry for More English." *Twenty Years of School and College English*. Ed. Adams S. Hill. Cambridge: Harvard UP, 1896. 6–16.

Hilliard, Asa. "Do We Have the Will to Educate All Children?" *Educational Leadership* 49.1 (Sept. 1991): 32–7.

Hillocks, George. *Research on Written Composition*. Urbana, IL: NCTE, 1986.

Hirsch, E. D. *Cultural Literacy: What Every American Needs to Know*. Boston: Houghton, 1987.

———. *The Philosophy of Composition*. Chicago: U of Chicago P, 1977.

Holbrook, Sue Ellen. "Women's Work: The Feminizing of Composition." *Rhetoric Review* 9 (1991): 201–29.

Hoover, Regina M. "Taps for Freshman English?" *College Composition and Communication* 25 (1974): 149–54.

Hoskin, Keith. "Education and the Genesis of Disciplinarity: The Unexpected Reversal." *Knowledges: Historical and Critical Studies in Disciplinarity*. Ed. Ellen Messer-Davidow, David R. Shumway, and David J. Sylvan. Charlottesville: UP of Virginia, 1993.

Hull, Glenda, Mike Rose, Kay Losey Fraser, and Marisa Castellano. "Remediation as a Social Construct: Perspectives from an Analysis of Classroom Discourse." *College Composition and Communication* 42 (1991): 299–329.

Integrity in College Curriculums. Washington: Association of American Colleges, 1985.

"Intellectual Property and the Construction of Authorship." Special issue of *Cardozo Arts and Entertainment Law Journal* 10.2 (1992).

Irlen, Harvey Stuart. "Toward Confronting Freshmen." *College Composition and Communication* 21 (1970): 35–40.

Jaeger, Richard M. "Weak Measurement Serving Presumptive Policy." *Phi Delta Kappan* Oct. 1992: 118–28.

Jameson, Fredric. "Postmodernism or the Cultural Logic of Late Capitalism." *New Left Review* 146 (1984): 53–93.

Jarratt, Susan C. *Rereading the Sophists: Classical Rhetoric Refigured*. Carbondale: Southern Illinois UP, 1991.

Jaszi, Peter. "Toward a Theory of Copyright: The Metamorphoses of 'Authorship.' " *Duke Law Journal* 2 (1991): 455–502.

Jaszi, Peter, and Martha Woodmansee. "The Law of Texts: Copyright in the Academy." MLA Convention. New York, Dec. 1992.

Johnson, Richard. "Ten Theses on a Monday Morning." *Education Limited: Schooling and Training and the New Right Since 1979*. Ed. Education Group 2, Cultural Studies, University of Birmingham. London: Unwin Hyman, 1991. 307–21.

Johnston, Peter. "Constructive Evaluation and the Improvement of Teaching and Learning." *Teachers College Record* 90 (1989): 509–28.

Jolliffe, David. "Three Arguments for Sophomore English." Presentation given at CCCC. San Diego, 2 Apr. 1993.

Jones, William. "Basic Writing: Pushing Against Racism." *Journal of Basic Writing* 12.1 (Spring 1993). Special Issue: 4th National Basic Writing Conference Plenaries. 72–80.

Kennedy, X. J., Dorothy M. Kennedy, and Sylvia A. Holladay. *The Bedford Guide for College Writers*. 3rd ed. Boston: Bedford, 1993.

Kidda, Michael, Joseph Turner, and Frank E. Parker. "There *Is* an Alternative to Remedial Education." *Metropolitan Universities* 3.3 (Spring 1993): 16–25.

Kirsch, Gesa. *Women Writing the Academy: Audience, Authority, and Transformation*. Carbondale: Southern Illinois UP, 1993.

Kirsch, Gesa, and Patricia A. Sullivan, eds. *Methods and Methodology in Composition Research*. Carbondale: Southern Illinois UP, 1992.

Kirsch, Sandra. "The Job Drought." *Fortune* 24 Aug. 1992: 62–74.

Kitzhaber, Albert R. "Death—or Transfiguration?" *College English* 21 (1960): 367–78.

Kraybill, Donald B. "Negotiating with Caesar." *The Amish and the State.* Ed. Donald B. Kraybill. Baltimore: Johns Hopkins UP, 1993. 3–20.

Kreisberg, S. *Transforming Power: Domination, Empowerment, and Education.* Albany: State U of New York P, 1992.

Kuhn, Thomas. *The Structure of Scientific Revolutions.* Chicago: Chicago UP, 1962.

Kytle, Ray. "Pre-Writing by Analysis." *College Composition and Communication* 21 (1970): 380–5.

Laird, Charlton. "Freshman English During the Flood." *College English* 18 (1956): 131–8.

Larson, Magali Sarfatti. *The Rise of Professionalism: A Sociological Analysis.* Berkeley: U of California P, 1977.

Lauer, Janice M., and J. William Asher. *Composition Research: Empirical Designs.* New York: Oxford UP, 1988.

Lederman, Marie Jean, Susan Ryzewic, and Michael Ribaudo. *Assessment and Improvement of the Academic Skills of Entering Freshmen: A National Survey.* New York: CUNY Instructional Resource Center, 1983.

LeFevre, Karen Burke. *Invention as a Social Act.* Carbondale: Southern Illinois UP, 1987.

———. "The Tell-Tale 'Heart': Determining 'Fair' Use of Unpublished Texts." *Law and Contemporary Problems* 55.2 (1992).

Lehman, Bruce A. *Intellectual Property and the National Information Infrastructure: A Preliminary Draft of the Report of the Working Group on Intellectual Property Rights.* Washington: GPO, 1994.

Lindholm, William C. "The National Committee for Amish Religious Freedom." *The Amish and the State.* Ed. Donald B. Kraybill. Baltimore: Johns Hopkins UP, 1993. 109–23.

Lloyd-Jones, Richard. "Who We Were, Who We Should Become." *College Composition and Communication* 4 (1992): 486–96.

Locke, John. *Two Treatises of Government,* 1690. Ed. Peter Laslett. London: Cambridge UP, 1967.

Lounsbury, Thomas R. "Compulsory Composition in Colleges." *Harper's Monthly* 123 (Nov. 1911): 866–80.

Lunsford, Andrea A. "Composing Ourselves: Politics, Commitment, and the Teaching of Writing." *College Composition and Communication* 41 (1990): 71–82.

———. "Reconstructing Authority and Intellectual Property." MLA Convention. New York, Dec. 1992.

Lunsford, Andrea A., and Lisa Ede. *Singular Texts/Plural Authors: Perspectives on Collaborative Writing.* Carbondale: Southern Illinois UP, 1990.

Lutz, William. "Making Freshman English a Happening." *College Composition and Communication* 22 (1971): 35–8.

Lytle, Susan, and Marilyn Cochran-Smith. *Inside-Outside: Teacher Research and Knowledge.* New York: Teachers College P, Columbia U, 1992.

LZB. "The Conversation Continues: *Voices in the Parlor." Rhetoric Review* 7 (1989): 407–8.

Mahin, Helen Ogden. "The Study of English Composition as a Means to Fuller Living." *English Journal* 4 (1915): 445–50.

Markoff, John. "Building the Electronic Superhighway." *New York Times* 24 Jan. 1993: sec. 3, pg. 1.

McClelland, Ben W., and Timothy R. Donovan. *Perspectives on Research and Scholarship in Composition*. New York: MLA, 1985.

McDonald, Robert L. "Interview with Gary Tate." *Composition Studies* 20.2 (1992): 36–50.

McHenry, Elizabeth, and Shirley Brice Heath. "The Literate and the Literary: African Americans as Writers and Readers, 1830–1940." *Written Communication* 11.4 (1994): 419–44.

McLaughlin, Milbrey W., Merita Irby, and Juliet Langman. *Inner-city Sanctuaries*. San Francisco: Jossey-Bass, 1994.

McRobbie, Angela. "Dance and Social Fantasy." *Gender and Generation*. Ed. Angela McRobbie and Mica Nava. London: Macmillan, 1984. 130–61.

Merges, Robert. "Review of Patenting/Licensing Laws as Related to Genome Research." Proceedings of a public meeting. Washington, DC, 21 May 1992.

Merton, Robert. *The Sociology of Science*. Ed. Norman W. Storer. Chicago: U of Chicago P, 1973.

Messick, Samuel. "Meaning and Values in Test Validation: The Science and Ethics of Assessment." *Educational Researcher* 18.2 (1989): 5–11.

Miller, Faye. "Literacy, Perception, and Mutual Support." Student paper, 1992.

Miller, J. Hillis. "Composition and Decomposition: Deconstruction and the Teaching of Writing." *Composition and Literature: Bridging the Gap*. Ed. Winifred Bryan Horner. Chicago: U of Chicago P, 1983. 38–56.

Miller, Susan. "The Feminization of Composition." *The Politics of Writing Instruction: Postsecondary*. Ed. Richard Bullock and John Trimbur. Portsmouth, NH: Boynton, 1991. 39–53.

———. *Textual Carnivals: The Politics of Composition*. Carbondale: Southern Illinois UP, 1991.

Mills, Barriss. "Writing as Process." *College English* 15 (1953): 19–26.

Monoghan, E. Jennifer. "Literacy Instruction and Gender in Colonial New England." *Reading in America: Literature and Social History*. Ed. Cathy N. Davidson. Baltimore: Johns Hopkins UP, 1989. 53–80.

Moss, Pamela A. "Shifting Conceptions of Validity in Educational Measurement: Implications for Performative Assessment." *Review of Educational Research* 62 (1992): 229–58.

Murphy, Sandra, et al. *Survey of Postsecondary Writing Assessment Practices*. Report to the CCCC Executive Committee, 1993.

Murray, Robin. "Fordism and Post-Fordism." *New Times: The Changing Face of Politics in the 1990s*. Ed. Stuart Hall and Martin Jacques. London: Verso, 1989.

Nabokov, Peter. "To Learn Another Way." *Native American Testimony: A Chronicle of Indian-White Relations from Prophecy to the Present, 1492–1992*. Ed. Peter Nabokov. New York: Viking, 1991. 213–31.

A Nation at Risk: The Imperative for Education Reform. Washington: National Commission on Excellence in Education, 1983.

Nelson, Marie Wilson. *At the Point of Need*. Portsmouth, NH: Boynton, 1991.

Newkirk, Thomas. "The Politics of Composition Research: The Conspiracy Against Experience." *The Politics of Writing Instruction: Postsecondary*. Ed. Richard Bullock and John Trimbur. Portsmouth, NH: Boynton, 1991. 119–35.

Newman, Katherine S. *Declining Fortunes: The Withering of the American Dream*. New York: Basic, 1993.

North, Stephen M. *The Making of Knowledge in Composition: Portrait of an Emerging Field*. Upper Montclair, NJ: Boynton, 1987.

Oakes, Jeannie. *Keeping Track: How Schools Structure Inequality*. New Haven: Yale UP, 1985.

Ogbu, John U. "Understanding Cultural Diversity and Learning." *Educational Researcher* 21.8 (1992): 5–14.

Ohmann, Richard. *English in America*. New York: Oxford UP, 1975.

Oja, Sharon Nodie, and Lisa Smulyan. *Collaborative Action Research: A Developmental Approach*. London: Falmer, 1989.

Olson, David R. "From Utterance to Text: The Bias of Language in Speech and Writing." *Perspectives on Literacy*. Ed. Eugene R. Kintgen, Barry M. Kroll, and Mike Rose. Carbondale: Southern Illinois UP, 1988. 175–89.

Parnell, Dale. *Dateline 2000: The New Higher Education Agenda*. Washington: Community College P, 1990.

Payne, William Morton, ed. *English in American Universities*. Boston: Heath, 1895.

Pearce, Fred. "Science and Technology: Bargaining for the Life of the Forest." *Independent* 17 Mar. 1991: 37.

Peck, Wayne C. "Community Advocacy: Composing for Action." Diss. Carnegie Mellon U, 1991. Abstract in *DAI* 431 (1992): 53/02A.

Peck, Wayne C., Linda Flower, and Lorraine Higgins. "Community Literacy." *College Composition and Communication* 46 (1995): in press.

Phelps, Louise Wetherbee. *Composition as a Human Science*. New York: Oxford UP, 1988.

Plato. *Symposium*. *The Collected Dialogues of Plato*. Ed. Edith Hamilton and Huntington Cairns. Bollingen Ser. New York: Pantheon, 1963. 526–74.

Porter, Dorothy. "The Organized Educational Activities of Negro Literary Societies, 1828–1846." *Journal of Negro Education* 5 (1936): 555–76.

Posey, Darrell Addison. "Intellectual Property Rights and Indigenous Knowledge: Problems of Implementing a Global Policy on Environment and Development." Conference on Cultural Agency/Cultural Authority: Politics and Poetics of Intellectual Property in the Post-Colonial Era. Bellagio, Italy, 8–12 Mar. 1993.

Pratt, Mary Louise. "Arts of the Contact Zone." *Profession 91*. New York: MLA, 1991. 33–40.

———. "Linguistic Utopias." *The Linguistics of Writing*. Ed. Nigel Fabb, et al. Manchester: Manchester UP, 1987. 48–66.

Pula, Judith J., and Brian Huot. "A Model of Background Influences on Holistic Raters." *Validating Holistic Scoring for Writing Assessment: Theoretical and Empirical Foundations*. Ed. Michael M. Williamson and Brian Huot. Cresskill, NJ: Hampton, 1993.

Puttenham, George. *The Arte of English Poesie*. Ed. Gladys D. Willock and Alice Walker. Cambridge: Cambridge UP, 1938.

Ravitz, Diane. "Launching a Revolution in Standards and Assessments." *Phi Delta Kappan* June 1993: 767–72.

Rice, Warner G. "A Proposal for the Abolition of Freshman English, As It Is Now Commonly Taught, from the College Curriculum." *College English* 21 (1960): 361–7.

RJC. "CCCC: Voices in the Parlor, and Responses." *Rhetoric Review* 7 (1988): 211–3.

Rodby, Judith. "Testing Our Ideas of Literacy." Unpublished MS. Department of English, California State U-Chico.

Rohman, D. Gordon. "Pre-Writing: The Stage of Discovery in the Writing Process." *College Composition and Communication* 16 (1965): 106–12.

Rohman, D. Gordon, and Albert O. Wlecke. "The Construction and Application of Models for Concept Formation in Writing." U.S. Office of Education Cooperative Research Project Number 2174.

Rose, Mark. *Authors and Owners: The Invention of Copyright*. Cambridge: Harvard UP, 1993.

Rose, Mike. "Education Standards Must Be Reclaimed for Democratic Ends." *Chronicle of Higher Education* 3 July 1991: A32.

——. "The Language of Exclusion: Writing Instruction at the University." *College English* 47 (1985): 341–59.

——. *Lives on the Boundary: The Struggles and Achievements of America's Underprepared*. New York: Free, 1989.

Rudolph, Frederick. *The American College and University: A History*. New York: Knopf, 1962.

Ruppert, Peter. *Reader in a Strange Land: The Activity of Reading Literary Utopias*. Athens: U of Georgia P, 1986.

Russell, David R. "Romantics on Writing: Liberal Culture and the Abolition of Composition Courses." *Rhetoric Review* 6 (1988): 132–48.

Sampson, Martin W. "The University of Indiana." *English in American Universities*. Ed. William Morton Payne. Boston: Heath, 1895. 92–8.

Samuelson, Pamela. "Writing As a Technology." Conference on Cultural Agency/Cultural Authority: Politics and Poetics of Intellectual Property in the Post-Colonial Era. Bellagio, Italy, 8–12 Mar. 1993.

Sandroff, Ronni. "The Psychology of Change." *Working Woman* July 1993: 52–6.

Schofield, Roger. "Dimensions of Illiteracy in England 1750–1850." *Literacy and Social Development in the West*. Ed. Harvey Graff. New York: Cambridge UP, 1981. 201–13.

Scholes, Robert. *Textual Power: Literary Theory and the Teaching of English*. New Haven: Yale UP, 1985.

Schuster, Charles I. "Toward Abolishing Composition." Presentation at CCCC. San Diego, 2 Apr. 1993.

Scribner, Sylvia, and Michael Cole. *The Psychology of Literacy*. Cambridge: Harvard UP, 1981.

Shepherd, Lucile. "Discussions: Prescribed English in College." *Educational Review* 46 (1913): 188–90.

Sherwood, John C. "The Oregon Experiment: A Final Report." *College Composition and Communication* 9 (1958): 5–9.

Siegel, Bernie. *Love, Medicine, and Miracles: Lessons Learned about Self-Healing from a Surgeon's Experience with Exceptional Patients.* New York: Harper, 1986.

Slevin, James. *The Next Generation: Preparing Graduate Students for the Professional Responsibilities of College Teachers.* Washington: Association of American Colleges, 1992.

Slosson, Preston William. "Discussions: Prescribed English in College." *Educational Review* 45 (1913): 407–9.

Smith, Page. *Killing the Spirit.* New York: Viking, 1990.

Smith, Ron. "The Composition Requirement Today: A Report on a Nationwide Survey of Four-Year Colleges and Universities." *College Composition and Communication* 25 (1974): 138–48.

Smith, William L. "Assessing the Reliability and Adequacy of Using Holistic Scoring of Essays as a College Composition Placement Program Technique." *Validating Holistic Scoring for Writing Assessment: Theoretical and Empirical Foundations.* Ed. Michael Williamson and Brian Huot. Cresskill, NJ: Hampton, 1993.

———. "The Importance of Teacher Knowledge in College Composition Placement Testing." *Reading Empirical Research Studies: The Rhetoric of Research.* Ed. John R. Hayes, et al. Hillsdale, NJ: Erlbaum, 1992. 289–313.

Smitherman, Geneva. *Talkin' and Testifyin': The Language of Black America.* Detroit: Wayne State UP, 1986.

Spellmeyer, Kurt. *Common Ground: Dialogue, Understanding, and the Teaching of Writing.* Englewood Cliffs, NJ: Prentice, 1993.

Stallman, Richard. "Against User Interface Copyright." *Communications of the ACM.* Nov. 1990: 15–18.

Stedman, N. A. "Discussions: Prescribed English in College." *Educational Review* 46 (1913): 52–7.

Sterling, Dorothy. *We Are Your Sisters: Black Women in the Nineteenth Century.* New York: Norton, 1984.

Strong, George. "Discussions: Prescribed English in College." *Educational Review* 45 (1913): 189.

"Study Says Half of Adults in U.S. Can't Read or Handle Arithmetic." *New York Times* 9 Sept. 1993: A1.

"Symposium on *The Teaching of College English.*" *English Journal* 24 [College Ed.] (1935): 573–86.

Taylor, Warner. "Should Freshman Composition Be Abolished?" *English Journal* 21 [College Ed.] (1932): 301–11.

Terrell, Mary Church. Manuscript Collection. Library of Congress.

Toffler, Alvin. "L.A.'s Lesson for the World." *World Monitor* 5.6 (June 1992): 13–6.

Trimbur, John. "Consensus and Difference in Collaborative Learning." *College English* 51 (1989): 602–16.

United States. *Biennial Survey of Education in the United States 1944–46.* Washington: GPO, 1950.

———. *The State of Small Business: A Report of the President.* Washington: GPO, 1990.

———. Dept. of Commerce. *Statistical Abstract of the United States, 1992.* Washington: GPO, 1992.

——. Dept. of Health, Education, and Welfare/Education Division. *Digest of Educational Statistics.* 1974 ed. Washington: GPO, 1974.

Voss, Richard. "Janet Emig's Composition Processes of Twelfth-Graders: A Reassessment." *College Composition and Communication* 34 (1983): 278–83.

Vygotsky, Lev S. *Mind in Society: The Development of Higher Psychological Processes.* Cambridge: Harvard UP, 1978.

White, Edward M. "An Apologia for the Timed Impromptu Essay Test." *College Composition and Communication* 46 (1995): 28–43.

——. "Assessing Higher-Order Thinking and Communication Skills in College Graduates Through Writing." *JGE: The Journal of General Education* 42 (1993): 105–22.

——. "Language and Reality in Writing Assessment." *College Composition and Communication* 41 (1990): 187–200.

——. "Portfolios as an Assessment Concept." *New Directions in Portfolio Assessment: Reflective Practice, Critical Theory, and Large-Scale Scoring.* Ed. Laurel Black, et al. Portsmouth, NH: Heinemann, 1994.

——. *Teaching and Assessing Writing.* 2nd ed. San Francisco: Jossey-Bass, 1994.

Williams, Raymond. *The Long Revolution.* New York: Columbia UP, 1961.

Williamson, Michael, and Brian Huot, eds. *Validating Holistic Scoring for Writing Assessment: Theoretical and Empirical Foundations.* Cresskill, NJ: Hampton, 1993.

Willinsky, John. *The New Literacy: Redefining Reading and Writing in the Schools.* New York: Routledge, 1990.

Wilson, David L. "Electronic Riches Are Free on the Internet, but Some Worry about the Consequences." *Chronicle of Higher Education* 28 July 1993: A18, A20–21.

The Wingspread Group on Higher Education. *An American Imperative: Higher Expectations for Higher Education.* Racine, WI: Johnson Foundation, 1993.

Witte, Stephen. "Context, Text, Intertext: Toward a Constructivist Semiotic of Writing." *Written Communication* 9.2 (1992): 237–308.

The Wizard of Oz. Dir. Victor Fleming. With Judy Garland, Frank Morgan, and Toto. MGM, 1939.

Woodmansee, Martha. "The Genius and the Copyright: Economic and Legal Conditions of the Emergence of the 'Author.' " *Eighteenth Century Studies* 17 (1984): 425.

"Workplace Literacy Gap." *Christian Science Monitor* 15 Oct. 1992: 9.

"Workshop Proceedings." Higher Order Thinking and Communications Skills Study Design Workshop. Arlington, VA, 17–19 Nov. 1991. Washington: U.S. Department of Education, Office of Educational Research and Improvement, 1991.

World Intellectual Property Organization. *Background Reading on Intellectual Property.* N.p.: n.p., 1988.

——. "General Information and Provisional Program." WIPO Worldwide Symposium on the Impact of Digital Technology on Copyright and Neighbouring Rights. Harvard University, 31 Mar.–2 Apr. 1993.

Young, Richard E. "Invention: A Topographical Survey." *Teaching Composition: Ten Bibliographical Essays.* Ed. Gary Tate. Fort Worth: Texas Christian UP, 1976. 1–43.

———. "Paradigms and Problems: Needed Research in Rhetorical Invention." *Research on Composing*. Ed. Charles Cooper and Lee Odell. Urbana, IL: NCTE, 1978. 29–47.

Zavarzadeh, Mas'ud, and Donald Morton. "A Very Good Idea Indeed: The (Post)Modern Labor Force and Curricular Reform." *Cultural Studies in the English Classroom*. Ed. James A. Berlin and Michael J. Vivion. Portsmouth, NH: Boynton, 1992.

Zigrosser, Carl. "Discussions: Prescribed English in College." *Educational Review* 45 (1913): 187–8.

Zook, Jim. "Washington Update." *Chronicle of Higher Education* 4 Aug. 1993: A20.

Contributors

David Bartholomae is a professor of English and former Director of Composition at the University of Pittsburgh. He is founder and coeditor of the Pittsburgh Series in Composition, Literacy, and Culture. He served as chair of CCCC and chaired the second MLA Literacy Conference. He has written widely on composition and the cultural and institutional contexts of English. With Anthony Petrosky, he is coauthor/editor of *Facts, Artifacts, Counterfacts: Theory and Method for a Reading and Writing Course* (1986), *The Teaching of Writing* (1986), and *Ways of Reading* (1993).

James A. Berlin was a professor of English at Purdue University. He taught elementary school and directed both the Kansas Writing Project and a composition program. His writing included two histories of *Writing Instruction in American Colleges, Nineteenth Century* (1984) and *1900–1985* (1987), and "Rhetoric, Poetic, and Culture: Contested Boundaries in English Studies" (1991).

Lynn Z. Bloom is a professor of English and holds the Aetna Chair of Writing at the University of Connecticut. She is past president of WPA. Her publications range from *Doctor Spock* (1972) to "Teaching College English as a Woman" (1992) and *Fact and Artifact: Writing Nonfiction* (1994).

Miriam T. Chaplin is a professor of English education at Rutgers University in Camden. She has been president of the National Council of Teachers of English and chair of the Conference on College Composition and Communication, as well as project director of the NCTE-sponsored Intercontinental Staff Development Program. She was a visiting scholar at the Educational Testing Service from 1986 to 1988. She has written *Reading Comes to College* (1978), contributed to *Tapping Potential: English Language Arts for the Black Learner* (1985), and coedited *Opening the American Mind* (1993).

Robert J. Connors, an associate professor of English at the University of New Hampshire, is the author of numerous articles on rhetorical history and theory and coeditor of the award-winning *Essays on Classical Rhetoric and Modern Discourse* (1984). He is coauthor of *The St. Martin's Handbook* (1989) and *The St. Martin's Guide to Teaching Writing* (1989). He has edited the *Selected Essays of Edward P. J.*

Corbett (1989) and is currently working on a book, *Composition-Rhetoric*, and an anthology of landmark articles in composition history.

Sharon Crowley is a professor of rhetoric at the University of Iowa. Among her publications are *A Teacher's Guide to Deconstruction* (1989) and *The Methodical Memory: Invention in Current-Traditional Rhetoric* (1990).

Donald A. Daiker teaches courses in composition, American literature, and the teaching of writing at Miami University. He is the coauthor/editor of *Sentence Combining: A Rhetorical Perspective* (1985), *Literature: Options for Reading and Writing* (1989), *The Writing Teacher as Researcher* (1990), *Handbook of Writing Portfolio Assessment* (1992), *The Writer's Options* (1994), and *New Directions in Portfolio Assessment* (1994).

Peter Elbow is a professor of English at the University of Massachusetts at Amherst. He has taught at MIT, Franconia College, The Evergreen State College, and SUNY at Stony Brook, where for five years he directed the writing program. At Stony Brook, he and Pat Belanoff pioneered the use of programmatic evaluation by portfolio. He is author of *Writing Without Teachers* (1973), *Oppositions in Chaucer* (1975), *Writing with Power* (1981), *Embracing Contraries* (1986), *What is English?* (1990), and (with Pat Belanoff) a textbook, *A Community of Writers* (2nd ed. 1995).

Linda Flower is a professor of rhetoric at Carnegie Mellon University and co-director of the National Center for the Study of Writing and Literacy at Berkeley and Carnegie Mellon. Her work in cognitive rhetoric explores the processes of planning, collaboration, and negotiation within academic discourse and community literacy. She is the author of *Problem-Solving Strategies for Writing* (1981) and *The Construction of Negotiated Meaning: A Social Cognitive Theory of Writing* (1994). Her coauthored works include *Reading-to-Write: Exploring a Cognitive and Social Process* (1990) and *Making Thinking Visible: Writing, Collaborative Planning, and Classroom Inquiry* (1994).

Sarah Warshauer Freedman is a professor of education and director of the National Center for the Study of Writing and Literacy at the University of California at Berkeley. Among her publications are three books: *The Acquisition of Written Language: Response and Revision* (1985), *Response to Student Writing* (1987), and *Exchanging Writing, Exchanging Cultures: Lessons in School Reform from the United States and Great Britain* (1994). She currently is working with teacher researchers in urban schools.

Anne Ruggles Gere, a professor of English and professor of education at the University of Michigan, is a past chair of CCCC. She has chaired the MLA Division of Teaching Writing and been a WPA consultant/evaluator for over a decade. Her publications include *Writing Groups: History, Theory, and Implications* (1987), *Writing and Learning* (1988), and *Into the Field: Sites of Composition Studies* (1993).

Carol Petersen Hartzog, Vice Provost, College of Letters and Science at UCLA, formerly directed UCLA's writing programs. Her publications include *Composition and the Academy: A Study of Writing Program Administration* (1986); related professional interests focus on educational reform and the challenges of late-20th-century academic administration.

Shirley Brice Heath is a professor of English and linguistics at Stanford University, with courtesy appointments in anthropology and the School of Education. Her research in language acquisition, sociocultural contexts for the development of literacy and literate behaviors, and relations between oral and written language is manifested in such publications as *Ways with Words: Language, Life, and Work in Communities and Classrooms* (1983), *The Braid of Literature: Children's Worlds of Reading* (coauthored, 1992), and *Identity and Inner-City Youth: Beyond Identity and Gender* (coedited, 1993).

Sylvia A. Holladay is Director, Communications Program, St. Petersburg/Gibbs Campus, St. Petersburg Junior College. She has written three freshman composition books and over 50 articles on composition and related professional issues. Her major interests are empirical research, instructional methods, curriculum development, and assessment.

Brian Huot teaches undergraduate and graduate courses in composition at the University of Louisville. He coedited and contributed to *Validating Holistic Scoring for Writing Assessment: Theoretical and Empirical Foundations* (1993). Most recently, he helped to found and coedit *Assessing Writing*, the only journal devoted to writing assessment.

Erika Lindemann, a professor of English and associate dean of the Graduate School at UNC at Chapel Hill, is the author of *A Rhetoric for Writing Teachers* (3rd ed. 1995) and past editor of the Longman and CCCC bibliographies of composition. She has directed writing programs at the universities of North and South Carolina.

Andrea A. Lunsford is Distinguished Professor and vice chair of English at The Ohio State University. With Robert Connors and Lisa Ede, she edited *Essays on Classical Rhetoric and Modern Discourse* (1984), winner of the 1985 MLA Mina Shaughnessy Award; with Lisa Ede, she has collaborated on numerous works, including the award-winning "Audience Addressed, Audience Invoked" (1984) and *Singular Texts/Plural Authors: Perspectives on Collaborative Writing* (1990). In 1984, she received the CCCC Exemplar Award.

Stephen M. North is an associate professor of English and former director of both the Writing Center and the Writing Program at SUNY at Albany. He is currently serving as NCTE's College Acquisitions Editor and as series editor for *Refiguring English Studies*. He is the author of *The Making of Knowledge in Composition: Portrait of an Emerging Field* (1987) and of many essays and articles in the field of composition. His current work involves the role of writing in English graduate education.

Charles I. Schuster served as Director of Composition and founded the graduate concentration in rhetoric and composition at the University of Wisconsin-Milwaukee. Currently WPA president, he has published on Mikhail Bakhtin, portfolio assessment, the politics of writing instruction, and nonfiction prose, particularly the writings of Richard Selzer and John McPhee.

James F. Slevin is a professor of English at Georgetown University, where he has chaired the department and directed the writing program. Active in professional organizations, including MLA and NCTE, he chaired the CCCC task force on professional standards that produced the "Statement of Principles and Standards for the Postsecondary Teaching of Writing" (1989). His recent publications include the coedited *Right to Literacy* (1990) and "Depoliticizing and Politicizing Composition Studies" in *The Politics of Writing Instruction* (1991).

Kurt Spellmeyer is an associate professor and the director of the Faculty of Arts and Sciences Writing Program at Rutgers University in New Brunswick, New Jersey. He has written *Common Ground: Dialogue, Understanding, and the Teaching of Composition* (1993) in addition to articles on composition, rhetoric, and the construction of knowledge.

Sandra Stotsky is a research associate at the Harvard Graduate School of Education and director of the Summer Institute on Writing, Reading, and Civic Education. Her research interests focus on reading/writing relationships, the teaching of writing, and the uses of writing for learning and for citizenship. She currently serves as editor of *Research in the Teaching of English*.

C. Jan Swearingen is a professor of English at the University of Texas at Arlington and Visiting Radford Chair of Rhetoric and Composition at Texas Christian University. Her *Rhetoric and Irony, Western Literacy and Western Lies* (1991) received Honorable Mention in the *Journal of Advanced Composition* W. Ross Winterowd Award for the best book published in composition theory in 1991. She is currently completing a book on multiculturalism and classical rhetoric as well as chapters for two collections on women in rhetoric.

John Trimbur is an associate professor of English and co-director of the Technical, Scientific, and Professional Communication program at Worcester Polytechnic Institute. He has published many articles on writing theory, collaborative learning, and cultural studies of literacy. The book he coedited with Richard Bullock and Charles I. Schuster, *The Politics of Writing Instruction: Postsecondary*, received the 1992 CCCC Outstanding Book Award.

Edward M. White is a professor of English at California State University at San Bernardino, former director of the WPA consultant/evaluator program, and past faculty coordinator of the CSU system's writing improvement program. His publications include *Developing Successful College Writing Programs* (1989), *Teaching and Assessing Writing* (2nd ed. 1994), *Assigning, Responding, Evaluating* (3rd ed. 1995), and coeditorship of *Inquiry* (1993) and *Assessment of Writing: Politics, Policies, and Practices* (forthcoming).

Index

abolitionist-reformist, 1–2, 47, 49, 51–54, 56–62, 72, 75, 277
Ackerman, John, 137
Adams, Peter Dow, 86–87
Adelman, Clifford, 103
Anderson, Melville B., 49
Anschluss, 77
Anya, Lilia, 254
"Apologia, An" (Edward M. White), 106
Applebee, Arthur N., 220
Arnold, Matthew, 220
Asher, J. William, 191
Asser, Paul Nijhoff, 264
assessment, 5, 82, 91, 101, 105–6, 108, 114, 116–19; alternatives, 112–15; basic writing, 93; beyond the classroom, 99; competence based, 95; crucial issues, 111; current, 146; elimination, 111; equivalency, 104; external, 102; future, 111–13; Holistic Scoring, 83, 85, 111; implications, 93; minimal competency, 84; multicultural, 84; national programs, 100; options, 94; performance, 108–13; placement decisions, 108–10; portfolio, 82–85, 89, 94–95, 112; practices, 112–13, 147; standardized objective tests, 163; statewide testing, 83; test conditions, 83; utopian, 82, 89, 94; validity, 113; yogurt model, 94
Association of American Colleges, 158
Association of Community and Junior Colleges, 33

Bachman, Susan, 242
Bailey, Dudley, 70
Bakhtin, Mikhail, 91, 184
Baldwin, James, 41
Barthe, Roland, 260–61
Bartholomae, David, 6, 11, 41, 87, 91, 269

basic writer, 87–88, 90
Beford Guide for College Writers, The (X. J. Kennedy, Dorothy M. Kennedy, Sylvia A. Holladay), 63–64
Belanoff, Pat, 85
Bell, Marvin, 67
Bellah, Robert N., 219
Berkenkotter, Carol, 138, 179, 192
Berlak, Howard, 113
Berlin, James A., 3, 127–28, 210, 220, 239–41
Bizzell, Patricia, 130, 191
Bledstein, Burton J., 116, 132
Blitz, Michael, 216
Bloom, Allan, 117
Bloom, Lynn Z., 268
Blumenthal, Sidney, 126
Bohman, Helen, 37
Bolter, Jay, 264
Book Lovers' Club, 221
Bourdieu, Pierre, 133
Bowles, Samuel, 134, 216
Boyle, James, 259, 262–63, 267
Braddock, Richard, 1, 189, 192–94, 200
Brandt, Deborah, 179, 244, 247
Bruffee, Kenneth A., 122, 167
Bruner, Jerome, 66, 68
Bryce, James, 206
Buber, Martin, 148
Burke, Kenneth, 78, 145
Burton, Dwight L., 191
Bush, George, 102, 161–62, 169–70

Caesar, Terry, 126, 265–66
Camp, Roberta, 112
Campbell, Oscar James, 53–54, 60
cartesian detachment, 42
Castellano, Marisa, 86
Chaplin, Miriam T., 4, 164, 172, 174
Charles, Ray, 168

301